L A N G U A G E   A C R O S S   C U L T U R E S

Proceedings of a symposium held at
St. Patrick's College, Drumcondra, Dublin

8 - 9 July 1983

Edited by

Liam Mac Mathúna and David Singleton

IRAAL

Irish Association for Applied Linguistics

Cumann na Teangeolaíochta Feidhmí

1984

LANGUAGE ACROSS CULTURES

ORGANIZING COMMITTEE

Sr. Marie de Montfort Supple
David Little
Liam Mac Mathúna (Chairman)
Clíona Marsh
David Singleton

SPONSORS / URRAÍ

The Irish Association for Applied Linguistics is very grateful
for the generous support which this Symposium received from
the following sponsors:

Ambassade de France en Irlande
An Comhchoiste Réamhscolaíochta
Bank of Ireland
Bord Fáilte
Bord na Gaeilge
Centre for Language and Communications
  Studies, T.C.D.
Coláiste Phádraig, Droim Conrach /
St. Patrick's College, Drumcondra
Comhar na Múinteoirí Gaeilge
Educational Company of Ireland
French Teachers Association
Institiúid Teangeolaíochta Éireann
The Linguaviva Centre
The National Dairy Council /
An Chomhairle Déiríochta
Údarás na Gaeltachta

Tá Cumann na Teangeolaíochta Feidhmí an-bhuíoch de na hurraí
thuasluaite as an tacaíocht fhial a thug siad don Siompóisiam seo

Irish Association for Applied Linguistics

© 1984

Cumann na Teangeolaíochta Feidhmí

ISBN   0   9509132   0   0

FOREWORD

The Republic of Ireland has two official languages which, in the words of Mrs. Gemma Hussey, Minister for Education, 'are the expression of two very different cultures'. This is a situation which is not unfamiliar also in other bilingual countries.

In the past, there has been a tendency to favour the narrow communicative aspects of language choice - the usefulness of a language for day-to-day business within and across the country's borders. More recently, we have come to realize that language serves a multitude of functions, and that the importance of a language stretches far beyond the function of carrying a certain number of bits of information.

One function of a language is to represent, and indeed to identify, shared cultural values. This aspect of the situation in Ireland was clearly brought home to us, in July this year, as participants at the International Symposium on 'Language Across Cultures' at St. Patrick's College, located on the outskirts of Dublin and surrounded by green pastures that lent the symposium the right Irish atmosphere, in addition to serving as a happy field of activity for the dedicated joggers on the International Committee.

On behalf of AILA, I want to take this opportunity of thanking the Irish Association for Applied Linguistics for generously hosting this year's meeting of the International Committee and for inviting us to the symposium; I also want to congratulate IRAAL on the splendid organisation of the symposium and on the publication of the papers in this volume.

I am convinced that these contributions will serve as a useful source of information on The State of the Art in some fields of Applied Linguistics and, in particular, on the linguistic and cultural situation in Ireland. These scholarly analyses will no doubt be felt to be relevant also to cultures and languages to be found far from the shores of Ireland.

October 1983

Jan Svartvik

President, AILA

CONTENTS

OPENING ADDRESS BY THE MINISTER FOR EDUCATION, MRS. GEMMA HUSSEY T.D.

Tá áthas orm bheith anseo libh inniu. Gabhaim buíochas libh as ucht cuireadh a thabhairt dom chun an siompóisiam seo a oscailt.

I am delighted to be here with you today. It gives me great pleasure to open officially this symposium on the theme 'Language Across Cultures'. I am very grateful to the Chairman of the Organising Committee for his invitation.

It is a real tribute to the work of IRAAL (The Irish Association for Applied Linguistics) that AILA (Association Internationale de Linguistique Appliquée) chose Ireland this year as the venue for the annual meeting of its International Committee. For this IRAAL symposium contributors over the two days will come from places as far apart as Texas, Turku and Tel-Aviv. To all these visitors to our shores I extend the traditional Irish 'Céad Míle Fáilte' or 'Hundred Thousand Welcomes'.

I must first of all congratulate you on your choice of title for this symposium. The word 'Linguistics' suggests to the layman the ivory tower of academic research. 'Language Across Cultures' has, however, very rich, recognisably human resonances. Within our own country, we have two official languages which are the expression of two very different cultures. The theme 'Language Across Cultures' suggests that this is not necessarily a barrier to communication; that cross-fertilization is made possible by purposeful dialogue and that language and the study of language can be a means of building bridges between cultures.

C'est bien évident que la langue et la culture sont étroitement liées, l'une à l'autre. Alors on pourrait dire que la langue est le moyen le plus important de transmettre la culture de - pour ainsi dire - père en fils; surtout ces aspects-là de la culture que l'on appelle, d'après l'UNESCO, le patrimoine non-matériel. C'est-à-dire les valeurs spirituelles, valeurs morales, valeurs esthétiques, voire même toute la mentalité des gens qui partagent la même langue. C'est pour ça que nous voulons garder les langues traditionelles, peu parlées, comme par exemple l'irlandais, en gardant tout de même le bon esprit pour les grandes langues, comme l'anglais, le français ou bien d'autres grandes langues européennes. C'est à cet égard que l'Association Internationale de Linguistique Appliquée peut jouer un rôle essentiel.

As I say AILA and IRAAL can play an essential bridge-building role within the academic world, where it could happen that research would be done in isolation and that would be expensive duplication of effort. It is an especially good example of fruitful dialogue between the various levels of education.

It is too easy for research in educational matters to sail along its own erudite course without reference to the realities of the 'chalk face'. IRAAL is interested in and has members from all general levels of the education system, as well as from specialized sectors such as speech therapy and training of the deaf. It involves teachers engaged in various levels of language remediation, as well as teachers of Irish, English and the continental languages.

On the home scene Linguistics as an area of study is now much more widely available than it was ten years ago. For example, the UCD Undergraduate and Master's programmes in Linguistics have existed for some years now. New arrivals are the part-time Diploma Course in Applied Linguistics offered by Kevin Street College of Technology and the courses in Communications and in Translating and Interpreting offered by NIHE, Dublin, both of which contain strong Linguistics/Applied Linguistics elements. A very important development for the study of Linguistics and Applied Linguistics in Ireland was the setting up of the Centre for Language and Communication Studies (CLCS) at Trinity College as a special project of the HEA. In October 1982 the first students enrolled for the CLCS Graduate Diploma Course in Applied Linguistics and Language Teaching.

Perhaps the clearest recognition by the Department of Education of the importance of linguistic study was the setting up of the Institiúid Teangeolaíochta Éireann which is currently fostering several linguistic research projects. Under the auspices of I T É the Modern Languages Syllabus Project for Post-Primary Schools evolved. This project was notable in the history of language-teaching in Ireland in that the researchers who set to work on a defined content syllabus for the teaching of Modern Languages in post-primary schools recognised at a very early stage that the valuable work could well be treated like just another hide-bound thesis if teaching materials were not developed simultaneously. Accordingly, a group of teachers began to hold weekly workshops under the guidance of the ITÉ Modern Language Advisers. They developed materials, tried them out in the classrooms, refined them further in the light of classroom use, and finally a French course for first-year pupils, based on the communicative approach to teaching, emerged.

Similar 'grassroots' work is under way in German, Spanish and Italian. For the teaching of Irish, a communicatively-oriented course called 'Mise agus Tusa' is at present being used in a number of schools. There again the initiative came from teachers themselves. This course has been developed under the auspices of ITÉ and of Bord na Gaeilge. I know that there are close links between IRAAL and these language-teaching projects: I am aware that individual members of IRAAL partici-pate in the ITÉ Modern Languages Project and that this overlap is not merely fortuitous but reflects many shared concerns and preoccupations.

IRAAL has, I know, helped to provide teachers with relevant theoretical insights. Other notable contributions of Linguistics to the use and teaching of Irish include a con-siderable volume of work on terminology in areas such as Dairying, Commerce and Business Studies and the course in Irish for weaker students developed as part of the Shannon project.

It is widely recognised that no matter what outstanding research is done in Linguistics and Applied Linguistics and no matter how many genuine efforts are made to bring the relevant insights into the classroom, the greatest motivator of teacher-behaviour remains the examination-paper. It is therefore imperative that our examinations reflect as far as is practicable the wisdom of modern research on the teaching of a subject. It may not always be true however that what is valid in linguistic theory can be applied in language-teaching. There are human factors involved; not all teachers may feel ready to embark on a kind of teaching for which their initial training did not equip them.

Given these very real deterrents to change I think that all those involved in Linguistics and language-teaching should welcome the changes which I have initiated in the Modern Languages examinations from 1985 onwards.

The candidates will now be set examination tasks which bear more resemblance to real-life tasks. They will be asked to write short passages of a functional nature in the target language. Passages of real, authentic language will be pre-sented for global comprehension. I would hope that the absence of set-texts in French and German will not lead to less reading in those languages. All too often the set-text was merely read aloud and translated. If even a fraction of the time given to this exercise were now devoted to silent reading of books of the pupil's choice the result for the pupil could be a very enriching introduction to journalistic/literary matter in the target language and for the teacher a much more economical use of valuable class-contact time.

The newest feature of the 1985 changes in Modern Language testing will be the introduction of a listening comprehension test. This, together with the emphasis on extensive reading, is in accordance with linguistic research which suggests that learners should be exposed to a much richer experience of the target-language than they are required to reproduce.

The examination syllabus offered to teachers for 1985 and subsequent years is a pragmatic compromise between the reassuringly familiar and the frighteningly innovative. Teachers' attention is being focused on the skills tested by the various tasks set in the examination, and guidance is given to them for the fostering of these skills in the classroom.

The fact that research moves quickly and tends to out-strip the national examination machine was brought home to me when I read the following excerpt from an abstract of one of your symposium papers: 'There are now indications on an increasing scale that, owing to the progress of cognitive-code learning theory, translation is re-establishing itself as a useful and legitimate tool of foreign-language teaching'. Plus ça change, ... plus c'est la même chose!

SOCIOSEMIOTICS ACROSS CULTURES

Wolfgang Kühlwein
University of Trier

I.   GENERAL

0. Language lends itself in various ways to investigation across cultures, ways which relate to our various modes of conceiving language and culture.

We can look at language (1) as a system
(2) as knowledge
(3) as behaviour.

We choose lexicology as a case in point. Within lexicology we shall limit our view to paradigmatic relations holding between so-called 'synonyms'.

1.   The mode of investigating language as a system and lexicology as one of its subsystems has yielded valuable but mostly self-contained lexical field studies since the days of lexical field study pioneers like Trier and Jolles, from the work done by Whorf and by German 'Sprachinhaltsforschung' (e.g. Weisgerber, Kandler, Gipper) to the more operationally oriented studies by Leisi, Lyons, Oksaar, Brekle, Ikegami, Kühlwein, Geckeler and others. Contrastive, cross-language lexicological studies have remained scarce, however, though there is a growing demand for them from both language typology and foreign language teaching. The proceedings of the 3rd International Conference of English (and other) Contrastive Linguistic Projects mirror this deficiency distinctly (Kühlwein - Thome - Wilss 1982). Why?

The basic problem underlying any systemic lexicological analysis is that of what should be regarded as semantic primes - and this problem has remained unsolved from the universalist approaches to language study in the 16th and 17th centuries to present linguistic theories. This desideratum called comparative/contrastive criteria to the attention of lexicologists (and lexicographers) from Leibniz (17th/18th centuries) to current linguistic theories. The ensuing contrastive lexicological studies, however, turned out to face at least two further problems:

(i)   the problem of tertium comparationis (TC) and along with it that of equivalence

(ii) the question as to which linguistic models and procedures are suited best for the study of languages across cultures.

5

Ad (i) : Type of 'equivalence' or discovery procedures	Problems remaining
FORMAL	based on linguistic structure exclusively
DERIVATIONAL-SEMANTIC	'How deep is deep structure?'; equivalence open to delicacy of derivational model
PARAPHRASE procedure	paraphrasing of paraphrase of ... yields regressum ad infinitum
TRANSLATIONAL procedure	fundamental limitations by truth conditions and cultural - institutional specificities
FUNCTIONAL-COMMUNICATIVE	mental processes of cognition; associative-connotative components, 'Verstehensuniversalien'

Ad (ii): Linguistic models and procedures	Problems and deficiencies for language comparison
CORPUS-BOUND procedures	TC unclear; mostly surface-structure-oriented
TRANSFORMATIONAL-GENERATIVE	TC : deep structure; sentence-based rather than text-based; register; linguistic variation
(GENERATIVE) SEMANTIC	TC conceptual; universal semantic grid
INTEGRATED VERBAL/NON-VERBAL BEHAVIOUR	behavioural universals; insufficiently developed
FUNCTIONAL-NOTIONAL-(REFERENTIAL)	basic notional grid; concept of 'function'

It follows from these (and other) limitations that contrastive approaches to lexicology, based on systemic properties
of language only, will remain open to doubt. As a consequence we are witnessing a widening of the scope of contrastive research beyond the confines of systemic linguistics into two further dimensions (Kühlwein 1983).

2.   Contrastive lexicological analysis is carried deeper,
to language as knowledge. This approach will certainly not
simply do away with older contrastive linguistic insights,
but it has to reinterpret them from a psycholinguistic
perspective. The basis of this perspective is conceptual
rather than formal/functional-grammatical. The conceptual
strategies which actively and passively interrelate with
the correspondingly different structures in different
languages (Dirven 1976) become the starting points of
research into language contact.

Theoretically this approach is the reverse of that of Sapir, Whorf and the German Sprachinhaltsforschung theorists, all of whom derived cross-language differences in conceptual systems from language specific formal/functional-grammatical systems; the extremes to which this line of inferencing had been carried (linguistically determined 'Weltanschauung', etc.) are well-known. In practical analysis, however, the two will converge: we do not have the underlying universal conceptual grid, which this psycholinguistically based approach needs as its TC - and the repeated onomasiological attempts to get one tell us a sad story throughout the history of language study. The basic conceptual grid can only be set up via the evidence of linguistic performance.

3.   Linguistic performance, however, can only be properly accounted for when seen within the intricate network of both verbal and non-verbal behaviour. If, however, we want to describe and teach differences of linguistic behaviour across cultures, their explanation via differing perceptual and conceptual strategies need not find its ultimate end in cognitive psychology. It has been suggested that one might base cross-cultural language description on an underlying pragmatic deep structure (instead of more syntactic or semantic deep structures) which should serve the purpose of a tertium comparationis (Spillner 1978):

$$\text{pragmatic DS } (=TC) \underset{\text{realization in } L_2}{\overset{\text{realization in } L_1}{\diagup\diagdown}} \text{contrasting}$$

We do, of course, not deny the obvious fact that pragmatics is involved in all these cases, but the construct of a universal pragmatic deep structure, to which higher language specific deviations could be traced down when we contrast language use,

(1) is an abstraction, and therefore rather the linguist's 'hocus-pocus' than 'God's truth';

(2) simply does not go 'deep' enough in explanatory power.

Often pragmatic accounts for cross-language differences are rather descriptive than explanatory. The question, why such differentiations exist leads to the intricate level of sociocultural, anthropo- and ethnolinguistic conditions, possibilities and contrasts.

Certain semiotic properties are inherent in any person, object or event about whom/which we are communicating; and it is among these semiotic properties that speakers of different societies make their choices in differing ways; thus a certain semiotic property of e.g. a specific person might strike speakers of one society as being highly

important, whereas its impact might be very low for speakers
of a different society. Let us call this the differing
'semiotic thrust' or 'semiotic impact'. If the semiotic
thrust of identical persons, objects, events, however,
varies across societies, corresponding differences will
result in naming these referents. Our decisions on
naming persons and things are determined by the different
ways in which they strike us, impress us - and as these
ways are (at least more or less) understandable among the
speakers of one society, they can neither be ultimately
caused psycholinguistically nor explained in individual
psycholinguistic terms only. Thus we end up with differences
among societies in the respective different processes of
semiotization. This is the sense in which we would like to
define the term <u>sociosemiotics</u>. Sociosemiotic processes and
their respective differentiations across cultures are not
abstract, are not the descriptive linguist's 'hocus-pocus',
but do exist. A <u>preliminary</u> model of what we are talking
about might look roughly like this:

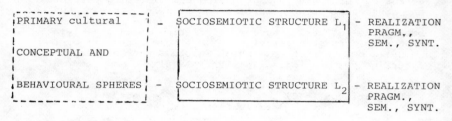

e.g. JUDGEMENT (ethic, aesthetic)
     'pragmatic universals',
     OCCUPATION/ACTIVITY,
     HOUSING, FRIENDSHIP, HOSTILITY,
     BEAUTY, UGLINESS, etc.

From a theoretical linguistic perspective this concept is
strengthened by the hypothesis of M.A.K. Halliday (from whom
I derived the term 'sociosemiotics'): we can only <u>say</u> what we
can mean, and we can only <u>mean</u> what we can <u>do</u>.

    With this behaviourally/sociologically determined
sequence Halliday opposed Dell Hymes's more psycholinguistically determined sequence. Thanks, however, to this con-
stellation of dichotomies (individual <u>vs.</u> social; psychological
<u>vs.</u> sociological; meaning <u>vs.</u> doing; knowledge <u>vs.</u> behaviour),
Halliday's concept of 'behaviour' and 'doing' ties in with
pragmatics all too nicely, actually equals pragmatics. It
will have become apparent from what has been said above

that we conceive of 'behaviour' and of 'doing' in a wider and less rigorous sense. We regard the differing ways according to which different societies cope with the semiotic thrust of their environment as part of 'doing' and 'behaviour'.

Admittedly this means that we come back after all to the notion of psycholinguistic processes - but only to the extent to which psycholinguistic processes are committal and representative not only for a particular individual but for all members of his/her group, speech-community, society. This perspective mitigates the confrontation psycho- vs. sociolinguistics; language use is both nature and nurture.

As for our concept of 'culture' we consequently hold that different languages are emanations of different cultures and that culture is everything one must know, feel and cope with, in order to be able to judge where members of a society in their various roles behave according to expectation or deviate, and to be able to behave according to expectations in the respective society if one is willing to (Göhring 1980, 73).

II. A SPECIFIC EXAMPLE

As an example we investigated BEAUTY (B) - as restricted to human beings - in English (E) and French (F) in order to find out

(a) the general inclination or disinclination towards or against attributing or expressing BEAUTY, i.e. its degree of impor- tance in different cultures;

(b) which sociosemiotic conditions must be met to assign BEAUTY to somebody in different cultures: the way a person looks, behaves, etc.;

(c) the language specific possibilities and habits of realizing and verbalizing these sociosemiotic processes.

We shall mainly concentrate on (a) and (b); for the semantics involved in (c) and for the numeric data cf. Nies (1979). The following tools and procedures were used:

0. Informants: 563 French, 773 English informants of all age groups (mainly 30 - 35 years). Age para- meter does not yield significant differences.

1. 'Synonyms' roughly grouped according to primary
   reference to clothing, primary reference to body,
   peripheric ones, and ones largely incompatible
   with either 'male' or 'female'

French		English		
beau		beautiful	I	♂
chic		chic	I	♂
coquet		comely	I	♂
élégant		dressy		
épatant		elegant		
(inélegant)		glamorous	I	♂
joli	I ♂	good-looking		
(laid)		gorgeous	I	♂
mignon	I ♂	handsome	I	♀
pimpant	I ♂	(inelegant)		
ravissant	I ♂	lovely	I	♂
		(plain)		
		pretty	I	♂
		smart		
		(ugly)		
		(unsightly)		

(...) = antonyms

I ♀ = largely incompatible with 'female'
I ♂ = largely incompatible with 'male'

Grouping according to results of opposition tests
(... not ... but ...), or (... not really ... but
only ...).

2. Parameters administered to these lexemes, e.g.
   [refined features] vs. [-refined features =
   coarse features]

3. Scale of evaluation (+2, +1, 0, -1, -2) for each
   lexeme along each parameter. (Established by 1,472
   test questions for French resp., 2,384 test questions
   for English, which equals 7,360 decision-making acts
   for French and 11,920 for English.)

4. Quantitative linguistic processing (factor analysis,
   x^2 tests, standard values, standard deviations,
   significant deviations, etc.)

The three most relevant criteria according to which
BEAUTY is assigned to persons in both languages seem to be:

1. semantic reference to clothing v̲s̲. body (P1-2)
2. aesthetic judgement as to constitution, perfection, harmony (P3-5)
3. non-aesthetic judgement as to physiological pre-conditions (age, sex typicity P6-7), psychological preconditions (vanity, warm-heartedness P8-9), psychosomatic impression (naturalness, seriousness P10-11)

The findings (cf. Kühlwein 1984) were compared with some evidence for German (G). Our respective G data are derived from a pilot study which, however, is much more limited (Fries 1982).

As a whole members of the French speech community (France) are more generous in attributing BEAUTY to persons than members of the English speech community (Great Britain). In both languages BEAUTY is attributed to females considerably more frequently than to males, but: the relation (+ BEAUTY) : (- BEAUTY) equals 2 : 1 for women in English, whereas it is 4 : 1 in French - and the only creature that ends up with a global dominance of (- BEAUTY) is the male in English. Thus the overall sequence is:

$$
\text{F female} \xrightarrow{\text{far ahead of}} \text{E female} \xrightarrow{\text{far ahead of}} \text{F male}
$$

$$
\xrightarrow{\text{somewhat ahead of}} \text{E male.}
$$

Our G data indicate a position between F and E : the overall relation (BEAUTY ♀) : (BEAUTY ♂) approximates to the one in F - 4 : 1; absolutely, however, the G scores are much lower than the F ones: similar to the E ♂ the G ♂ also ends up with a global dominance of (- BEAUTY).

P (1 and 2) [± well-dressed] vs. [± good physical appearance]

F ♀ vs. E ♀ : For F females adjectives which primarily refer to being well-dressed can at the same time more easily evoke the impression of physical B than their E counterparts. The same tendency is evinced even more clearly by F adjectives primarily denoting physical B of a woman when they come to be used for being well-dressed.

F ♂ vs. E ♂ : For males adjectives primarily referring to being well-dressed evoke the impression of good physical appearance also more easily in F than in E, but the difference is a slight one only; there is, however, a greater reluctance in F than in E to use adjectives which primarily refer to physical B of the male to refer simultaneously to male dress.
It seems that on the whole the semiotic impact of good clothing is related more closely to that of good physical appearance in F than in E, in particular for females.

F ♀ vs. F ♂ : The above-mentioned association of good physical appearance triggered by adjectives that primarily refer to being well-dressed is stronger for females than for males in F. The analogous tendency is even stronger with adjectives that primarily refer to physical B in F. They allow to associate being well-dressed much more easily for the female than for the male.

E ♀ vs. E ♂ : In E adjectives primarily used to indicate a state of being well-dressed for the female may be used to refer to physical B just a little bit more easily than this is the case with males; when it comes to the effect of adjectives primarily referring to physical B upon the associating of a state of being well-dressed as well, there is no distinction between female and male in E. Obviously sex-specificity plays a more important role in this respect in F than in E.

P 3 : Constitution [refined vs. coarse features]

F (vs. E) is rather strongly inclined towards attributing B-adjectives which primarily refer to physical appearance on the basis of refined features; with coarse features, however, F tends towards attributing B-adjectives which primarily refer to clothing - whereas in E B-adjectives which primarily refer to clothing are used to an equal extent irrespective of refined or coarse features; on the other hand E is more inclined towards attributing B-adjectives which primarily refer to physical appearance despite coarse features (with the exception of beautiful, however). Obviously the distinction refined vs. coarse features is more important in F.

P 4 : Perfection [± consummate outer appearance]

Perfection seems to be more important in F than in E for the attribution of B-adjectives which primarily refer to clothing. But the chances of being assigned B-adjectives which primarily refer to physical appearance are higher for a perfectly appearing person in E (especially for the E man) than in F.

P 5 : [± harmony of appearance]

This feature turns out to be much more relevant for the conception of B in F than in E, especially as regards clothing; in E even lack of harmony can well go along with B-adjectives which primarily refer to clothing fairly easily, whereas in F lack of harmony more or less excludes B-adjectives which primarily refer to clothing; in the latter respect both F and E are somewhat more lenient with men than with women.

P 6 : Age [± looking one's age (middle-age)]

F is very generous in assigning B-adjectives -
especially those which primarily refer to clothing -
to women who look their age, E being particularly
harsh towards women who endeavour to look younger than
they are.

P 7 : Sexually typical appearance [± feminine/masculine looking]

For females : no B-adjectives if no sex-typicity in
both languages; for males : distinctly male appearance:
easy evocation of B-adjectives primarily referring to
the body in both languages; only slight evocation of
adjectives primarily referring to clothes with E males;
for the F woman this feature in addition evokes B-
adjectives primarily referring to clothing fairly easily.

P 8 : Vanity [the intention to impress by a good appearance]

Both languages - and F more than E - react to this
criterion mainly within the area of B-adjectives
which primarily refer to clothing, the sequence of
importance of this criterion being (from strongest
to weakest) F woman, F man, and, almost irrelevant
for the E woman and E man.

P 9 : Warm-heartedness [± amiable, warm-hearted, friendly]

The impact of this feature is fairly low in both
languages. It has a slightly positive effect on the
evoking of B-adjectives which primarily refer to
physical B for the F woman, followed by the F man,
followed in turn equally by the E man and woman.

P 10: Naturalness [± natural, unassuming vs. well-groomed,
     cultivated]

On the whole F reacts more sensitively towards both
natural and cultivated appearance. Above all,
cultivated appearance has a highly positive correlation
with B-adjectives which primarily refer to clothing
particularly for the F woman. As for adjectives
which primarily refer to physical B, there is also a
remarkably high correlation with both natural and
cultivated appearance for the F woman; for the F man,
the E woman and the E man these adjectives go with
'cultivated' more easily than with 'natural', but
the respective correlations are weaker than the one
for the F woman.

P 11: Seriousness [+ serious, earnest vs. cheerful, serene]

Altogether the correlation is low. Though both a
serious and cheerful nature induce B-adjectives
slightly more easily in F than in E - especially for
the F woman, for whom a cheerful disposition con-
tributes towards the use of adjectives mainly referring
to physical B to a much higher degree than for the E.

Cross-language comparison of sociosemiotic properties

Both groups of adjectives which we distinguished on the basis
of compatibility (compatible with ♂ and ♀ vs. (largely)
incompatible with one of them) can be evoked by a far
greater variety of features for the F woman than for anybody
else. Within the group of those adjectives which are compatible with both male and female, the feature of being
well-dressed dominates in both languages, followed for the
E woman by the physiological feature 'looking one's age'
(for the F woman appearing only at rank 5!), whereas rank
2 is occupied for the F woman by the psychosomatic impression
'cultivated and well-groomed appearance' (for the E woman
rank 4). Rank 3 is occupied in both languages by the
noticeable wish to impress by a good appearance. 'Perfection
of outer appearance' ranges somewhat higher for the E woman
than for the F woman within this group of adjectives as well
(rank 5 vs. rang 6); for this group of adjectives the feature
'physical beauty' is much more important for the E woman than
for the F woman (rank 6 vs. rank 16).

What is especially striking within this area of top
criteria of the first group (compatible!) is that for the F
woman it contains fairly oppositive criteria : thus 'natural
and unassuming disposition' (rank 5) does not cause
considerably more difficulties to attribute these B-adjectives
than 'well-groomed, cultivated appearance' (rank 2)
is doing; similarly we find both 'harmony of appearance'
(rank 8) and its counterpart (rank 4) fairly high on the list;
the F woman is even pardoned for lacking 'perfection of outer
appearance' (rank 12 after '+ perfection of outer appearance':
rank 6); F is also more lenient towards the woman who tries
to hide her real age (rank 10 after 'looking one's real age':
rank 7); even the F woman who does not endeavour to impress
by a good appearance stands a fair chance of being attributed
this group of B-adjectives (rank 15 after 'noticeable wish

to impress by a good appearance': rank 3). Lacking
human warmth and having coarse features are also less
serious obstacles against the attribution of these
B-adjectives for the F woman. Obviously F allows
for the attribution of B-adjectives marked as compatible for the woman within a far wider scope of
aesthetic and extra-aesthetic (physiological, psychological and psychosomatic) judgements.

Thus in E the attributing of these B-adjectives seems
to follow a more clearly profiled image of the woman,
whereas in F it seems to be much more strongly oriented
according to the specific person concerned.

For those adjectives which are (highly) incompatible with male, 'sexually typical feminine appearance'
ranges highest for the F woman, followed by 'refined
features'; in E 'perfection' of outer appearance ranges
highest for these adjectives, followed by 'sexually
typical appearance'; in both languages the 'impression of
being nicely dressed' occupies rank 3 and 'physical
beauty' rank 5, 'harmony of appearance' occupying rank
4 for the F woman, which is occupied by the noticeable
'wish to impress by good appearance' for the E woman;
'refined features' merely occupy rank 6 for the E woman,
which is occupied by a 'serene disposition' for the F
woman, for whom on the other hand 'perfection of outer
appearance' occupies only rank 7, followed by 'well-
groomed and cultured appearance' and the noticeable 'wish
to impress by a good appearance'.

Altogether psychosomatic features rank considerably
higher for the F ♀ than for the E ♀ in this group of
adjectives. As for males, aesthetic features rank higher
for the F ♂ than for both E ♂ and ♀.

Our preliminary data for G (still leaving aside the
compatibility grouping and negatively marked features
like [- perfection]) reveal : for women the top rank
is occupied by [+ well-dressed] (=clothing), for men
by [+ consummate outer appearance] (=perfection); for
both men and women [+intention to impress by good
appearance] (=vanity) ranges second; for women [+ refined
features], [+ good physical appearance], [+ sexually typical
appearance] follow, for men [+ looking one's age] , [+ amiable,
friendly, warm-hearted], [+ well-dressed] follow. At the
lower end of the scale we find for women [+ harmony of
appearance], [+ natural, unassuming] , [+ amiable, friendly,
warm-hearted] , [+looking one's age] , [+ serious, earnest]

and at the bottom [+ consummate outer appearance] ; for
men the lower end of the scale shows [+ natural,
unassuming], [+ good physical appearance], [+ sexually
typical appearance], [+ harmony of appearance],
[+ refined features], [+ serious, earnest].

We conclude that among the aesthetic properties
[+ consummate outer appearance] (= perfection) seems to
be extremely important for attributing B to G men - much
more important than for both F and E men -; but it is
next to unimportant for G women, - strikingly less important than for E and F women ; on the other hand other
aesthetic features like 'constitution' and 'harmony' range
higher for the G women than for G men. There are no
significant G male/female differences as regards psychosomatic properties; among physiological properties Germans
seem to be fairly harsh in assigning B to middle-aged
females who look their age (contrasting with E and
strikingly contrasting with F), but very lenient towards
middle-aged men who look their age; 'sex-typicity' ranges
fairly high with G women, fairly low with G men as a
determining factor for the assignment of B. Among the
psychological features 'warm-heartedness' is more important
for a G man who wants to be assigned B than for F men,
E men and F, E and G women.

III. CONCLUDING REMARK

Such or similar cross-language sociosemiotic
observations yield an encompassing background against
which an actual speech utterance can be put into relief;
in traditional terms of lexical field study one might
say these sociosemiotic observations provide an overall
onomasiological basis (with a corresponding extension
of the term 'onomasiological', however) for each specific
proper semasiological assessment. E.g. semantically very
much alike as elle est une femme tres élégante / il est
un homme tres élégant and she is a very elegant woman /
he is a very elegant man may be, a considerable difference
will become apparent on the ground of the different
sociosemiotic loads of the two utterances, as soon as one
is prepared to consider that overall + B is assigned to
females twice as generously in the French speech community
as compared to the English one, and that in particular
terms which denote B as primarily referring to clothing
(e.g. élégant / elegant) simultaneously evoke the
association of B as referring to one's physical

appearance, to the body, much more easily in French for a woman than for a male as well as considerably more easily than in English for both the male and the female. What I 'do', e.g. which criteria I (consciously or subconsciously) regard as being sociosemiotically relevant within my speech community, determines what I mean and what I say, e.g. when attributing a specific 'synonym' denoting B.

REFERENCES

a) Historical background

Brekle, H.E. (1963), 'Semantische Analyse von Wertadjektiven
    als Determinanten persönlicher Substantive in William
    Caxtons Prologen und Epilogen', dissertation,
    University of Tübingen.
Brekle, H.E. (1972), Semantik, München.
Ikegami, Y. (1970), The semiological structure of the
    English verbs of motion, Tokyo.
Jolles, A. (1934), 'Antike Bedeutungsfelder', PBB 58,
    pp. 97-109.
Kühlwein, W. (1967), Die Verwendung der Feindseligkeits-
    bezeichnungen in der altenglischen Dichtersprache,
    Neumünster.
Kühlwein, W. (1968), Modell einer operationellen
    lexikologischen Analyse : Altenglisch 'Blut', Heidelberg.
Leisi, E. (1961), Der Wortinhalt : Seine Struktur im
    Deutschen und Englischen, Heidelberg.
Lyons, J. (1963), Structural semantics: An analysis of
    part of the vocabulary of Plato, Oxford.
Gipper, H. (1963), Bausteine zur Sprachinhaltsforschung,
    Düsseldorf.
Kandler, G. (1959), 'Die "Lücke" im sprachlichen Weltbild.
    Zur Synthese von "Psychologismus" und "Soziologismus"',
    in H. Gipper (ed.), Festschrift für L.Weisgerber,
    Düsseldorf, 1959, pp. 256-270.
Oksaar, E. (1958), Semantische Studien im Sinnbereich der
    Schnelligkeit : Plötzlich, Schnell und ihre Synonymik
    im Deutsch der Gegenwart und des Früh-, Hoch- und
    Spätmittelalters, Stockholm.
Sapir, E. (1921), Language, New York
Trier, J. (1932), 'Sprachliche Felder', in Zeitschrift für dt.
    Bildung 8, pp.417-427.
Whorf, B.L. (1956), Language, thought and reality, ed.
    J. Carroll, New York.
Weisgerber, L. (1954), 'Die Sprachfelder in der geistigen
    Erschliessung der Welt', in B. von Wiese (ed.),
    Festschrift für J. Trier, Miesenheim, pp. 34-49.

b) Contemporary

Dirven, R. (1976), 'A redefinition of contrastive linguistics',
    IRAL 14, pp. 11-13.
Dirven, R., W. Hünig, W. Kühlwein, G. Radden, J. Strauss (1976),
    Die Leistung der Linguistik für den Englischunterricht,
    Tübingen.
Fries, R. (1982), Eine kontrastive Analyse von Schönheits-
    adjektiven im Deutschen und Englischen, Trier (mimeo).
Göhring, H. (1976), 'Interkulturelle Kommunikationsfähigkeit',
    in H. Weber (ed.), Landeskunde im Fremdsprachenunterricht :
    Kultur und Kommunikation als didaktisches Konzept,
    München, pp. 183-193.

Göhring, H. (1980), 'Deutsch als Fremdsprache und interkulturelle Kommunikation', in A. Wierlacher (ed.), Fremdsprache Deutsch 1, Heidelberg, pp. 70-90.
Halliday, M.A.K. (1978), Language as social semiotics, London.
Kühlwein, W.,G. Thome, W. Wilss, (eds.), (1981), Kontrastive Linguistik und Übersetzungswissenschaft: Akten des Internationalen Kolloquiums Trier/ Saarbrücken September 25-30, 1978, München.
Kühlwein, W. (1983), 'Pedagogical limitations of contrastive linguistics', in J. Fisiak (ed.), Contrastive linguistics: Prospects and problems, The Hague (in press).
Kühlwein, W. (1984), 'A sociosemiotic approach to contrastive lexicology: "BEAUTY" in English and French', in Proceedings of the XIIIth International Congress of Linguists, Tokyo (in press).
Nies, G. (1979), Onomasiologisch-semasiologische Analyse ausgewählter französischer und englischer Schönheitsadjektiva, 3 Bdd. Diss. Trier.
Spillner, B. (1978), 'Methoden der kontrastiven Linguistik in der Frankreichkunde', in H. Arndt, F.R. Weller (eds.), Landeskunde und Fremdsprachenunterricht, München.

TRANSLATION ACROSS LANGUAGES
OR ACROSS CULTURES?

Albrecht Neubert
Karl-Marx-Universität
Leipzig

It has become one of the commonplaces in the study of
translation that we do not translate words, but ideas. The
competent translator tries to recapture the content of the
source in a target version. Phrased in the context of the
symposium 'Language Across Cultures', the business of the
translator could be likened to a messenger who carries
'cultural goods' from one speech community to another. And
his great achievement appears to be his ability to make the
readers of his art forget that they speak a language
different from that of the writer whose ideas are presented
in words familiar to their way of thinking. Foreign or distant cultures have been transported into their homes. Germans
have come to experience Shakespeare in translations which are
closer to their language of today than Shakespeare's idiom is
to present-day speakers of English. The great authors of
antiquity, of Greek and Latin culture, ring true in the verna-
culars of contemporary nations. The Bible has been translated
into almost every language and is instrumental in the propagation of the Christian religion, although the new versions no
longer represent the 'original word'. The works of the founders
of revolutionary movements of today, notably Marx, Engels and
Lenin, have been rendered into more than a hundred languages
and serve as up-to-date guidelines for the building of a new
political and social world.

The history of translation and in particular the pheno-
menal exchange of information brought about by the media bear
witness to the general feeling of an unlimited receptiveness
of one's mother tongue. As a result the language of origin
of a particular piece of information becomes more and more
irrelevant. The assimilation of the cultures of the world,
past and present, feeds the illusion that one language, of
course one's own, is perfectly sufficient to enable a person
to become acquainted with, be entertained by and, in fact,
feel at home in a multitude of cultures, close and distant.

Can we draw the conclusion, then, that languages do not
act as barriers between cultures, but that, on the contrary,
cultures can, so to say, step out of their respective
linguistic guises and take on any linguistic shape whatever
without giving up their intrinsic or indigenous quality? I
think such a conclusion, although it seems to be warrantable
for the masses of unilingual consumers of translations from
whatever culture, is quite unwarrantable if we take into
account the actual experience of the translator who grapples
with the only too well-known problems of dissociating the
semantic context of the source expressions from the linguistic

structure in order to carry them across into another cultural
and linguistic environment where the message to be conveyed
will by no means fit easily and smoothly into a new verbal
dress without evoking, at least for the knowing translator,
unwanted associations caused by the original linguo-semantic
ties of the source language. It was Jacob Grimm who found
for the translator's plight a most memorable analogy:

> Was übersetzen auf sich habe, lässt sich mit demselben
> Wort, dessen Akzent ich bloss zu ändern brauche, deutlich
> machen: übersetzen ist übersetzen, traducere navem. Wer nun
> zur Schiffahrt aufgelegt, ein Schiff bemannen und mit vollem
> Segel an das Gestade jenseits führen kann, muss dennoch
> landen, wo anderer Boden ist und andere Luft streicht.

An attempt to put Grimm's words into English is in
itself an illustration of our problem. Here is my version:

> The whole point about translation can be cleared up by
> a simple paraphrase: translate means put over, traducere
> navem. Whoever is about to set sail, to man a ship and
> to take her under full sail across to unknown shores
> should not be surprised to arrive in another land where
> another wind blows.

I think this is a very apt way of putting what constitutes
the issue of our symposium. The idea put forward by Jacob
Grimm becomes immediately clear. It remains transparent whatever words we use to express it. Thus the German distinction
which depends on the potential stress variations between underlying form and prefix such as übersetzen/übersetzen (cf. über-
rennen/überrennen, überlegen/überlegen etc. - a fairly systematic contrast!) can - quite easily - be reconstructed by an
analogous English contrast between (anglicized) loan and
phrasal loan translation. Thus semantic content is saved,
although with different linguistic form. The crucial point
raised here, raised by generations of translators, is the part
language, linguistic structures, play in the constitution of
messages. Or more specifically, does any single language
leave its unique imprint on the propositional content of a
piece of connected discourse? Even if it is true that we do
not translate words but ideas, is there such a thing as a
verbal shell around an idea, or are ideas perhaps intrin-
sically permeated by verbal arteries which pump the blood of
life into the flesh of thought?

I think there are at least 4 areas where the original to
be translated may be thought to be bound up within the framework of the source language and the communicative community.
These four areas act as constraints upon any translation into
another language and for another addressee.

First, and perhaps most importantly, languages represent historically grown systems of form/meaning relationships. The restricted repertoire of phonetic/phonological, grammatical and lexical components and distinctions is exploited in discreet rule-governed ways to express an unlimited meaning potential in unique language-specific ways.

Secondly, in the course of their historical and social development, communicative communities (my term for speech communities) have codified their experiences differently, stressing, in their communicative activities different aspects of reality as socially relevant. Although in principle unrestricted in their potential cognitive powers, communicative groups have always tended to single out certain semantic frames and their respective components as more important than others.

Thirdly, since people live under different geographical and climatic conditions they have come to take for granted that certain reflections of their natural environment should find their way into their natural manner of speaking. Their natural surroundings colour their linguistic expressions.

Fourthly, and perhaps most difficult to pin down, any linguistic utterance is part and parcel of a particular communicative situation determined by the particular needs and interests of the communicative partners. Languages have evolved in response to such types of communicative situations. In other words, speakers, writers, and readers alike have developed, and got used to linguistic conventions characterizing and characteristic of textual types in typical situations.

These four criteria, in short, the language system, the social history, the natural environment and the communicative situation, interact to produce, to repeat Grimm's metaphor, the impression of 'another land where another wind blows'.

It is, in fact, the cumulative effect of all four factors which is responsible for the translator's everlasting struggle to do his or her job to the satisfaction of the many unilingual recipients whose linguistic singlemindedness, as I said at the beginning of my talk, requires that they be left undisturbed by any 'translational noise' whatsoever. For the translator, however, the four factors, no doubt, restrict or condition translatability. Restricted or conditioned translatability, then, can be measured on a multidimensional scale with the four types of criteria as basic yardsticks. Some examples should make the point a bit clearer.

1. Examples of systemic contrasts are of course legion. The most striking of these are tense/aspect distinctions, e.g. English simple or progressive forms, Russian fully-fledged aspectual classifications, German tenses, to give only some more generally known problem areas. As soon as we leave the Indo-European languages we come across many more 'unexpected', 'unfamiliar' syntactic regularities. I am thinking e.g. in terms of the entirely aspectual verb classifications of American Indian languages such as Hopi studied by B.L. Whorf and his followers. Other examples are supplied by the incidence of grammatical 'gaps' in the target language. Or take the opposite case, when the target version cannot avoid grammatical distinctions non-existent in the source language. Closely connected with these grammatical (syntactic/morphological) 'imbalances' is the subtle interplay of grammatical and lexical representations, i.e. purely lexical substitutions of grammatical distinctions or the grammatical reconstruction of lexical expressions. The above example of übersetzen/ übersetzen rendered by translate/put over illustrates the substitution of morphological (derivational) by phrasal means. Other contrasts stem from differing pronominal systems which make it imperative that reference takes different routes from language to language. Imagine, for instance, the English rendering of the du/Sie relationship in German or rather the 'lexical substitution' of the 'sudden' change from polite/ formal Sie to familiar/intimate du in a German novel. The opposite direction is just as difficult, demanding the replacement of one pronoun by the other (Sie - du) in German, although there is no pronominal clue in the English you-only original.

2. Whereas systemic differences, however striking they may be, need not necessarily be imbued with cultural meanings in the substantial sense of the word, but act rather as formal markers of a particular 'linguistic culture', the second type of constraint is nearly always culturally meaningful, i.e. it represents an historical stage in the consciousness of the respective communicative community. It is mostly bound up with the 'lexicalization of reality' or rather the way speakers of a language have come to single out certain conceptualizations as worthy of deserving a particular 'name' which they store in their social memory beyond an ephemeral communicative situation. The vocabulary of politics is a case in point. The sociopolitical institutions in a country are couched in a historically developed terminology that differs significantly, even among states of similar or identical socio-economic structure. The vocabularies covering institutional terms in a socialist state differ markedly from the labels naming the 'corresponding' institutions in a capitalist country. Translations of texts dealing with economic, political and even cultural events between English and German prove immensely more difficult than translations of corresponding texts from, say, Russian into German or v.v. although in a systemic-'innerlinguistic'-comparison, English and German turn out to be much closer than Russian and German.

Let me give you one example of what I mean by linguistic channeling of social experience. In the Guardian Weekly (8-5-83) we read about American reactions to a particularly aggressive speech by President Reagan: 'Senator Paul Laxalt sounded a warning note about the President's approach. "I suppose", he commented, "one risk would be that the speech is so bellicose that it may make some of the undecided people say, Hey, this is going too far: don't Vietnam us"'. The Vietnam experience has affected the American mind so deeply that the concept of an undeclared war forced upon the nation has triggered off the use of the transitive verb 'to Vietnam' meaning to involve the country in another act of aggression against a small so-called 'communist-infiltrated' country which may be anywhere. Here it happens to be in Central America, more specifically El Salvador. Findlandization or Balkanization are earlier examples of this semantic process of singling out what happened to one region and making it stand for a more general process. In any event, historical or social experience of a particular kind leaves its imprint upon the language, thus constraining any attempt to translate the label into another language whose speakers have not had the same experience and who will find it difficult to 'have a word for it'. Reading the daily papers provides a mass of data illustrating the ongoing process of naming our experience, new facts, new ways of looking at them, new ways of looking at previous conceptualizations and so on, with either new linguistic labels or rather new shades of meaning attached to old words. This phenomenon is definitely 'culture bound', i.e. it takes different verbal routes in different linguistic cultures thus creating ever-new translational problems.

Take a recent headline 'Decision day on wash-up time strike' with an explanatory passage 'Failure to accept the management diktat of ending the "washing up time" involving working an increased half hour on the present 38½-hour week ...'. Here again quite an involved sequence and relationship of social data have been condensed into the noun phrase 'wash-up time strike' meaning a strike against the management's decision to deduct the time needed by the car workers to wash up after work from the paid working hours, thus forcing them to work longer hours than before. Incidentally, the use of the German work 'diktat' is another case in point with the spelling k as additional marker. Language, words in particular, crystallize multipartite experiential complexes into communicable lexical patterns. These relatively simple lexical items, which may consist of nominalized multiword-lexical units, do not only stand for larger frames but also evoke all the connotations linked to the larger, developed frame of experience.

Perhaps the most typical cases of those 'lexically frozen' chunks of experience are what are called realia, language-specific lexemes which reflect life and manners of the communicative community which has coined and developed them. They may refer to concrete items of the speakers' environment as well as to specific concepts, ways of looking at life, habits, norms and ideals etc. They may stand in the centre of a community's ideology or

rather at the fringe. The former are the keywords of a
culture. Raymond Williams once collected slightly more than
one hundred keywords which he called a vocabulary of culture
and society. For him those terms – among them alienation and
art, bourgeois and bureaucracy, capitalism and class, democracy
and dialectic, elite and equality, down to theory and
tradition, wealth, welfare and work – 'are significant, binding
words in certain activities and their interpretation; they are
significant indicative words in certain forms of thought.
Certain uses bound together certain ways of seeing culture and
society.' (Williams 1976, 13). These keywords represent 'a
crucial area of social and cultural discussion, which has been
inherited within precise historical and social conditions and
which has to be made at once conscious and critical – subject
to change as well as to continuity...' (Williams 1976, 21-22).

If these keywords occur in texts which have to be translated into very different cultures they tend to lose the
cultural and social aura. Within closer cultural circles
embraced by communicative communities which share significant
historical and social and thus cultural experiences, these
'alienating' effects should be much rarer. But there may be,
on the other hand, quite decisive contrasts within the speakers
of one single language if I think, for instance, of the
ideological differences between the speaker of German in the
GDR and the Federal Republic, although the same words may be
used. We have reached the extreme pole of the language-culture
dichotomy aptly conceptualized by the theory of the two cultures
within one nation or rather one speech community. It may
require 'translation' within the speakers of one language. In
fact, this 'translation' has always been with us if we think of
the reinterpretation of words whose meanings have changed considerably over the centuries. Think only of the meaning Queen
Victoria associated with the word democracy. When she had
heard about her son's, the Prince of Wales's, escapades with Lady
Mordaunt, she wrote to the Lord Chancellor, Lord Hatherlay, in
1870 saying 'the fact of the Prince of Wales's intimate acquaintance with a young married woman being publicly proclaimed, will
show an amount of imprudence which cannot but damage him in the
eyes of the middle and lower classes, which is deeply to be
lamented in these days when the higher classes, in their frivo-
lous, selfish and pleasure-seeking lives, do more to increase
the spirit of democracy than anything else.' (Royal Archives
Z 449/80, quoted by Sir Philip Magnus, King Edward the Seventh,
1964). Her use of democracy is reminiscent of Burke's usage
almost a century earlier. The connotation was definitely
negative. When it comes to the translation of lexical terms
which deviate from the modern norm in the source language the
translator is no more at a loss than a present-day reader of
the original.

In my treatment of the uniqueness of semantic configu-
rations within a particular language I have so far said very
little about the multitude of socially and culturally conditioned events, states and objects which are typical of the
communicative activity of the users of a language. In fact,
social life is inextricably bound up with linguistic labels.

British higher education cannot be understood without knowing about UCCA, GCE, JMB, LEA, UGC, etc. More concretely, from the Chancellor to the Student Union, the admissions tutor to the careers service, honours to ordinary degree, everything in a British university has a specific name linked to a hierarchy of domains. Other countries have organized their higher education differently and - this is my point - have not only given it target language names, as is natural, but also target-culturally shaded meanings with a contrasting hierarchy of relationships among them.

3. In addition to this social systematicity characterizing the semantics of our conceptualization of social reality there is a further area or rather group of areas where language takes on a shape which makes it unique. Imagine the translation of Shakespeare's sonnet VIII 'Shall I compare thee to a summer's day?' into a language whose speakers think summer the most unbearable season of the year. Or translate Goethe's poem 'Über allen Gipfeln ist Ruh; In allen Wipfeln spürest du kaum einen Hauch' - for readers who have never seen a forest, let alone magnificent pine trees towering and unmoved by the hustle of hectic life - Goethe's poem is a cry for rest and relaxation. He was a very busy minister in Weimar. Or Goethe's poem 'Dem Schnee, dem Regen, Dem Wind entgegen, Im Dampf der Klüfte Durch Nebeldüfte ... Wie soll ich fliehen? Wälderwärts ziehen.', will embarass the translator into a language system in the desert where the words for snow or a densely wooded gorge steaming with fog, typical of the Thuringian pine forests, are just not available. The lack of expressions for non-existent things and, for that matter, states and processes of another natural environment is, of course, compensated for, if I may say so, by a wealth of words representing the respective geographical and climatic milieu of the target language culture. The enormous variety of words and their shades or nuances of meaning for snow in the Eskimo-Aleut or the multitude of names for palm trees in African languages, on the other hand, are well-known examples for the 'embarras de richesses' of a translator into European languages. Along with the distinctly local colours these terms convey there are also close links between words for natural objects and their figurative senses. Take for instance the imagery of English sea and sailing terms.

In actual fact, the essence as well as the examples given in this third section of constraints upon translation tie in with what I called contrasting semantic codifications of reality under my heading number 2. In both cases, the speakers of the source language - in contrast to those of the target language - have developed either historical, social 'preferences' or 'habitual ways of speaking' which have become profoundly characteristic of their stock of words as a whole.

4. The fourth aspect of translational inadequacy is of quite a different nature. It is a feature of what I could call a different 'speech culture'. The term is vague enough to include the culturally conditioned occasions for communicative behaviour. Let me give a very simple explanatory example by referring to my present activity, i.e. the reading of a paper. In German I would use the pronoun _wir_ ('we') whereas in English I have made a point of using _I_. Thus there is a contrasting textual convention - and not only one - governing the writing up and reading of a scholarly paper. Similar occasions result in different textual arrangements making even quite related languages differ markedly in their stylistic surface structures. Sometimes the variations are very subtle, almost unnoticeable to the careless observer. Take the use of the imperative in English in all kinds of directions, i.e. in so-called directive texts, from the Highway Code to the instruction manual, and listen to the infinitives in, shall I say, equivalent German texts. Then again the textual 'deviations' may be quite striking in official, business and scientific writing. But also everyday conversations may turn out to be worlds apart from language to language. Even what is called phatic communion, the small talk serving no other means than keeping contact, is largely determined by unwritten conventions of source and target languages. A learner of a foreign language is very often awkwardly aware of his isolated position among native speakers who engage in a seemingly meaningless exchange of what are, however, socially very meangingful linguistic signals. I would go so far as to say that even the repair mechanism of an error in speaking occurs in language-specific correction rules. So even making a mistake betrays the native speaker as native speaker. In other words non-native speakers make other, 'funny' mistakes.

The constraints lumped together under this heading of textual specificity as a result of unique communicative situations are in fact, a follow-up to the systemic contrasts of below-sentence level. They refer to the 'grammar of the paragraph' or perhaps the textuality of a whole piece of discourse. It is true they are much more difficult to categorize. They are also not outright mistakes from the point of view of the native speaker who may be puzzled or somehow intrigued by the wording or a translation that is not really incorrect, but he or she just would not express it in this way. The reason why textual constraints upon a translation are almost never fully taken into account by the translator is that there are no hard and fast rules he can follow, the range of variations, rare, possible, frequent, preferable, adequate, optimal, ideal - note the scale - being very often so broad that the choice is left to his or her discretion when no exhaustive analysis of contrastive source and target language textual type, i.e. no contrastive textology, is yet available.

In the light of what the four constraints on translation so far discussed suggest about the links between structures, meanings and texts on the one hand and the 'neutral' propositional content of the messages to be conveyed on the other hand, I should like to make a few remarks in conclusion. I am now in a somewhat better position to compare the two seemingly conflicting points of view. (1) Translations make us forget cultural distinctions; (2) languages are rooted in their speakers' cultures and form in fact unsurmountable barriers for translation. I think the two views are but half-truths. Translations rather demonstrate that languages are neither neutral carriers of information nor unique views of the world. Translators are neither mere mouthpieces, mechanical information processors nor traitors, neutralizers of cultural values. Translation is rather a highly typical though unique example of the subtle and continually vacillating dialectic between cultural specificity and human universality. Languages are both dividing lines and bridges between cultures. It is, in fact, the translator's brave attempt not to disregard the above-mentioned four constraints but to take them fully into account that ensures not always, it is true, but in his best products a highly satisfying approximation to an equivalent exchange of what users of different languages have experienced in their respective cultural environments, their individual and social histories, their particular times and places, and last but not least, within the framework of their specific interests and value systems. The last point is, I think, decisive. Translations never occur in a social vacuum as a translation exercise in class tends to make us believe. In other words, we never translate languages as such. They are untranslatable. We also do not translate cultures, they are as such unique systems. What we do translate is a linguistic product of a culture, a text, for which - and this is most important - there is a more or less pressing need among members of the target culture. It is this means/end relationship which makes translation not only possible but highly rewarding. Translations, then, are quite natural extensions of source texts under the linguistic, semantic, social, historic, geographical, and textual constraints of a target audience. It is this extension, the new dimension of the source text under the 'sun of the target culture', that makes translations unique means of communication among different cultures. Translations under pressure to fill a particular need develop unforeseen means. They always enrich and at the same time distinguish cultures. They represent unity in diversity.

Olga Mišeska Tomić
University 'Kiril i Metodij'
Skopje

Throughout the life of language grammatical notions and
their formal exponents have been changing. The changes
have usually been common for a given language family, though
with variations in scope and strength. In areas of intensive interlanguage contacts, however, linguistic features
have frequently crossed cultural boundaries, so that
grammatical properties which a given language shares with
its respective genetic relatives have been relaxed and
shifted more often than elsewhere, while 'alien' properties
have been acquired. We shall be specifically concerned
with the intercultural influences upon the grammatical
categories operating in the verbs of the languages of
Europe. The term 'grammatical category' here refers to those
formal properties of linguistic units which are morphophono-
logically expressed.

The central reference point in the verbal systems of
the Indo-European languages is the fundamental point in
every speech situation - the moment of speaking. The forms
referring to the future are originally present forms that
do not denote actions but obligations, desires or intentions
of actions which suggest that the actions themselves will
take place after the moment of speaking, i.e. in the future.
The past tense, in its turn, is perpetually nourished by
forms which originally had denoted a present state
resulting from a previous action.

Through internal reconstruction one is led to deduce
that Proto-Indo-European had only two sets of verbal forms:
Present and Aorist. Very likely, the original distinction
between them had been a distinction of aspect, similar
to the one now obtaining in a number of West African
languages. Time reference has actually developed as a
consequence of aspectual distinctions. At an inter-stage,
the same set of forms had probably incorporated both Past
Tense and Perfective Aspect functions, as do the forms in
present-day written Arabic, referred to by Comrie (Comrie
1976). When the Imperfect came into existence (in most
but not all Indo-European languages - the Germanic languages
lack it, for example), the Aorist got established as a Past
Definite Tense, aspectually distinguished from the Imperfect,
which referred to a past action lasting over a period of
time.

Subsequently, the European verbal system was enriched
with another set of forms - those of the Perfect.
(According to Kurylowicz, 1971) the Perfect has been going
through four stages of development: (1) present state
(result of previous action), (2) action previous to the
moment of speaking (with present result), (3) past action
referred to the moment of speaking (anteriority), (4) past
action. Most Indo-European languages have gone through
stages 1 to 3 but not all of them have reached stage 4.
Whether and to what an extent a language reaches this
stage depends, however, not only on the relative closeness of genetic relations but also on cross-cultural
contacts with genetically more remote or totally alien
languages.

In most of the Romance languages, at least in their
colloquial registers, the Perfect has reached stage 4.
Thus, whereas written French maintains the difference
between the Past Definite, the Indo-European Aorist
(e.g. Jean lut le livre, 'John read the book') and the
Past Composite, the Indo-European Perfect (e.g. Jean a
lu le livre, 'John has read the book'), in the spoken
language the former does not appear, the Perfect forms
having lost their aspectual meaning of present relevance of a past situation and assuming the function of
the Indo-European Aorist. In Spanish and Portuguese,
however, the distinction Aorist:Perfect has persisted
in the colloquial language, as well. And these are
the Romance languages which, more than the other
languages of that family, have been in contact with
genetically unrelated languages in which aspectual distinctions are prominent (Basque and Arabic).

In German, the Preterite - a simple past tense in
which the functions of the Slavonic and Romance Aorist
and Imperfect are combined - is gradually becoming
obsolete; in the South German and Swiss German dialects
it has been completely lost and replaced by the Perfect,
which, in its turn, has lost its aspectual features.
But in English - a Germanic language extensively exposed
to alien influences - the Perfect has become firmly
established as an aspectual category whose exponents combine with exponents of other verbal categories (tense
being only one of them) to produce a well-balanced,
symmetric system.

The origin of the English Perfect is to be found in
the changes of the word order of the so-called causative
constructions (such as She has the dress made.). When
word order became fixed, former communicative variants
acquired differential semantic values. So, while in
She has the dress made, has is a full verb and made
reflects a state resulting from a previous action, in
its word order variant She has made the dress, has is
an auxiliary and made refers to the previous action
inherent in the result. Subsequently, the have + past

participle construction became grammaticalized and began
to be used not only where change of previous state was
assumed but also where the action had no pre-existing
object. Thus, alongside <u>She has made the dress</u> we have
<u>She has suffered great pain.</u>[1]

At the early stages of its existence, the English
Perfect followed the pattern of the present day German
or French perfects - it was formed with the forms of
either <u>have</u> or <u>be</u>, depending chiefly upon the transitive or intransitive character of the respective verb.[2]
Subsequently, <u>have</u> came to be the only auxiliary and
the English Perfect became a completely developed
aspectual category, which spread over the whole English
verb system with remarkable regularity. This development - unique in the Germanic languages - was most
probably influenced by the cross-cultural contacts of
English with the Celtic languages, which embody pronounced aspectual distinctions.

In Irish, Scots Gaelic and Welsh these distinctions
are not completely grammaticalized. Perfective Aspect
is there marked through periphrastic expressions
containing temporal prepositions just as Progressive
Aspect is signalled by periphrastic expressions including
locative prepositions. Thus, the Welsh equivalent of the
English sentence <u>I have written a letter</u>, <u>Yr ydwin i wedi
ysgrifenn'r llythyr</u>, literally means 'am I after writing
the letter', while the word for word reading of the Irish
equivalent of <u>He is coming</u>, <u>Tá sé ag teacht</u>, is 'is he at
coming'. The only pure grammatical aspectual signal in
Celtic is the North Welsh Imperfect denoting Habitual
Aspect. Nevertheless, the notional meanings of the aspectual categories in Irish, Scots Gaelic and Welsh are
very distinct and the oppositions with non-aspectual
constructions are regular enough to have helped the
English Perfect get established as a fully fledged
aspectual category, denoting relevance of a preceding
action at a given point of time, and to sponsor the
development of the category of Progressive Aspect,
reflecting the lasting of an action over a time span[3]
as well as that of Habitual Aspect, signalling the
usual occurrence of a past action.

Let us now turn to the Slavonic languages, in some
of which (but definitely not in all) the Perfect has
gone through all Kurylowicz's stages of development and
beyond. So, in Russian, a Slavonic language which has
been developing relatively independently of alien
influences, the Aorist has completely vanished and past

actions are denoted by remnants of the Perfect signals –
the active participle constituents of the former auxiliary
byt, 'be', + active participle constructions, which have
lost their aspectual values. (E.g. Petja napisal pis'mo,
'Petja wrote a/the letter', literally 'Petja written a/the
letter'.) In this language the Imperfect has also
disappeared but the contrast between the former Aorist
and Imperfect is expressed by the presence or absence of
the affixal markers of the Durative Aspect, the aspectual
category par excellence, so characteristic of all modern
Slavonic languages. Thus, while Petja napisal pis'mo means
'Petja wrote a/the letter', Petja pisal pis'mo reads
'Petja was writing a/the letter'.

The West Slavonic languages, whose contacts with 'aliens'
have been moderate, have also lost their respective Aorists
and Imperfects and use the former Perfect forms to refer to
past actions (not without the auxiliary, though, except in
the third person). In the Slavonic languages which take
part in the Balkan Sprachbund, however, the Aorist and
Imperfect are still living; not equally well in all of
them, it must be admitted.

Though all grammars of Serbo-Croatian list the complete paradigms of the Aorist and the Imperfect, not all
speakers of Serbo-Croatian use them. In fact, usage of
these 'past tenses' is restricted to specific dialectal
areas. Most educated speakers born since the Second
World War would be able to tell you what videh ('see',
Aor.) and vidjah ('see' Imp.) are. (They learnt it at
school!). Nevertheless, not only in their conversations
but also in their writing, they would use video sam
('saw' Non-durative Perfect) and vidjao sam ('see'
Durative Perfect). The Perfect is very rapidly becoming
the only past tense, the past tense, which assimilates
the markers of the former Aorist/Imperfect distinction
and transforms them into markers of Durative Aspect.

In Bulgarian, at least for the time being, no bell
has finally tolled for either the Aorist or the Imperfect;
they are still there. Yet, because of the interplay with
the abundance of affixes marking the Durative Aspect,
their functions get twisted. Both the Aorist and the
Imperfect, as well as the Perfect, can combine with both
Durative and Non-durative Aspect markers, yielding
Durative or Non-durative Aorist, Durative or Non-durative
Imperfect and Durative or Non-durative Perfect. (The verb
hodi, 'go', has the following past forms, for example:
hodi (Durative Aorist), nahodi se (Non-durative (refl.)
Aorist), hodeše (Durative Imperfect), hodil səm (Durative
Perfect), nahodil səm se (Non-durative (refl.) Perfect).
The exponents of the Perfect – various forms of the verb

səm, 'be', + active participle - have acquired the function of denoting unwitnessed actions or states, developed under the influence of Turkish.

While as an exponent of the 'classical' Perfect səm + active participle functions only in reference to past events, as an exponent of unwitnessed actions or states it refers to present, future and conditional events as well. This differentiation of usage and a slight formal variation consisting in the absence of the auxiliary in the third person singular and plural in the case of unwitnessed action or state as opposed to its presence otherwise, have led many grammarians to set up two parallel paradigms of 'past definite' and 'past unwit- nessed', 'tenses', respectively, which differ only in the presence or absence of the auxiliary in only one person. The justification for this analysis does not hold, however. The omission of the auxiliary is a regular feature of the verbal expressions with double time reference in the Balkan Slavonic languages in general. The extension of usage, in its turn, has come about with the extension of the functional load of the given formal markers. The Bulgarian Perfect has simply undergone a major shift of scope of re- ference and thus has become a paradigm in relation to which the paradigm of the Aorist, with its restricted function of denoting an action or state that takes place at a certain past point of time, is marked.

In Macedonian the Imperfect has become the past tense par excellence. The Aorist appears only in certain set expressions, while the exponents of the Perfect - various forms of the verb sum, 'be', + active participles - are gradually being transformed into exponents of the category of Modality, which combine with the exponents of all other verbal categories without restrictions. Thus, under the influence of Turkish, the Perfect has turned off the path it has been following in the other Slavonic languages. Instead of developing into a past tense, it has provided formal devices for expressing a modal category. The category of Perfective Aspect is not lost, however. Under the influence of the Perfect in Albanian, Aromanian and Greek, the Macedonian Perfect is being reactivated through new exponents - forms of the verb ima, 'have' + dever- bative adverbs and forms of the verb sum, 'be' + passive participles. The distribution of these exponents is not even. Ima + deverbative adverbs universally represent the Perfect of Experience, which denotes that the given event happened at least once up to the moment to which it refers (e.g. (a) Vakva riba nemam jadeno dosega, 'Such a fish I haven't eaten until now', (b) Vo ovaa kuḱa imam dojdeno poveḱe pati, 'In this house I have been more than once'); with transitive verbs it also denotes the perfect of result, which indicates that the given state is a result of a previous event (e.g. <u>Knigata veḱe ja imam pročitano</u>, 'The book, I have read it already'). <u>Sum</u> + passive participle has a much more restricted usage - it signals the Perfect of Result with intransitive verbs (e.g. <u>Jadena sum</u>, 'I have eaten', literally 'Am (f.) eaten').

Several things should be remarked in connection with the new Macedonian Perfect. First of all, the Perfect of Result (formed with the passive participle, without an auxiliary) exists in the East and West Slavonic languages, as well; though only with transitive verbs. (E.g. Rus. <u>Dom postrojen</u> means 'The house has been built' and not 'The house was built', which is the equivalent of an auxiliary + past participle construction - <u>Dom byl postrojen</u>). Thus, <u>Jadena sum</u> and similar constructions are a Slavonic development which in Macedonian, under the influence of contacts with Albanian, Aromanian and Greek, has become part of a well-developed system.

Second, the Perfect of Experience, with the equivalent of <u>have</u> + passive participle as exponents, has made an effort to get into the verbal system of another Slavonic language - that of Czech. Nevertheless, there it has not gone further than stage 2 of Kurylowicz's four stages; sentences like <u>Ja mám úkol udelan</u>, 'I have the task done', denote actions previous to the moment of speaking with present result. Obviously, the aspectual value of the German Perfect, under the influence of which the new Czech Perfect has tried to develop, had weakened before the latter got established, and further advancement had been hampered. This was not the case with the new Perfect in Macedonian, since the aspectual values of the Albanian, Aromanian and Greek Perfects are still strong.

Third, when translating the new Macedonian Perfect into Turkish, in which the function of the Perfect has never been grammaticalized, bilingual speakers (Turks living in Macedonia) use signals of unwitnessed modality. There are no indications that the function of these signals will be extended, yet one cannot but compare that usage with the way unwitnessed modality was introduced in Macedonian - through the signals of the old Perfect. This suggests that there is some affinity between the function of unwitnessed modality and that of perfective aspect.

Fourth and last (but not least!), the new Perfect has not spread throughout the territory of the Macedonian language community. The contacts with Turkish had been even and the need to grammaticalize unwitnessed modality is felt in all Macedonian dialects and registers. The contacts with Albanian, Aromanian and Greek, for their part, have been perspicuous only in the Western and Southern parts of the territory; so the new Perfect got established as a category only in the Western and Southern dialects and in the standardized language of educated speakers who come from the West or the South. A considerable portion of Macedonian speakers use the old Perfect to express both perfective and unwitnessed actions. Thus, in Macedonian we have an intersection of two verbal systems. One of them has two past tenses: a Simple Past Tense (the former Imperfect) and a Composite Past Tense (the former Perfect, which, in addition to its traditional functions, signals unwitnessed actions). The other system has only one past tense, whose exponents are in interaction with distinct exponents of more than one aspectual and modal category. Thus, in the sentence Do sega ḱe te imal naučeno da plivaš, 'He says he would have taught you to swim by now', ḱe is a modal particle most often used to express futurity, ima + -eno denotes the Resultative Perfect, -l - Unwitnessed Modality (in the third person without the auxiliary sum), while the prefix na- signals Non-durative Aspect. The exponents of individual categories have well defined, fixed places in the verbal expression, very much like the signals in English.

In areas of close cross-cultural contacts the development of the grammatical categories of a language often diverges from the general trend taken by the grammatical categories of the language family to which it belongs. Thus, the Indo-European Perfect has been moving in the general direction of the Aorist. In the language communities which have been developing relatively independent of alien influences it has ousted the latter and has become the past tense par exellence. In the language communities whose boundaries intersect with those of alien language communities, however, this has not been the case. So, the Indo-European Perfect has been gradually becoming the only past tense of the respective verbal systems. Nevertheless, in the insular and peninsular Western and Southern fringes of Europe, where inter-cultutal contacts are intensive, it has become the marker of an aspectual category denoting relevance of an anterior action in a given moment, which combines with quite a number of signals of other categories (tense being only one of them) to yield a rather analytic verbal system.

Intensive cross-cultural contacts can lead a language towards the grammaticalization of conceptual categories which are not grammaticalized in the languages with which it is genetically bound. The character of the grammatica-lization depends not only on the specificities of the source and target languages, but also on the contacts of the target language with other languages. The Turkish category of Unwitnessed Modality has influenced the verbal systems of both Bulgarian and Macedonian. But whereas in Bulgarian it has led to the extension of the scope of an existing paradigm (that of the Perfect), in Macedonian, because of

the parallel formation of a new Perfect (under the
influence of Greek, Albanian and Aromanian), the old
Perfect paradigm is gradually becoming free to act
exclusively as an agent of the newly acquired category of Unwitnessed Modality.

As the cross-cultural intersections do not spread
uniformly over a given language area, there are variations
in the grammaticalization of given conceptual categories
that create subsystems within a given language system.
These are most often related to individual dialects.
Nevertheless, in languages with recent or flexible standardization, like Macedonian, the dialectal grammatical
subsystems sponsor or set off the use of individual
standardized structures and tend to form subsystems
within the standard language itself. This tendency indicates that it might be necessary to reexamine our
present conceptions of standard language, dialect and
register.

NOTES

1. Note that She has suffered great pain has no
   'causative' counterpart.

2. Expressions like He is come and He is gone are
   residuals from those stages.

3. Initially, the English Progressive also included
   a locative proposition. Consider the somewhat
   obsolete He is a-coming.

REFERENCES

Andrejčin, L. (1938), Kategorie znaczeniowe koniugacji bulgarskej, Cracow: Polska Akademia Umiejtności.

Aronson, H.I. (1977), 'Interrrelationships between aspect and mood in Bulgarian', Folia Slavica 1, pp. 9-32.

Comrie, B. (1976), Aspect, Cambridge: Cambridge University Press.

Friedman, V.A. (1977), The Grammatical Categories of the Macedonian Indicative, Columbus: Slavica.

Friedman, V.A. (1978), 'On the semantic and morphological influence of Turkish on Balkan Slavic', Papers from the Fourteenth Regional Meeting, Chicago Linguistic Society, pp. 108-118.

Gola,b, Z. (1960), 'The influence of Turkish upon the Macedonian Slavonic dialects', Folia Orientalia, 1, pp. 26-45.

Greenberg, J. (1966), Language Universals, Janua Linguarum, Series Minor, The Hague: Mouton.

Grickat, I. (1954), O perfektu bez pomoćnog glagola u srpsko-hr-vatskom jeziku i srodnim sintaktičkim pojavama, Beograd: Srpska akademija nauka.

Jakobson, R. (1932), 'Zur Struktur des russichen Verbums', Charisteria G. Mathesio, Prague: Cercle Linguistique de Prague, pp. 74-84.

Jespersen, O. (1924), The Philosophy of Grammar, London: George Allen and Unwin.

Klein, H.G. (1974), Tempus, Aspekt, Aktionsart, Tübingen: Niemeyer.

Koneski, B. (1967), Gramatika na makedonskiot literaturen jazik, Skopje: Kultura.

Kurylowicz, J. (1964), The Inflectional Categories of Indo-European, Heidelberg: Carl Winter.

Kurylowicz, J. (1971), 'The evolution of grammatical categories', Esquisses Linguistiques 2, München: Wilhelm Fink, pp. 38-54.

Lyons, J. (1968), Introduction to Theoretical Linguistics, Cambridge: Cambridge University Press.

Lyons, J. (1977), Semantics, Cambridge: Cambridge University Press

Panevová, J. (1980), Formy a funkce ve stavbě české věty, Praha: Akademia.

Panevová, J., E. Benešová and P. Sgall, (1971), Čas a modalita v češčině, Praha: Universita Karlová.

Palmer, F.R. (1965), A Linguistic Study of the English Verb, London: Longman.

Quirk, R., S. Greenbaum, G. Leech, J. Svartvik (1972), A Grammar of Contemporary English, London: Longman.

Tomić, O.M. (1982), 'Linguistic features and grammatical categories' Folia Linguistica (to appear).

ON TAKING LANGUAGE TESTS: WHAT THE STUDENTS REPORT[1]

Andrew Cohen
Hebrew University of Jerusalem

There is a small but growing literature on how students go through the process of taking language tests - i.e., the steps that they take to arrive at answers to questions. Such research has generally focused on the testing of native language skills, and it has come to encompass second-language testing as well. The purpose of such research has been to explore the closeness of fit between the tester's presumptions about what is being tested and the actual processes that the test taker goes through. The findings have been revealing, both for what has been learned about weaknesses in tests and for what has been learned about successful and unsuccessful test-taking strategies.

Regarding weaknesses in tests, for example, it has been found - through looking closely at the performance of native 3rd grade test takers - that the test passages such students are requested to read may be seriously flawed (Fillmore 1981). Such passages have been referred to as 'a new genre for English written language' - with unnatural requirements of lexical choice, grammatical structuring, and syntactic alterations to test particular vocabulary items. Regarding the strategies of test takers, it has been found that poor native and non-native readers contort test material in both a semantically unnatural and a grammatically awkward way to fit their schemata or cultural background knowledge (Fillmore and Kay 1980, Laufer and Sim 1982). Research has also revealed 'mainline' vs. 'fragmented' reading of test questions. Whereas in mainline reading, the respondent quickly gets the main idea and uses this as a point of departure, in fragmented reading, the reader refers primarily to words in the immediate vicinity of the question or to some very strong concept in the text (Dollerup et al. 1981). Likewise, poor performers on cloze tests have been found to be those who among other things do not use 'forward reading' (i.e., utilizing the context following the blank) to find clues for supplying the missing word (Homburg and Spaan 1981).

Furthermore, respondents have been found to do surface matching between information in the text, in the item stems and in the multiple-choice alternatives - without processing any of these stimuli for meaning. Respondents have also been found to perform

tasks by analogy to previous tasks without noticing
what may be slight changes in the response procedures
(Fillmore and Kay 1980, Hosenfeld 1976, Cohen and
Aphek 1979).

The outcome of these various strategies may be that
respondents get items wrong for the right reasons or
right for the wrong reasons. In other words, a good
student may produce a wrong answer as a result of an
adventurous inference, while a weak student may choose
the appropriate alternative despite faulty reasoning
(Mehan 1974, MacKay 1974, Dollerup et al. 1981). Thus,
due to flaws in the test or due to certain test taking
strategies, students may not be displaying a representative performance of their language competence.

The principal purpose of this paper is to discuss
methods for obtaining verbal report data on second-
language test-taking strategies, to report on some
of the types of findings obtained, and to look at the
implications of the findings for prospective test
takers and test constructors. The findings will be
drawn from a series of unpublished studies conducted
by university students - studies dealing with how
language learners take reading tests, especially of
the cloze and multiple-choice varieties.

METHODS FOR OBTAINING VERBAL DATA

We will first describe some of the types of verbal
data that can be collected, and then will describe some
ways that these data can be collected.

Types of Verbal Data

There are at least two types of verbal data available
- those regarding the process of responding and those
regarding reactions to items and subtests.

The Process of Responding   First, there are data
concerned with the process of responding to test
items and procedures - i.e., how the respondents went
about it. For example, did they read the instructions
and pay attention to special procedures associated
with the given testing format? For example, if they
were requested to first read a passage (with or without
deletions) from beginning to end, did they do it or did
they read only parts of it and/or jump around?
Similarly, if respondents were requested to read all
multiple-choice alternatives before answering a given
item, did they, in fact, do this?

In their effort to understand passages and items, did
the respondents translate as they read (either in
their heads or in writing)? How did they go about
answering questions? Did they do so systematically -
eliminating unreasonable choices? For example, did
they guess in a calculated way based on inferences or
did they guess impulsively? In filling in cloze items,
did they make use of the context preceding and following
each blank in choosing an appropriate word? If the
students were allowed to use a dictionary while completing the test, did they actually use it and if so,
how? Finally, did they copy from another respondent's
test paper?

Reactions to Items and Subtests   Respondents can report
on the ease or difficulty with which they read a given
passage, answered particular questions, or performed
certain tasks like taking a dictation, giving a
short speech, and the like. They can also report on
their attitudes toward a certain testing format, such
as the cloze test, or toward a certain type of item -
e.g., one that calls for inference as opposed to one
which is based on information readily available in the
text.

How the Verbal Data are Obtained

How the data are obtained is a major issue regarding all research in this area of verbal report. First, do we want to obtain 'think-aloud' data (simply letting the thoughts flow verbally without trying to control, direct, or observe them) or self-observational data (where there is limited or more extensive analysis of thoughts and abstraction about those thoughts)? Self-observational data constitute either introspection (if they relate to thoughts within 10-20 seconds), immediate retrospection (within minutes of the thoughts), or delayed retrospection (after an hour, a day, a week) (Cohen and Hosenfeld 1981). (Ericsson and Simon (1980) have a somewhat similar break-down between 'think-aloud' data and data reflecting what they call 'concurrent' and 'retrospective verbalizations'). Sometimes we want spontaneous, unanalyzed report, while other times we want the learners' reflective observations on what they did.

Secondly, do respondents write their replies or are they given orally - possibly to be audio- or video-taped? If respondents write down their thoughts, then some material is invariably lost in the writing process. They may not express in writing what they would have said. However, by having respondents write down their thoughts, it is possible to obtain data from large groups of respondents at the same time. Oral responses generally call for small-group or individual sessions, unless the respondents are seated, say, in booths in a language lab and asked to record their replies.

Thirdly, do we obtain the data while the test is actually going on or at some time after the testing session has ended? For example, it is possible to inter-sperse within a test questions that test language per-formance with questions that call for verbal report about the test itself. Such questions could appear at the end of each subtest. A problem in collecting data this way is the interventionist effect of the verbal report questions. Yet a problem in waiting until after the test is over to ask questions is that some of the most interesting data may no longer be recoverable in that the respondents may have forgotten the processes that they used and the reasoning behind what they did. It is also possible to have the test itself constitute a measure of test-taking strategies. For example, the successful completion of a test could indicate that a respondent was utilizing a given set of strategies.

A case in point would be giving respondents multiple-choice questions without giving them the passage upon which the questions are based (an approach to be reported on below). Then calculated guessing could be assessed.

SOME OF THE DATA OBTAINED

The following are illustrative of possible data that can be obtained using procedures such as those outlined above. The findings are all drawn from student course papers. Two of these studies looked specifically at strategies in taking cloze tests - one involving 25 Israeli 9th-grade EFL students taking a regular and a discourse cloze (Emanuel 1982), and another one involving 22 Israeli 12th-grade EFL students and four native English speakers taking a regular cloze (Hashkes and Koffman 1982). In these two studies, students were asked questions about how they took the cloze tests - immediately following the tests themselves. In another study, 45 Hebrew University EFL students were given a test comprising a reading passage with multiple-choice and open-ended questions, and a cloze test constructed from a summary of the passage (Roizen 1982). In this study, the students were asked to react in their native language to each subtest of the test as they completed it.

The final two studies investigated the taking of multiple-choice reading comprehension tests. In one of the studies, 40 ESL students at the University of California, Los Angeles, were asked to describe how they arrived at answers to a 10-item multiple-choice test based on a 400-word reading passage (Larson 1981). Seventeen signed up in groups of two or three to meet with the author of the test within 24 hours after the test. Twenty-three students met in groups of five or six led by an interviewer four days after taking the test. In the other study, 32 intermediate and 25 advanced Israeli EFL students were given a title and just the first paragraph of a passage appearing on the previous year's exemption examination, and then were asked to answer twelve questions dealing with the portion of text not provided. Two weeks later they were given the text in full along with the questions and once again were asked to respond (Israel 1982).

The Process of Responding

The Cloze   Although the instructions on the cloze
test request that the respondent read the entire
passage through before answering, only up to one-
quarter of the respondents in the cloze studies
indicated doing this (Emanuel 1982, Hashkes and
Koffman 1982).   The purpose of this request was to
have the students benefit as much as possible from
the surrounding context.   Moreover, as many as 16%
of the students indicated not using the context of
the preceding or following sentences to find clues
for filling in the blank at hand.   The bulk of the
students did this 'part of the time', and about a
third to a half as many did this 'all the time'.
When taking the discourse cloze, students reported
using context more than with the regular cloze - as
would be expected, since the discourse cloze involves
pronominal reference, lexical substitution, and the
like.   The majority (64%) of the respondents said
that they were most likely to look for a clue to the
answer in the same sentence containing the deletion
(Hashkes and Koffman 1982).

When students were asked what they did when they
did not know how to fill in a blank, poor students
indicated that they just left the space blank - that
they were reluctant to guess.   The better students
reported that they were more likely to guess.   Most of
these guesses (82%) were based on the immediate or
micro-context (Hashkes and Koffman 1982).   Another
strategy that respondents used was that of translation.
Twenty-seven percent reported translating parts of the
text as they went along, while 18% said they regularly
translated the immediate sentence of the blank.   The
researcher found that those who reported translating
while doing the cloze also got poorer scores (Hashkes
and Koffman 1982).

The investigators were also interested in whether
successful performance on the cloze indicated that the
student had understood the passage.   Accordingly,
students were requested to give a summary of the passage
in their native language.   There was found to be a low
correlation (r = .24) between these summaries and performance on the cloze (Hashkes and Koffman 1982).
This finding seems to be in keeping with some of the
recent literature (Alderson 1979, Klein-Braley 1981)
suggesting that the 'classical' cloze test is more of a
measure of word- and sentence-level reading ability
than of discourse-level reading, as was originally
claimed.

46

The Hashkes and Koffman study also investigated whether native students filled in blanks on the cloze test in a way different from non-natives. They found that the natives used the context as much as possible to find clues to missing words, more so than most of the non-natives. This often involved rereading the sentences several times. This strategy was used extensively by the one native who correctly supplied the _exact_ word for all 20 deletions.

Multiple-Choice Reading Comprehension Tests

Whereas the instructions asked students to read the passage before answering the questions, students reported either reading the questions first or reading just part of the article and then looking for the corresponding questions (Larson 1981, Roizen 1982). Respondents were also advised to read all the alternatives before choosing one as the correct answer. Larson's study found that students would stop reading the alternatives as soon as they found one that they decided was correct. Larson also found that students would use a strategy of matching material from the passage with material in the item stem and in the alternatives. They preferred this surface-structure reading of the test items to one that called for more in-depth reading and inferencing. It was found that this superficial matching would sometimes result in the right answer.

One example involved the following item from the Larson study:

5.   The fact that there is only one university in Filanthropia might be used to show why......

    a. education is compulsory through age 13.
    b. many people work in the fishing industry.
    c. 20% of the population is illiterate.
    d. the people are relatively happy and peaceful.

Students were able to identify (c) as the correct answer by noticing that this information appeared earlier in the _same_ sentence with the information which appeared in the _item_ stem:

...The investigating travel agency researchers discovered that the illiteracy rate of the people is 20%, which is perhaps reflective of the fact that there is only one university in Filanthropia, and that education is compulsory, or required only through age 10.

They assumed that this was the correct answer without understanding the item or the word 'illiterate'. They were right.

In another example, students did not have to look in the text for surface matches. They were able to match directly between the stem and the correct alternative:

2. The increased foreign awareness of Filanthropia has.......

   a. resulted in its relative poverty.
   b. led to a tourist bureau investigation.
   c. created the main population centers.
   d. caused its extreme isolation.

Students associated 'foreign' in the stem with tourist in option (b), without understanding the test item.

It was also found that more reasoned analysis of the alternatives - e.g., making calculated inferences about vocabulary items - would lead to incorrect answers. The following item provided an example of this:

4. The most highly developed industry in Filanthropia is......

   a. oil.
   b. fishing.
   c. timber
   d. none of the above.

This item referred to the following portion of the text:

...most (dollars) are earned in the fishing industry... In spite of the fact that there are resources other than fish, such as timber in the forests of the foothills, agriculture on the upland plateaus, and, of course, oil, these latter are highly underdeveloped.

One student read the stem phrase 'most highly developed industry' and reasoned that this meant technologically developed' and so referred to the 'oil industry'. He was relying on expectations based on general knowledge rather than on a careful reading of the text. The point is that his was a reasoned guess, not that of, say, surface matching, as in the previous example.

In another study, students reported being able to answer questions correctly on the basis of their prior knowledge of the topic and their general vocabulary knowledge (Roizen 1982). In fact, this is what the student in the above example about developed industries was trying to do. Moreover, in the study where the students were purposely not given the passage to work with (Israel 1982), the rate of success on the multiple-choice items was still surprisingly high - 49% for the

advanced group and 41% for the intermediates. These
results are far better than the 25% success rate that
would be expected on the basis of chance alone.[2]
When the students were given the test with the complete
passage and questions two weeks later, the advanced group
now scored 77% and the intermediates 62%. The score
necessary for exemption from further EFL study was 60%.
The fact that the average performance on the test was
low even when the passage was provided makes the
results without the passage that much more striking.

Other Processing Issues   Roizen (1982) found 17%
of her sample reported cheating. This was on a test
that was anonymous, not counting toward their grades.
Perhaps this is why cheating went on, or perhaps it
simply reflected that cheating was a regularly used
strategy for a small subsample of the group. On
another issue, since students were allowed to use
dictionaries on that same test, Roizen asked students
whether they actually used their dictionaries (Hebrew-
English) and if so, how often. She found that three-
quarters needed to refer to the dictionary to get
through the passage, about one-quarter looked up 10
words or more, and some looked up more than 20 words.
What might such extensive use of the dictionary suggest
about the respondent's test taking strategies? It is
likely that excessive use of the dictionary is a sub-
stitute for contextual guessing, and most likely an
unproductive strategy, when used extensively.

Reactions to Item Types   Sometimes respondents
were relatively uniform in their reactions to item
types. For example, they generally felt that it was
harder to answer multiple-choice items based on
reading passages than open-ended questions (Roizen 1982).
They also did not like items that involved inferencing
or in which the original text was disguised through
the use of paraphrase (Larson 1981). In other cases,
the students were more or less split in how they
reacted to items or subtests. For example, 60% of
the respondents in the Roizen study did not like the
cloze. They said that it made them nervous, that it
required too much patience and concentration, and that
it did not help them comprehend the text. The other
40% liked it because it required thinking and logic.
A recent study by Madsen (1982) also found that the
cloze was a high anxiety-producing test.

    Another interesting split in attitudes was over
items testing for anaphoric reference. Some respondents (55%) felt that these items helped with

their overall comprehension of the passage because the
items made them return to certain words and structures,
causing them to link sentences and ideas. Others (45%)
found that looking for specific points distracted them
from the larger context. They felt that they could
only understand such questions if they understood the
entire text, and that if they understood the entire
text, then such questions were a waste of time. They
felt that questions like, 'What does the "it" in line
7 refer to?' were only testing grammar, not reading
comprehension (Roizen 1982).

DISCUSSION

There are some basic problems with self-report
approaches to understanding the test-taking process. One
problem is that the most authentic data are obtained for
tests which really count. But on such tests respondents
may be unwilling to supply honest information out of the
fear that this information might adversely affect their
grade. And if the tests are not for credit (as in the
case of all but the Larson study above), then perhaps
we are not obtaining a true picture of how a student
takes a test when it does count (David Nevo, personal
communication). There is a further problem that some
of the information is already at a level of generalization
removed from the actual completion of the item or task.
In other words, if I really wanted accurate information on
how a student fills in blanks on a cloze test, I would need
the respondent to report on how each blank was filled in,
immediately after that blank was filled in. One way to
obtain some information on the answering of multiple-choice
items is to have the respondent indicate why alternative
responses were rejected. But this still would not
necessarily get at all the processes leading to the selection of a multiple-choice alternative.

Despite the reservations associated with this line of
investigation, there do appear to be some implications of
the work to date. One message to test takers would be to
read all instructions very carefully. The implicit
message here is that somehow by doing exactly what the
instructions call for, the respondents will do the best
job on the task at hand. Thus, the message is also directed
at the test constructors - namely, to make sure that the
instructions reflect the most efficient approach to taking
the particular test. For example, perhaps respondents should
be encouraged to read the multiple-choice questions before

reading a test passage. As a teaching strategy, we often ask questions before having students read a passage in order to motivate the students in their reading. Respondents could also be given several questions after a short portion of text as a way of dealing with this issue. With respect to the issue of students not reading all the alternatives, it would be possible to have the students indicate their rationale for rejecting the alternatives that they do not select (see Cohen 1980, pp. 24-26).

It would also appear that students need to be taught how to take a cloze test. A research study some years ago found that practice sessions in how to complete cloze tests did not produce significantly greater improvement among those receiving the sessions than among control-group students (Kirn 1972). Klein-Braley (personal communication) suggests that the lack of significant improvement was due to substantial differences in the behaviour of the individual cloze tests. She found that the reliability and validity of $\underline{n}$th deletion cloze tests vary greatly from one test to the next (Klein-Braley 1981). Assuming we obtained reliable and valid cloze tests, perhaps we could then train people to take such tests more successfully. For example, students could be offered techniques for how to read a passage that has a series of blanks in it. Special attention could be given to the use of preceding and following context - and not just within the sentence containing the deletion. Respondents could be shown how to guess contextually, using all the available clues. Perhaps such sessions could now be made effective enough to produce significant results.

In summary, then, this paper has demonstrated ways that we can obtain verbal report data on second-language test-taking strategies, and has illustrated some of the types of data obtainable. The main conclusion seems to be that there is value in striving for a closer fit between how test constructors intend for their tests to be taken and how respondents actually take them. This may involve changing the format of the test or training the respondents to deal with that format more effectively. An avenue for further research would be to explore the effects of training in taking different types of language tests.

NOTES

1.   Revised version of a paper presented at the Second
Meeting of the Israeli Academic Committee for Research
on Language Testing (ACROLT), Kiryat Anavim, January
4-5, 1983.   My thanks to David Nevo, Bernard Spolsky,
Chris Klein-Braley, and Joan Abarbanel for their comments
on the original version.

2.   A study conducted with 1,200 native elementary-school
readers of English found that the probability of correct
response on four-choice items from five standardized
tests without the passage ranged from .32 to .50 (Tuinman
1973-74).   Another study with 101 second-quarter college
freshmen and 17 English Department faculty members found
that freshmen got 52% correct and faculty 75% correct on
five-choice items from a scholastic aptitude test without
the passage (Fowler and Kroll 1978).   Thus, the results
for the non-natives are consistent with results for natives.

REFERENCES

Alderson, J. C. (1979), 'The cloze procedure and proficiency in English as a foreign language', TESOL Quarterly 13.2, pp. 219-227.

Cohen, A. D. (1980), Testing language ability in the classroom, Rowley, MA: Newbury House.

Cohen, A. D. and E. Aphek (1979), 'Easifying second language learning', a research report under the auspices of Brandeis University and submitted to the Jacob Hiatt Institute, Jerusalem, ERIC ED 163 753.

Cohen, A. D. and C. Hosenfeld (1981), 'Some uses of mentalistic data in second language research', Language Learning 31.2, pp. 285-313.

Dollerup, C., E. Glahn, and C. Rosenberg-Hansen (1981), 'Reading strategies and test-solving techniques in an EFL-reading comprehension test - A preliminary report', Copenhagen: Dept. of English, University of Copenhagen.

Emanuel, E. (1982), 'The use of the cloze technique - regular cloze and discourse cloze - in the teaching of Hebrew as a mother tongue', course paper, School of Education, Hebrew University of Jerusalem (in Hebrew).

Ericsson, K. A. and H. A. Simon (1980), 'Verbal reports as data', Psychological Review 87.3, pp. 215-251.

Fillmore, C. J. (1981), 'Ideal readers and real readers', in D. Tannen (ed.), Georgetown University round table on languages and linguistics 1981, Washington, D.C.: Georgetown University Press, pp. 248-270.

Fillmore, C. J. and P. Kay, (1980), 'Progress report: Text semantic analysis of reading comprehension tests', Berkeley: Dept. of Linguistics, University of California, Berkeley.

Fowler, B. and B. M. Kroll (1978), 'Verbal skills as factors in the passageless validation of reading comprehension tests', Perceptual and Motor Skills 47.1, pp. 335-338.

Hashkes, B. and N. Koffman (1982), 'Strategies used in a cloze test', course paper, School of Education, Hebrew University of Jerusalem.

Homburg, T. J. and M. C. Spaan (1981), 'ESL reading proficiency assessment: Testing strategies', in M. Hines and W. Rutherford (eds.), On TESOL '81, Washington, D.C.: TESOL, pp. 25-33.

Hosenfeld, C. (1976), 'Learning about learning: Discovering our students' strategies', Foreign Language Annals 9.2, pp. 117-129.

Israel, A. (1982), 'The effect of guessing in multiple-choice language tests', course paper, School of Education, Hebrew University of Jerusalem.

Kirn, H. E. (1972), 'The effect of practice on performance on dictations and cloze tests', M.A. Thesis, ESL Section, Department of English, University of California, Los Angeles.

Klein-Braley, C. (1981), 'Empirical investigations of cloze tests: An examination of the validity of cloze tests as tests of general language proficiency in English for German university students', unpublished doctoral dissertation, University of Duisburg.

Larson K. (1981), 'A study of student test-taking strategies and difficulties', course paper, ESL Section, Dept. of English, University of California, Los Angeles.

MacKay, R. (1974), 'Standardized tests: Objective/objectified measures of "competence"', in A. V. Cicourel et al. (eds.), Language use and school performance, New York: Academic Press, pp. 218-247.

Madsen, H. S. (1982), 'Determining the debilitative impact of test anxiety', Language Learning 32.1, pp. 133-143.

Mehan, H. (1974), 'Ethnomethodology and education', in D. O'Shea (ed.), The sociology of the school and schooling, Washington: NIE.

Roizen, M. A. (1982), 'The population explosion: Test taking strategies project', course paper, School of Education, Hebrew University of Jerusalem.

Tuinman, J. J. (1973-74), 'Determining the passage dependency of comprehension questions in five major tests', Reading Research Quarterly 9.2, pp. 206-223.

LANGUAGE AND CULTURAL IDENTITY:
THE CASES OF IRELAND AND ROMANIA

Martin J. Croghan
NIHE, Dublin

In this paper I want to look at the relationship between language and cultural identity, but in particular to examine how this relationship has operated in the context of both Ireland and Romania, countries which have had long histories of colonization. Each of the two countries has been independent for only about sixty years.

For the context of this discussion culture is regarded as the symbolic organization of space by a group. In another context I might use the famous Tylor (1874, 1:1) definition of culture as '...that complex whole which includes knowledge, belief, art, morals, law, custom, and any other capabilities and habits acquired by man as a member of society'. Or, for example, the Sapir definition (1970:218) of culture: 'what a society does and thinks'. Sapir wanted to deny any causal relationship between language and culture and the next sentence contains a definition of language: 'Language is a particular how of thought'. Sapir's definitions were obviously useful for this purpose in that particular section of this exposé but it must be borne in mind that Sapir a few pages before (215) said '...there must be some relationship between language and culture and between language and at least that intangible aspect of race that we call "temperament"'. Sapir was anxious to define culture and language in such a way as to deny a precise causal relationship between them.

Sapir's use of the term 'race' highlights one of the principal difficulties in talking about the relationship between language and culture and that is the lexicographical problem: we do not have the terms to refer to the phenomena found in different circumstances in different parts of the contemporary world. The terms we do possess - race, nation, tribe, ethnic group, caste, clan, people - often create new problems rather than throw any light on the phenomena. These terms were used as an intellectual framework in an age that was both racist and imperialist, when anthropologists were almost exclusively representative of the 'Great Powers' and the study of 'culture' was often the study of 'exotic primitives'. Generalizations were made which were not valid but there were no 'primitive' intellectuals in academia who could explain the sensitivities and sensibilities of their own group. In the context of the present paper which deals

in part with Ireland an extract from Sapir, which appears
only a few pages away from the extracts above (209-210),
illustrates the point: 'If by "English" we mean also
Scotch and Irish...'. In my definition of culture
as the organization of space, the organization is by
the group and so the group's sensitivities and sensibilities are an important part of this organization.
But just as dictionaries are a cultural manifestation of
a prestige social class as shown in the last century by
Lafargue's seminal study (Gambier and Mercellesi 1979)
of French, then also the terms existing in English,
French and German are terms primarily suited to intellectual
representatives of 'Great Power' nations.

    This sensitivity of the group itself is especially
important because frequently it is these very sensitivities
which are not known to outsiders or are ignored or held
up to ridicule. Jessel's book on The ethnic process
(1978) illustrates how sensitive the discussion of
ethnicity can become, for example, when the book is written
by an 'ethnic insider'. The term 'ethnic' culture used in
the US (Di Pietro 1978) is often used politically to refer
to groups which are not regarded as belonging to the
mainstream in-power group. The term 'ethnics' is used in
other national contexts to refer to marginals (Janos 1971)
or sub-nationals (Anderson et al. 1967). But using the
generic term 'ethnics' to refer to politically non-prestige
groups should make the term suspect in an academic context which should endeavour not to use insult terms (just
as we might avoid, in our non-academic language, terms
such as 'Paddy', 'wog', 'spic' and 'nigger').

    Traditional 'Great-Power' intellectuals were operating
from their own social base, a prestige grouping from
within a nation-state. Because of this legacy it has
become difficult to reinstate the study of culture to its
legitimate place. Because we have neglected to study
culture at-home as it were, we have seriously falsified
our analysis of social class, for example, and an important factor in the analysis of culture is the consideration
of the social-class dynamic in generating cultural values.

    It is the contention of this paper that many cul-
tural anthropologists and sociologists have implicitly
reflected Great Power interests through the intellectual
framework underlying their approach to the study of
culture and social dynamics. The basic assumption for
much of anthropology and sociology is that there is a
high degree of order and rationality in cultural and
social systems, and that the duty of the scientist is
to discover what this social and cultural order into
which the individual is socialized is (the replication

of uniformity: Wallace 1970). But to postulate that
there is a shared cognitive map and a shared set of
values and goals (Wallace 1970:26) is not a very
scientific approach to the analysis of culture and
society. From summary observation it is obvious that
what does exist is a high degree of diversity.

The refusal to admit diversity and to acknowledge
contradiction, in Western intellectualism is bitterly
catalogued by Hsu in his Psychological anthropology
(1961:Ch. 4). Wallace in his Culture and personality
(1970:25) lists Erich Fromm ('a nuclear character structure must be shared by 'most members of the same culture"
in order for the culture to continue... socialization must
make people "want to act as they have to act"'), and Mead
('Margaret Mead has carried the argument to the point where
cultural heterogeneity is conceived as almost ipso facto
pathogenic') among others, who fail to see that a culture
is indeed complex as Tylor said. This complexity
frequently contains contradictions and sometimes the
contradiction may indeed lead to individual and group
breakdown. But not necessarily. Examples from Ireland
would be where the 'woman' is both a sacred personage and
a non-prestige citizen at the same time, or where violence,
politically, can be both heroic and sinful.

I am using the term 'diversity' rather than 'pluralism'
because many ideologists (religious and political in
Ireland, and political in Eastern Europe) find the term
threatening. But the general problem is simple: if you
think a grouping such as a nation shares a common cognitive map and a common set of values, the burden is
on you, logically, to prove this. For example, the fallacy
in asking how an Irish Catholic nun can be a Marxist is
the fallacy of regarding our cognitive maps and values as
algebraic systems; asking the question in fact is semantically an intimation of disapproval. The burden on the
social analyst is to investigate how the nun combines
elements of Marxism and her religion into a framework,
cognitively and behaviourally.

In sociology as in anthropology, the conservative-
liberal-radical traditions have all been imposers of
order:

> Contemporary industrial society is integrated
> theoretically through the imposition of con-
> ceptual models of the 'rational society',
> bringing together democracy and utilitarianism
> on a supposedly scientific basis. Variations
> in this theorizing process are evident,
> dependent upon the operation of particular
> ideologies: Differences in philosophy, methods,

rationality types, and proposed solutions are
evident, dependent upon whether society is
viewed as located within nature, history, or
individual reason - the conservative, radical
and liberal reactions to economic change.
Particular ideologies influence the theorizing
process; nevertheless, imposition of system
rationality in one form or another remains
sociology's major concern.(Kinloch 1981:177)

Someone may argue that a Durkheim solution (1964:55)
should be applied: 'We shall call "normal" those social
conditions that are most generally distributed and the
others "morbid" or "pathological".' But this proposal
should also include a discussion of sub-group dominance (as
the paper will develop later with concrete examples). But
it is important to stress that the traditions of Marx, Weber,
and Durkheim, while they may differ on many important items,
generally operate in their analysis of social dynamics as
seekers after rational order.

Someone else may wish to argue that a society should
have, must have, common values or 'common sentiments' to
use the Durkheim phrase, if it is to exist optimally as a
group. That is a discussion of a legitimate but different
logical order that belongs in moral philosophy where one
chooses a value or a cluster of values. A social scientist
is better employed trying to find out 'what is'.

In the tradition of sociology and anthropology
great damage has been done in neglecting to consider the
importance of certain aspects of culture and the cultural
manifestations of class. Marx, for example, failed to
see religion as culture and the USSR itself has probably
done more harm to groups seeking liberation by failing to
understand that religion can be accommodated within
different types of ideologies: in the US Cardinals carry
out religious rituals at the launching of submarines and
the atom bomb mission to Japan went with the benefit of
sacerdotal blessing. Inconsistencies within culture
become a problem when they are made a problem. In con-
centrating on one important aspect of class dominance
through economic power we have almost totally failed to
understand how it is that the cultural manifestations of
the dominant class have become the aspiration of the non-
prestige classes. In the understanding of the dialectic
between labour and capital, it is important to realise
that the cultural manifestations of the prestige class have
become the values of the non-prestige classes, because the
latter have accepted the 'forms and relations' between men
and things' (Marcuse 1954:113ff.), which the prestige class
has adopted; this happens in most countries of the world
independently of ideology and/or religion. Many Westerners,

for example, profess genuine shock that the Party and State
Élite in Eastern Europe exhibit many of the cultural
manifestations of the prestige groups in Western Europe.
Western academics create complicated models ('administered
societies', 'mobilization systems', 'a mobilizational model',
'movement regimes', 'totalitarian models' - Bertsch 1974:54)
to explain politics in Eastern Europe; the attainment and
retention of power can be adequately explained in the context of the acquisition, retention and transmission of the
cultural manifestations of the prestige class similar to
the situation in Western societies. This model of prestige cultural capital does not explain every aspect of
socio-political dynamics in Eastern Europe - it is only
a model - but it does seem to explain more adequately
that the above models the retention/transmission aspects,
particularly. And as a model it is of wider application
than the models catalogued by Bertsch, above.

   But in the examination of society from the point
of view of class, there is the additional problem that
many academics and intellectuals in Europe want to behave
culturally as members of the prestige class and at the
same time want to feel guilty about this association (but
not the behaviour, however), as they attempt to expiate
their guilt in attacking the culture of their own sub-
group. Using pejorative terms such as 'bourgeois' and
'petit-bourgeois' does not help us understand the complex
whole of social dynamics or cultural values and
manifestations. Guilt, however assuaging of the individual and academic conscience, is not likely to generate
science. If we are to begin to understand the relationship between language and culture in the sense of
language and identity we must consider capital as being
cultural as well as economic (Bourdieu 1979, 1980).
Language is cultural capital.

   Ireland and Romania are two nation states where
language in itself, for different reasons, constitutes
an important element in national identity. But language,
if it is to be considered as cultural capital, must be
considered within the totality of cultural identity.
Our identification may seem to be inconsistent but, just
as in the case of the self, 'it is not assumed that
'inconsistency' is necessarily problematic or that
'human nature abhors incongruity - dissonance - imbalance
... in some contexts, an inability to withstand imbalance
might itself be seen as pathological' (Honess 1982:42).
Examples of seeming inconsistency from Ireland and
Romania would be where in the case of Ireland any seeming
interference on sovereignty from Britain is intolerable
but is welcomed from the Vatican (even though it was a

Pope who first instructed an English King to invade Ireland
in the middle of the 12th Century, so 'that the people of
the land, shall receive you with honour and revere you as
their lord' (Curtis and McDowell 1943:17); Romania
jealously guards her sovereignty with the principle,
'non-interference by outsiders in internal affairs', but
also positively boasts of its dominance by and racial and
linguistic links with the Roman colonists, insisting, for
example, that the name of the country is spelled 'Romania'
rather than 'Rumania' (Rosetti 1973). The Romanian
language, it is insisted (Dumitrescu and Mancas 1978), has
remained par excellence the Latin language despite the
influence of Slavic languages, in particular, as well
as Turkish and Greek through invasion and colonization and
despite the fact that the first instances of written
Romanian were even in the Cyrillic script. The dominance
by the Roman Empire becomes not only accepted but welcomed
as a mark of identity (in this instance, particularly,
non-Slavic identity).

Group and national identity then does not form a
rational or consistent pattern. The inconsistency
applies diachronically and synchronically. Some signals
of identity lie dormant and may be resurrected (as has
happened with Irish music over the last twenty years).
The hierarchical scaling of signals of identity also changes
over time: Romania now on a popular level, but also
officially, ranks national sovereignty over the inter-
nationalism posited by the offical ideology (Ionescu 1972).

We are frequently unaware of the factors which contribute to our group/national identity and sometimes are
only made aware of them by influences outside our group.
We may consciously disavow a group identity and yet this
disavowal may not be fully possible; this becomes true
expecially when a group is unsure of its identity (as
with Catholics and non-Catholics in Northern Ireland as
identified each by the other and not necessarily by
religious criteria).

In the following taxonomy of national identity there
is no intention of imposing a closed semantic analysis:
linguistics has consistently failed to operate with an
open-ended semantic model which could cope with synchronic
inconsistency and radical changes diachronically in
hierarchical scaling. Group identity is not necessarily
communicative and hence can only be modelled very inadequately
by formal semantic analysis, French-type structuralism or
transformational generative semantics (Kielstra 1974).
Because factors in group identity are not necessarily static,
rational or capable of being conceptualized (and hence
verbalized), the boundary concepts of 'not', 'zero', and
'identity' adapted from artifical systems are not necessarily
applicable to the examination of national identity; but
logical operations of any kind are not necessarily applicable,
by definition, to material which may or may not be verbalized
and certainly not to material which cannot be expressed

60

explicitly in language. Cultural manifestations are
meaningful and are structured, but not statically in a
system (Hermand 1975): they are not necessarily cognitive
or capable of linguistic expression (and the laws of
identity, contradiction and excluded middle are not
necessarily applicable, which makes the application of
linguistic models to non-linguistic cultural manifestations
a game of chance).

Applying a common-sense taxonomy as I am now doing,
however, to national identity probably means that I am to
some extent failing to meet a cultural academic requirement.
But the schema, though simple, is both heuristic and
analytic (the use of brackets means that the item may or
may not be operative).

```
(Music-Craft-Art-                    Sovereignty    Media    Myths        (Dress)
 Literature)
                                          National Identity

             (Language)   (Ancestry)   (Ideology)   (Religion)
```

By sovereignty I mean territorial sovereignty which
is recognized in some fashion internationally so that
the territorial entity is classified as a nation-state.
Both Ireland and Romania are to some extent unstable
territorially as is common in post-colonial contexts.
Ireland in its constitution makes a claim to the whole
of the island; but while 70% of the Republic regard the
unification of the country as something to hope for, less
than 50% think this is likely in the next 50 years (MRBl
Poll, The Irish Times, 1983). In the case of Romania,
Hungary claims part of the territory of Transylvania and
Bulgaria a section of territory along the Black Sea;
Romania maintains a claim to a strip of territory along
the North-East frontier with the USSR.

But the striking difference between Romania and
Ireland is in the instance of language as a factor of
cultural identity. In the process of colonization the
Romanian language was under threat from invasion and
colonization (the latest attempt was after 1944 with
the introduction of Russian at all levels within the
educational system), but the Latinate language sur-
vived from the Daco-Roman period. The Transylvanian
School began the historical study of the language in
the eighteenth century as an integral part of their aim

to have both a free Romania and a peculiar Romanian identity.
Romania has always had since the 1800s an indigenous
intelligentsia who were able to provide the literary and
ideological-linguistic service so that the language had
a base for survival. Romanian intellectuals always
rejected the adjacent countries as a culture-ally and
chose France as the Romance-culture link. The 'national
language', a term used since 1826 in Romania (Nicolescu
1958), has since the mid-fifties become more Latinized
phonologically and orthographically under the direction
of the Romanian Academy (Iordan 1974). Some linguists
in Romania are national figures and their works are used
as texts throughout the school system. Emphasis is
continually put on standardization (for the written
language there is a 'literary' standard and in the case
of spoken language dialects, it is said, are disappearing).
The standardization is not based on research; it is by
decree, popularly accepted by all. The emphasis on
standardization allows linguists to make a statement en
passant that, due to the effects of the Communist ideology,
the spoken language has become standardized as differences
between the peasants, workers, and intellectuals wither
away under Socialism. In a country where there are large
numbers of minority-language users empirical sociolinguistics is not encouraged (despite the fact that,
in general, Romania has had a generous policy, linguistically, to Hungarian and German speakers, in particular).
Language in Romania is the official and popular signal
of unity for people who consider themselves Romanian.
Attempts were made after 1948 to ideologize the Romanian
language with the advent of Socialism. The Slavic
Tovaras/Tovarasa meaning 'comrade' (the Romance-root
could not be used because the Fascists had used the term
Kamerad) was introduced to displace Domnul/Doamna (Mr/
Mrs) which were regarded as class markers. The term was
quickly regarded as a symbol of Russian hegemony and is
now also the symbol of the Communist regime. Communism,
because of the influence of Marx and Stalin, has always
been conscious of language and linguistics, but Romania
retained for example, its complex pronominal and address
system to express class distinction (Croghan 1976), and
Tovaras is now used sometimes as a joke or an insult term.

But despite the clumsy attempts at linguistic
engineering, the Romanian language itself, as a Romance
language, is a most important signal of national
identity for Romania, situated as it is within a complex
of Slavic-speaking countries (and in territorial dispute with two of these), and with Hungary also as a
neighbour (with which it is also in dispute).

But though Romania was colonized for centuries it
possessed a Romanian-speaking, native intelligentsia in
the 19th century. The intelligentsia in Ireland,
however, were for the most part Anglo-Irish and English-
speaking. Ireland had been partially Anglicized in
the medieval period but this influence had declined in
the 15th century. It was in the second half of the
16th century that the second phase of Anglicization

began. This brought with it the almost total destruction of the educational system for the native Irish with consequent illiteracy in Irish. The study of the social sciences, for example, in Ireland has not yet recovered to any European-type level. The work on the Irish language in the 19th century was done by foreign academics. The Irish language coming into this century did not have a contemporary literature, an agreed orthography or an official standard. The standardized literary dialect in use from the 12th to the 17th century was by 1900 far removed from the spoken language. In the 19th century the native-Irish intelligentsia, both clerical and lay, did not develop a cultural bulwark for the Irish language. Since its re-establish-ment in Ireland, clerical education has always used a foreign literature in a foreign language for the education of students. The native Irish lay intelli-gentsia were preoccupied with commerce and politics, but the culture of politics in the 19th century in Ireland was primarily a British inspired culture (O'Day 1977), whose language was English.

The Irish language failed because it did not have a support system to meet culturally the needs of a population in the 19th century who were being educated and who were emigrating (to English-speaking countries). But more importantly, there was already in place a cultural support system which met educational, economic, political and linguistic support standards of the highest order, if one were to function in the English language. Literacy and upward mobility demanded English. The Anglo-Irish tradition, in English, was not only the only model available but was a model of world standing in some aspects of its cultural manifestations, and had been for centuries.

But from the medieval period (Cosgrove 1979:2-12; Curtis and McDowell: 52-59) the Irish were regarded by some English and Anglo-Irish as 'degenerate' and 'wyld'. Watson in his Irish identity and the literary revival (1979:13-34), catalogues the racist and insulting language used in the modern period by the English and Anglo-Irish - such as Bishop Berkeley, Disraeli, Matthew Arnold, Lord Salisbury, J.P. Mahaffy (the Provost of Trinity College, Dublin), Waugh - about the Irish as lazy, dirty, violent, drunk, superstitious, bigoted, idolatrous, apes, white chimpanzees, unstable, childish, insane, aborigines ('...anthropological studies in "Victorian" England... gave a new "scientific" impulse to the simianisation of Paddy':289). Swift had regarded the sound of Irish as canine.

In the period 1850-1920 the native Irish population needed a language for education, commerce, emigration and politics; the language would have to have a written counterpart (books for education, newspapers, leisure reading etc.). There was in the island itself and in Britain (Ireland and Britain were a political unit in the 19th century) a model for upward mobility and a language in place, English. The people chose English.

At the turn of the last century in Ireland, a movement was launched to foster the Irish culture and language; this movement also became highly politicized and participated in the struggle for independence from 1914-1922. With independence the Irish language was adopted officially in the educational system but for various reasons the language never became the language used by a significant number of people in a variety of social and cultural functions. The reasons include the lack of the necessary cultural infrastructure for a language; the lack of political will among most of the leaders; the lack of academic support from the intelligentsia (there was no significant number of 'native' Irish intelligentsia who were not clerics); and the lack of support from the 'native' church. But the most important reason for the failure of the new Republic of Ireland to re-develop its native language was that the Anglo-Irish culture remained, and is still, the dominant model.

In the years following independence there was no social revolution in Ireland of any kind to match the violent revolution which had achieved independence for part of the island. On the national level the political focus was on attaining and retaining power; there has never been since independence a political leader who was other than a variety of laissez-faire, socially and culturally. The leaders of the majority Church (the 'native' church), were advocates of the status quo, politically, both before and after the revolution, and concentrated its energy on controlling education on all levels for the native Irish, controlling the social ideology, and the creative cultural manifestations such as writing and the visual arts. Clerical education and the general orientation of the Catholic Church, politically and culturally, was that of a foreign church but the energy of the Church at all levels was on the control of ideas, beliefs and behaviour and not on creativity or the development of an intellectual clerical

64

culture which would in any sense be Irish.

The cultural model for the native Irish remains the Anglo-Irish culture (despite the development and continued existence of the 'native' Irish-language culture as a minority movement: the latest figures show that 4% - + 3% - can function normally through Irish: MRBI 1983). Ireland is now, linguistically, a British province showing all the characteristics of a Yorkshire, for example. There are two reasons for this development: the Anglo-Irish model has (particularly in the upper echelons of commerce, in sections of one of the major political parties and in the areas of Third Level education which are of high prestige, socially) always contained within its speech varieties a social dialect which was phonologically similar to the social dialect of Britain; and secondly, through the influence of the British media (in particular BBC radio and more recently the availability of British television for the majority of the Irish population either directly or by re-transmission on the Irish television service). Ireland is exposed continuously to the speech patterns of England.

Ireland now has a dialect situation in which there are geographical variations but there is also, in a state of advanced development, a prestige social dialect which is tending to operate socially as RP does in England and whose phonological tendencies are similar to those of RP. I prefer to use the word 'tendency' because the dialect situation has not yet settled completely: there are people who use this social dialect in Ireland uni-dialectally but there are also people in Ireland who are bi- and tridialectal because they still operate socially in two or even three different environments, making it important culturally to be able to blend and adapt across class and occupational divides. The principal phonological characteristics of this social dialect of Hiberno-English are contained in Appendix 1 (Croghan 1983).

While Ireland is a sovereign nation-state, one of its primary signals of national identity is dissatisfaction with its sovereignty because of its official and popular (although the strength of the latter is now debatable) claim to full sovereignty over the whole island, inclusive of Northern Ireland. The only other native-Irish signal of identity which has some popularity is Irish music. But Irish music receives minimal official support and little or not support from institutions such as Third Level Institutions. It could be argued that the revival of Irish music as a vibrant, even though minority interest,

in the last twenty years owes a great deal to the revival
of interest internationally in folk and ballad music.

The electronic media in Ireland have been state-
run, centralized media giving no opportunity to the
development of local culture and, particularly in the
case of language, giving no opportunity for the acceptance
of local dialects. Because the media in Ireland have been
highly centralized, the attention by government has
frequently been an emphasis on control, and not a creative
and cultural emphasis.

In general, then, Ireland's culture is a British
culture, apart from its concern with sovereignty. But
because Ireland is a sovereign nation it has two choices
if it is to live in any kind of harmony with itself:
it should seek a realignment with Britain constitutionally,
or it should plan a cultural development based on its
native Irish traditions and forge new cultural
manifestations.

Appendix I

The Phonology of the Social Dialect within Hiberno-English

The following is a summary of the phonological tendencies of the social dialect within Hiberno-English. The phonology reflects the British Received Pronunciation system. (As RP is popularly referred to as BBC-, Oxford English etc., I would suggest that the term 'Trinity English' be used to refer to the HE social dialect). I use the terminology of traditional articulatory phonetics only because I find it the simplest analytic model in sociophonology. I am presenting the results in taxonomic fashion because the research is still at the taxonomic stage. I also use the taxonomic mode of presentation to stress that the empirical work has come before the conclusions contained in the paper.

The social dialect (SD) system of Hiberno-English monophthongs does not match the RP system perfectly but the tendencies are similar:
1.1 While· many HE dialects use a short, front half-open vowel in words such as 'bath','grass', the SD tends to use a longer, more open, central to back position. This happens particularly in words such as 'after', 'aunt' (V + Fricative or Nasal, as in RP).
1.11 This also tends to happen in words such as 'Arts' (V + r + C, where the post-vocalic 'r' is or may be omitted, adding length to the vowel if the post-vocalic 'r' is omitted).
1.2 In the SD there is a tendency, as in RP, not to pronounce 'r' in final position in words such as 'father', 'mother'.
1.3 There is a tendency in the SD not to pronounce 'r' in contexts such as 'earth', 'bird', 'worm' and to use the distinctive RP central vowel (with lips in a slightly spread, neutral position) for all of the (V + r) context.
2 There is a tendency in the social dialect (SD) of HE towards diphthongization where other dialects are inclined to use monophthongs (the diphthongs used mirror the RP system phonologically):
2.1 The SD uses an RP-type diphthong, /ou/, in the pronunciation of words such as 'no', 'show'. Most other dialects in HE use a half-closed back monophthong of varying length (and similar to CV 7).
2.2 The SD uses an RP-type diphthong, /ei/, in the pronunciation of words such as 'hay', 'they'. Most other dialects in HE use a long, front, closed - half-closed monophthong or a somewhat more open, front, long monophthong.
3. In the case of consonants, the social dialect (SD), avoids the following which are all found in some or many different dialects of Hiberno-English (the SD, as will be seen from the second half of each section aligns itself systematically with the RP consonantal

system). Many of the following are regarded by non-Irish speakers of English as 'typically Irish' (sic):

3.1 The tendency towards dentalization in (t or d + V) or (s + t or d + V) or ((V) + n + (V) or (C)) contexts: the SD uses the alveolar or even a post-alveolar position in phrases such as 'toe', 'do-re-mi', 'stand', 'as down they went', 'on no account', 'on cattles' backs'.

3.11 The tendency towards dental and alveolar affricatization in (t or d + r + V) or (t or d + V) contexts respectively: the SD uses the alveolar position in words such as 'tripe', 'drisheen', 'tea', 'Dublin'.

3.2 The tendency towards reducing aspiration in (p or t or k or h + V) contexts: the SD does not reduce aspiration in words such as 'pity', 'Timothy', 'Kitty', 'cold', 'happy'.

3.3 The tendency towards some degree of palatalization with laterals, alveolar nasals, alveolar fricatives, and palato-alveolar fricatives: the SD tends not to exhibit palatalization in words such as 'Liam', 'no', 'slow', 'shape'.

3.31 The tendency towards post-velarization/uvula-rization in the case of the velar stops and velar nasals: the SD uses a velarized sound in words such as 'Cait', 'goat', 'song'.

3.32 The tendency towards using an alveolar nasal in final (-ing) positions: the SD uses a velar nasal in words such as 'singing'.

3.33 The tendency towards using a very clear /l/ in initial position: the SD does not use a clear /l/ in words such as 'lily', not a very clear /l/, that is.

3.34 The tendence towards syllabification with (bilabial or alveolar) nasals or laterals in final position: the SD tends not to use syllabification in these contexts, in words such as 'film', 'cotton', 'couple'.

3.5 The tendency to use /hw/ or the voiceless allophone of /w/ in certain (wh + V) contexts such as 'when', 'which': the SD uses /w/ or the voiced allophone of /w/ in these contexts.

3.6 The tendency towards using a labio-dental stop in (f or v + V) contexts: the SD uses a labio-dental fricative in words such as 'fine' and 'vicious'.

3.61 The tendency towards using a dental or alveolar stop in (th + V) contexts: the SD uses a dental fricative in words such as 'thigh', 'this', 'that'.

3.62 The tendency towards using a palato-alveolar fricative in (s + t or tr or k or m or n or l or w + V) contexts: the SD uses an alveolar fricative in words such as 'stand', 'strand', 'skill', 'scan', 'small', 'snow', 'slow', 'swipe'.

3.7 The tendency towards using an alveolar or den-talized tap, or a post-alveolar continuant with a certain amount of friction, or a lingual roll, in (r) contexts: the SD tends to use a post-alveolar continuant with little or no friction in words such as 'tripe'.

Bibliography

Anderson, C.W. et al. (1967), Issues of political development, Englewood-Cliffs, N.J.: Prentice-Hall.

Bertsch, G.K. (1974), Value change and political community: The multinational Czechoslovak, Soviet and Yugoslav cases, London: Sage Publications.

Bourdieu, P. (1979), La distinction-critique sociale du jugement, Paris:Minuit.

Bourdieu, P. (1980), Le sens pratique, Paris:Minuit.

Cosgrove, A. (1979), 'Hiberniores Ipsis Hibernis', in A. Cosgrove and D. McCartney (eds.), Studies in Irish history. Dublin:UCD, pp. 1-14.

Croghan, M.J. (1976), 'Kinship and ideology: terms of address in contemporary Romanian', Northwestern University: Chicago (mimeo), 35pp.

Croghan, M.J. (1983), 'The phonology of the social dialect in Ireland', NIHE:Dublin (mimeo), 56pp.

Curtis, E. and R.B. McDowell (1943), Irish historical documents, 1172-1922. London:Methuen.

Di Pietro, R.J. (1978), 'Culture and ethnicity in the bilingual classroom', in Georgetown University Round Table on Languages and Linguistics, pp. 504-516.

Dumitrescu, F. and M. Mancas (1978), 'History of Romanian', Revue Roumaine de Linguistique 23, pp. 1-4, 7-70.

Durkheim, E. (1964), The rules of the sociological method, New York: The Free Press.

Fromm, E. (1949), 'Personality', in S.S. Sargant and M.W. Smith (eds.), Culture and personality, New York: Viking Fund.

Gambier, Y. and J.B. Marcellesi (1979), 'French Revolution', Philologica Pragensia 22. 4, pp. 194-204.

Hermand, J. (1975), 'French Structuralism from a German point of view', Books Abroad 49(2), Spring, pp. 213-221.

Honess, T. (1982), 'Accounting for oneself', British Journal of Medical Psychology 55, pp. 41-52.

Hsu, F.K. (ed.) (1961), Psychological anthropology: Approaches to culture and personality, Homewood, Illinois:Dorsey Press.

Ionescu, G. (1972), Comparative Communist politics, London:Macmillan.

Iordan, I. (1974), 'Limba Noastra in epoca actuala', Limba Romana 23. 4, pp. 263-266.

Janos, A.C. (1971), 'Ethnicity, communism and political change in Eastern Europe', World Politics 23 (April), 493-521.

Jessel, L. (1978), The ethnic process, Mouton: The
     Hague.
Kielstra, N. (1974), 'A critique of the epistemological
     backgrounds of formal semantic analysis',
     Communication and Cognition 7(3-4), pp. 437-453.
Kinloch, G.C. (1981), Ideology and contemporary sociological
     theory, Englewood Cliffs, New Jersey: Prentice-Hall, Inc.
Marcuse, H. (1954), Reason and revolution. Boston:Beacon Press.
Mead, Margaret (1947), 'The concept of culture and the
     psychosematic approach', Psychiatry 10, pp. 57-76.
MRBI Poll, The Irish Times (June 27, 1983), p. 6.
Nicolescu, A. (1958), 'Despre primele atestari ale
     terminului limba nationala' in Omagiu lui Iorgu
     Iordan, Bucharest: A.R.P.R.
O'Day, A. (1977), The English face of Irish nationalism,
     Dublin: Gill and Macmillan.
Rosetti, A. (1973), Brève histoire de la langue roumaine
     des origines à nos jours, The Hague: Mouton.
Sapir, E. (1970), Language. London: Granada.
Tylor, E.B. (1874), Primitive culture, vol. 1, New York.
Wallace, A.F.C. (1970), Culture and personality,
     New York: Random House.
Watson, G.J. (1979), Irish identity and the literary
     revival, London: Croom Helm.

SOME SOCIOLINGUISTIC IMPLICATIONS OF VIETNAMESE
LEARNING ENGLISH IN IRELAND

Miriam Dean
University College
Dublin

The dramatic relocation of numbers of displaced persons
from a Vietnamese/Chinese cultural environment to a Western
environment has occasioned most host countries considerable
anxiety. The amount of thought devoted to resettlement
programmes has varied from country to country but, in most
cases, preliminary ideas regarding methods of resettlement
have been, necessarily, reassessed. It is therefore useful, during this period of reassessment, to study some of
the cross-cultural problems that have arisen from the viewpoint of sociolinguistics, both in terms of problem
diagnosis and problem solving; the latter being rather
more taxing.

There are some aspects of the Vietnamese resettlement
programme which are common to most of the host countries
involved. However, each country adds to or subtracts from
its own administrative infrastructure in its approach to
the problems encountered in resettlement, and Ireland is
no exception. Similarly, the Vietnamese will each react
in their own idiosyncratic way to the particular environment in which they find themselves and, at times, make
comparisons, for instance, not only of their present
standard of living with that in Vietnam prior to 1975,
but also of the seemingly limitless opportunities
available to their counterparts elsewhere.

These are particularly relevant factors to take into
consideration with regard to Ireland which, like other,
less affluent countries, is in a state of economic
crisis - a condition which creates numerous financial
difficulties for all concerned in the planning of a
programme of resettlement. However, despite the burden
of unemployment and the pressures of protecting a
relatively small population, there is a tremendous
response in Ireland to any initiative shown by the
Vietnamese.

The first group of Vietnamese to arrive in Ireland
came in 1979. Two agencies, the Vietnamese Resettlement
Committee and the Irish Episcopal Commission for
Emigrants Refugee Section were given the task of settling
and, eventually, integrating the newcomers into the Irish
community. Various auxiliary and voluntary organisations

also offered their services, which were gratefully accepted. The number settled in Ireland to date is in the region of 291 persons i.e. approximately 60 families. It is not the intention, at present, to give a detailed account of the socio-economic or linguistic profile of each member of the group, but rather to give an overview of some of the more easily identifiable profiles.

Although described as Vietnamese, the newcomers are not an ethnically homogeneous group, being of Chinese as well as of Vietnamese origin and in some cases a mixture of the two. It would appear to be germane to any studies on the integrative process to make some reference to the migrants' place of origin. Whether, for instance, the newcomers have originated from a rural or a metropolitan environment and, a crucial point, whether the host country is using these and subsequent distinctions in cross-cultural terms in order to plan an appropriate programme. When planning the resettlement of Vietnamese another factor to take into account is the possible antipathy between those originating from North Vietnam and those originating from the South.

Further socio-economic observations which may be relevant include factors such as age, education, previous occupations and points of relocation.

As may be expected, the age range of the group covers a wide spectrum - from babies born in Ireland to the very elderly paterfamilias. The educational profile is equally varied. For the ethnic Chinese, especially from South Vietnam, education has been a rather haphazard experience. Accustomed to their own Chinese schools, many lost opportunities for further education when, in 1975, the communists closed these schools. Some from both ethnic groups came from the rural areas, where educational opportunities were limited and all except the elderly have, in some form or other, followed their studies under the shadow of armed conflict. The majority speak both Vietnamese and a Chinese dialect and some are literate in one or the other of these languages or both. A few speak only one of these languages whilst some are not literate in either. Contact with the Indo-European family of languages appears to have been limited. Some of the older members of the group have a slight knowledge of French whilst some of the younger members had acquired a modicum of English, usually the American version.

The occupational range is, despite the relatively small population, also quite varied. It includes, jeweller, acupuncturist, hairdressers, soldiers, amongst others, and a core of semi-skilled and unskilled whose occupations had been determined by their indigenous socio-economic setting.

The majority have settled in the greater Dublin area with a smaller concentration in Cork. A few are dispersed over various parts of Ireland in towns such as Tralee, Dundalk, Sligo and Dungarvan. The tendency has, however, been for them to move to areas more accessible to their own cultural cluster units.

English language classes were offered to the Vietnamese at the time of their arrival, but proved to be ineffective in some cases. Since then, classroom orientated teaching has been established in one or two centres and a pilot project of home based language teaching was initiated in Dún Laoghaire in October, 1982. The project was established under the aegis of the Dún Laoghaire Vocational Education Committee, headed by Michael Riordan and Father Pelly, director of the Episcopal Commission for Emigrants Refugee Section. It was hoped to give teachers a unique opportunity to take a more flexible and perceptive approach to the task of integrating the two communities, Irish and Vietnamese, than had been possible previously.

The objectives of the project were for the teachers to make direct contact with the students in their respective dwellings and to develop a language programme to suit the students' abilities and needs. Should the teacher-student relationship expand and include wider responsibilities then clearly the project would be of even greater value in the resettlement process.

It is necessary, at this point, to emphasise that the enterprise described has not been designed as a research project but essentially as a rescue operation. Nevertheless, quite useful inferences can be drawn from the experience gained over the past eight months. Thus it may be useful to outline some of the difficulties encountered in the integrative process, both by the students directly involved in the project and other members of the group not directly involved, i.e. families and friends.

Some Problem Areas

The socio-economic environment is probably the most significant factor in the adaptive process and one in which the acquisition of the English language plays an intrinsic role. For many, the deliberate acquisition of language beyond the legal limit of compulsory education is a wasteful luxury that can only hinder the consolidation of the family unit. The main task is economic survival.

This attitude to language learning is particularly manifest amongst ethnic Chinese and Vietnamese from North Vietnam, where consolidation of the political doctrine of communism allied to military activity took precedence over education beyond the meagre minimum. Any effort to resettle this group with the tools of language, must also take cognisance of their socio-economic profile, not only at the purely geographical level, but also should take into account the impact of change encountered when moving from a small highly stratified rural socio-economic unit to that of the larger urban technological environment of Ireland. For the urbanised of South Vietnam, these distinctions are not as dramatic. Nonetheless, members from both groups will, to some extent, suffer from symptoms of disorientation.

The Vietnamese are all very much aware that Ireland is undergoing a period of financial stringency and that, inevitably, they will find themselves in competition for resources with their Irish neighbours, who are not additionally handicapped by their lack of cultural and linguistic uniformity. Job opportunities are, therefore, limited, low in status and lacking in promotional incentives within the immediate future. Consequently, if an opportunity for financial advancement occurs, then it must take precedence over time and energy spent on linguistic activity. Even if the student has the optimal requisites for successful language learning, i.e. motivation, ability, personality etc., that potential is likely to be at risk during this period of pro-longed instability. This lack of economic security can also affect the tenor of cross-cultural interaction, especially since, in physiological terms, the Vietnamese are easily identifiable as an alien group often competing with Irish nationals and thereby engendering a certain amount of hostility.

Under such difficult conditions, it is not sur-prising to find that most Vietnamese, when learning English on an informal basis, tend to acquire a very restricted verbal repertoire. (I use this term in a rather wider sense than Bernstein (1973), who was primarily concerned with a monolingual society.) Those living in deprived neighbourhoods and working in the kitchens of canteens and hotels experience verbal exchanges which tend to be limited to the scatological. Neighbourhood contact is minimal and exchanges tend to be on an extralinguistic basis with the result that both communities are prolonging the social distance

existing between them. It is not always easy to bridge
this cultural gap, especially as the trauma of dislocation can have such a devastating effect on the
self-esteem of the newcomer; the need for a period of
readjustment in psychological as well as social terms
must therefore also be considered.

'Speaking an unfamiliar language is equivalent to
entering into a new psychological situation. Directions
are uncertain ...' (Herman 1972, p. 501). Sometimes
these uncertainties stem directly from the immigrants'
geographical dislocation and at other times they can
exacerbate problems which are already an inherent part
of a migrant's personality.

For the latter, problems in communication can, not
only increase behavioural problems, but also inhibit
the alleviation of these and other problems, when the
culturally familiar communicative support system is
absent. Another consideration is the tremendous
psychological pressure felt by those who are still in
the process of reuniting the various family members
with each other, especially with those still in Vietnam.
The feelings of panic engendered when faced with the
language of bureaucracy are not difficult to imagine.

There are also problems experienced by various
members of the community, when they realign their
relationships as in the case of marriage or when they
find that there is a need to reassess their socio-
economically conditioned expectations, as they must do,
for example, on starting a business. In both cases,
the lack of a culturally determined advisory support
system could be detrimental to their mental health.

Then, there are the problems caused by role
reversals, when younger members of the family unit
possess greater authority than their elders by virtue
of the superiority of their communicative skills, a
situation which can ofter create a sense of redundancy
amongst the older members of the group.

At the same time, the younger members of the group
also come under pressure as possession of these skills
requires them to take on responsibilities greater than
those normally associated with their stage of maturity.
There is also the fear that as the children acquire
greater skills of communication they will gradually
be alienated from their cultural inheritance and will
ultimately reject the authority of the family unit.

A further problem period, still not sufficiently
explored, occurs when the normal patterns of development
in language acquisition are subject to interruption,
leaving a language 'hiatus' before entry into the next
language mode. School-children are particularly
vulnerable to this form of dislocation as their developmental progress is still calculated on a chrono-
logical scale. During their travels, the opportunity for
them to develop their linguistic skills in Vietnamese,
Chinese, or both, become extremely limited. Without
formal teaching in these skills in Ireland the acquisition
of these languages will develop at a slower rate than
that experienced by their elders. Meanwhile they are
also acquiring the English language at a rate different
to that of their Irish peer group. Thus, they may
find that they are in danger of suffering from language
deprivation at both ends of the scale (Weinreich 1964,
p. 109), during this interregnum.

These are just some of the psychological and social
problems encountered which affect, in some degree, the
kind of language teaching programme the Vietnamese
students can and will use.

Factors Influencing Teaching Strategies

The Dún Laoghaire project is relatively unusual in
that the teaching-learning process takes place in the
students' homes. Whilst home-based teaching could
create or intensify tensions within the learning process,
advantages would appear to far outweigh disadvantages.
There is the advantage, for instance, that time, a
scarce commodity, can be more easily controlled when
the timetable is set by mutual agreement. Also, members
of the community, like young mothers, who are prevented
by family responsibilities from attending formal classes,
appreciate the opportunity for alternative access to the
learning process. Thus the attention span between
student and teacher can be extended to allow for greater
development at both the formal and the informal level
of teaching and learning.

There are also some students who have suffered a
certain loss of self-esteem, and learning in a classroom
location can sometimes reinforce this sense of loss.
Consequently, lessons held on the students' territory
can often help to re-establish that self-esteem and
avoid possible ridicule. Some of the locations have
been distinctly uncomfortable, but this shared dis-
comfort has often been instrumental in creating a

sense of solidarity between student and teacher. Indeed, the home-bound location is of invaluable assistance in establishing a strong teacher-student relationship.

A breakdown of some of the borders of authority gives both parties a much greater opportunity to open informal communication networks. However, it is necessary to emphasise that this relationship can also be fraught with difficulties. It is not always easy to discriminate in which areas a teacher's intervention, as a social agent, is necessary and whether this intervention is deemed acceptable.

Another delicate cross-cultural element, in home-based teaching, is the relationship of the students with their kith and kin and the consequent effect of these relationships on the teacher's role. A pertinent factor, as far as the teacher is concerned, is the attitude of the kin group to the integrative process in general.

However, even if relationships and attitudes are of a positive nature, a sensitive situation could still arise where the head of the family might feel that his traditional role was being threatened by the intrusion of a member of an alien culture. Any conflict in this area could easily cause hostility and subsequently create intractable obstacles in the teaching process. On the other hand, in the home-based situation it is much easier to exchange cultural rituals: Christmas cards with Chinese New Year cards, chopsticks with knives and forks, noodles with potatoes. Relevant topic material for teaching purposes is, thus, easily at hand.

The development of reading and writing skills in the English language presents a variety of problems. Where it is necessary to teach a student who has had no previous experience in writing, then the strategies used for an Indo-European language environment can be incorporated into the teaching programme. However, special attention will be necessary in transcription exercises from spoken to written language when unfamiliar phonological dispositions can cause difficulties. Similarily, unfamiliarity with certain phonological elements in the English language can cause transcription difficulties for students already literate in Vietnamese, which has, incidentally, been romanised. Students literate in Chinese present a different problem. Their patterns of learning to read and write an ideogrammatic form predisposes them to use the same techniques for English; substituting the word or phrase form for the ideogram. Some members of this group will, however, have acquired reading and writing skills in Vietnamese, though at different levels of competence.

However, not only is it necessary to identify the problems and influences which could complicate the cross-cultural learning process, but it is also necessary in this context to identify and reconcile the language learning objectives both of the host country and the immigrant community.

In Ireland, language planning issues tend to be restricted to debates on the appropriate use or, on occasions, non-use of the Irish language. Consequently, a language planning policy outside the orbit of the Irish/English debate has probably never been developed; nor has it been necessary to give any consideration to widening the issue until a relatively short time ago.

Although the Vietnamese community in Ireland remains numerically smaller than that of neighbouring Britain, estimated in 1982 to be in the region of 20,665 (Simsova 1982, pp. 61-2), the number is increasing and it would be useful if there were an official forum to assist in resolving some of the linguistic/cultural differences between the Irish and Vietnamese communities. Meanwhile objectives can only be stated in implicit rather than explicit terms.

Where the migrant unit is proportionally small, objectives tend to be geared to linguistic assimilation to the major language of the host country on an ad hoc basis.

In the first stages of resettlement objectives are reasonably easy to discern in that emphasis is placed on the acquisition of 'survival English'. The term 'survival English' was developed to highlight the distinction between courses for students who choose to study the language in order to enhance expertise and students for whom a mastery of English, perfect or imperfect, is no longer a matter of choice, but rather of survival. Consequently, the objectives of both the Irish and the Vietnamese communities would appear to be united in the need for a programme of survival English as a preliminary means of communication.

Evolving a Teaching Programme

It is not proposed, in this paper, to elaborate on actual teaching practices, but rather to highlight some of these differences between teaching English as a second language to speakers of the Indo-European family of languages, often on an ephemeral basis, and teaching survival English to students who cannot share this 'areal affinity' (Halliday 1978, p. 199), and who are no longer socially mobile.

It may be noted at this point that when 'little
time can be devoted to language learning, the most
suitable method may be the one with the minimum
learning load and the maximum range of meaning and
expression, in other words, the one with the greatest
relative productivity' (Mackey 1974, p. 328). Whilst
agreeing with these objectives in principle, I feel
it is necessary nonetheless to pause and take into
account the enormous difficulties Vietnamese students
encounter when taking their first steps in the
acquisition of the English language, namely, phonological intelligibility. Programming at this level
has been particularly taxing as appropriate remedial
material has not, as in so many cases, been readily
available. Both Vietnamese and Chinese speakers,
especially the adults, have some difficulty, for
instance, with consonant clusters, distinguishing vowel
length and recognising certain consonants in the final
position. Since their native languages are tonal and
monosyllabic, English stress, intonation and rhythm
patterns can also cause them a great deal of confusion.
Inadequate guidance in these areas can give rise to,
not only a· lack of intelligibility, but also
unacceptability. A string of remorselessly 'fast
staccato syllables' (Kaldor 1970, p. 217) could easily
be interpreted by the English speaker/hearer as a hostile
act. Unless a comprehensible sound system is established, communicative exchange is limited. Failure
at this level could jeopardise the whole process of
language integration.

With reference to printed materials available,
most have been prepared for the ephemeral student of
the English language, and are therefore not relevant
to the needs of the Vietnamese in their choice of
priorities at the Topic level. In any case, material
suitable for Britain, America or Australia is not
necessarily relevant to Ireland. Although the English
language is in majority use, in most parts of Ireland,
cognisance must be taken of the role of Irish. It is
part of the language of survival for students in
Dublin, for example, to know that when they see 'An
Lár' on a bus, it usually means that it is going into
the centre of Dublin.

Devising and selecting the most appropriate images
for 'survival' reading and writing skills is probably
one of the major tasks under consideration when
planning a teaching programme. 'Many of the books
written for native speaker literacy students are likewise unsuitable for ESL learners' (Lessons from the
Vietnamese, p. 69). This point may also be extended to

include purely pictorial materials, part of the audio-
visual armoury. In the anxiety to produce material
which is both relevant and stimulating, it is easy to
forget student input. A number of the students came
to Ireland from a predominantly rural environment
where technological development has been sparse and
where fewer consumer goods have been available. Due
to some unfamiliarity with many of these items, when
they are used for illustrative purposes and consequently presented for teaching, there is a danger
of the picture, literally, distorting the reality.

Most of the points made so far relate to the
initial stages of the language teaching-learning
process. However, difficulties can still arise
after the acquisition of survival tactics. Adult
students are students in a hurry and often accumulate
imperfect language skills which may require remedial
treatment. One has also to be reminded that, however
stimulating and flexible the programme, external
demands on the students' time and energy will take
precedence over the language learning process. It
is for this follow-on period that it is most difficult
to organise. Failure to consolidate and develop the
integrative process at this most vulnerable stage can
lead to a complete breakdown of cross-cultural
communication with ever increasing problems for the
future.

Incidentally, failure to consolidate may not
entirely be due either to a change in attitude by
the student, or to the host country's inability to
contribute any further to their integration, but
rather to a combination of the two. Frequently,
however, the fault arises because of a lack of dialogue.
Unfortunately, the tendency has been for Western
governments to resettle the Vietnamese without adequate
consultation. Host countries are often unaware that
whilst they have perceived their objectives, the
Vietnamese cannot identify theirs unless they too can
have a period of sociolinguistic learning. It is then
hoped that when they have expanded their knowledge base,
they will be in a better position to participate in the
integrative process. There are, of course, many more
aspects of the resettlement programme which it has
not been possible to comment upon at present. Meanwhile
it is hoped that the Dún Laoghaire project will be
allowed to continue, despite stringent financial constraints, for it gives a unique insight into the conditions under which the Vietnamese are trying to
re-establish themselves.

'At this point, it is necessary to take note of a theoretical issue ... namely that there does not at present exist any framework within which cross-cultural/ cross-status group comparison and typology of findings from the various studies of communicative norms can be placed. This means that investigators ... tend to study each reference group in terms peculiar to themselves or to their own society' (Milroy 1980, p. 87). The writer encountered similar difficulties in placing the subject under discussion into the appropriate framework.

It will be interesting though, at a later date, to develop some of the points that have emerged in this preliminary study and, perhaps, find an appropriate framework.

REFERENCES

Bernstein, B. (1973), <u>Class, codes and control: 1.</u>
<u>Theoretical studies towards a sociology of</u>
<u>language,</u> St. Albans, Herts.: Paladin.
Halliday, M.A.K. (1978), <u>Language as social semiotic:</u>
<u>The social interpretation of language and</u>
<u>meaning,</u> London: Arnold.
Herman, S.R. (1972), 'Explorations in the social
psychology of language', in J.A. Fishman (ed.),
<u>Readings in the sociology of language,</u> The
Hague: Mouton.
Kaldor, S. (1970), 'Asian students and Australian English',
in W.S. Ramson (ed.) <u>English transported: Essays</u>
<u>on Australian English,</u> Canberra: Australian National
University Press.
<u>Lessons from the Vietnamese</u> (n. d.), Cambridge: National
Extension College.
Mackey, W.F. (1974), <u>Language teaching analysis,</u> London:
Longman.
Milroy, L. (1980), <u>Language and social networks,</u> Oxford:
Blackwell.
Simsova, S. (1982), 'Library needs of the Vietnamese in
Britain', Research Report 10, School of Librarianship
and Information Studies, Polytechnic of North London.
Weinreich, U. (1964), <u>Languages in contact: Findings and</u>
<u>problems,</u> The Hague: Mouton.

FOLKLORE, LINGUISTICS AND BILINGUALISM

Owen Egan
Educational Research
Centre
St. Patrick's College
Dublin

I want to examine the simplest models of the influence of one language on another, in particular, models
which are suitable for application in large-scale
educational studies. Afterwards, I will outline a more
complex model which I feel is appropriate for our
situation here in Ireland, where the older national
language, Irish, is taught in the schools to a population of students which is now almost entirely
English-speaking.

1. Elementary models of interference and transfer

In polemical writing about bilingualism it is easy
to distinguish two models of inter-linguistic dependence,
one favoured by proponents of uniculturalism, and one
favoured by proponents of biculturalism or multiculturalism. In the uniculturalist view it is
suggested that the first language cannot attain its
optimal level of development while part of its territory
is still occupied by traces of other languages. In the
multiculturalist view it is suggested that languages enrich
each other, and in fact that the first language will not attain
its optimum development $\underline{without}$ the presence of other languages.

The models can be easily put into a mathematical
format. If $X(L1)$ represents a score or a datum of
some sort for the first language (a measure of linguistic
achievement, for example, or the amount of time allo-
cated to L1 in the school curriculum), and $X(L2)$ is
the corresponding figure for the second language, then
the uniculturalist hypothesis may be written

$$(1) \quad X(L1) + X(L2) = k$$

where k is a constant. The model says that any
increment in scores for L2 must be accompanied by a
corresponding decrement in L1, or, in a looser version
of the hypothesis, by $\underline{some}$ decrement in L1. I will
refer to this as the interference hypothesis. It has
also been called the balance hypothesis, or the
deficit hypothesis.

The multiculturalist hypothesis can be introduced
by first rewriting (1) as

$$(1a) \quad X(L1) = k - X(L2)$$

where k may be thought of as the maximum value which
L1 would attain on X if L2 could be reduced to zero.
Reversing the sign on X(L2) gives a contrary hypothesis

$$(2) \quad X(L1) = k + X(L2)$$

which is that L1 will increase from a constant value k
on X according as L2 achieves non-zero values on X.
Every increment on the X(L2) axis now entails an increment on the X(L1) axis also. I will refer to this
hypothesis as the transfer hypothesis, broadening
the term to cover not only cognitive phenomena but
also the alleged transfer of resources, emphasis,
attention, and so on, from one language to the other.

While I will stress the wide range of interpretations for interference and transfer hypotheses,
and the possibility that 'interference' is true in
one domain (allocation of teaching time) and
'transfer' in another (metalinguistic awareness) it
turns out that a very simple statistic, the linear
correlation of X(L1) and X(L2), will provide a rough
and ready test for all interference and transfer
hypotheses, however we interpret them. It will have a
value of -1.00 if (1) is exactly true, and a value of
+1.00 if (2) is exactly true, and will tend towards
one or other of these extremes according as one
hypothesis is more true than the other. Since the
correlation arbitrarily equalizes units of measurement
it tests the increment and decrement hypotheses only
in the looser sense referred to above, i.e. in the
sense that an increment on one axis is accompanied
by some increment on the other, and so on.

2. Fitting the models to language scores

In large-scale educational surveys there is a
saying that 'everything correlates with everything'.
This is true enough for achievement scores obtained at
one point in time. Here the pervasive influence of
factors such as home background and general aptitude
will mean that the student doing well in one subject
is probably doing well in others also. English and
Irish are no exceptions to this rule. Standardized
tests in the two languages, with the traditional
subtests on Vocabulary, Comprehension, Spelling, etc.,
typically show correlations in the order of .60 or
.70 between the two languages, right from age 6 through
to 15. Correlations of the same order are found between
each of the languages and mathematics, and since
educationalists tend to interpret the latter

correlations partly in terms of shared skills, one might
interpret the former in this way also. However, the gross
correlation of achievement measures obtained in a single
time-slice is largely a measure of the larger influences
we mentioned, and since there is no plausible method
of isolating the alleged transfer effect which is hidden
behind them, they do not constitute very strong evidence
for transfer.

The matter can be pursued a little further if longitudinal data are available. When beginning and end
of year scores are available for each student, it is
possible to look at the gains made during the school
year, a procedure which removes most of the long-term
influences from the analysis. Data based on gain-
scores are a good deal more salient for transfer and
interference hypotheses, since it is not at all
implausible to think of the motivation of teachers
and pupils as a finite quantity, represented by k in
(1), for which the two languages are competing. In
fact, however, a strong transfer effect still persists
in the analysis of language gains. Data from a study
done here in Dublin on a sample of 4th standard
students (aged 10 and 11) in 1979 and 1980 show a
correlation of .40 between gains for classgroups in
English and Irish during one school year. (Data
for 1,083 students from 38 classrooms were available
for this analysis. For more details see Egan 1982.)
The teachers who teach L1 more effectively than their
colleagues do likewise with L2, and vice versa, while
losses in one language are accompanied not, as the
interference hypothesis would suggest, by gains of
the other language but by losses on it too.

As it happens the overall figure of .40 conceals
a teacher effect which, I believe, is important for
the teaching of second languages generally. The
figure rises to a remarkable .80 for teachers who
adopt an informal, child-centred approach, with an
integrated curriculum and an emphasis on affective
materials, such as music and poetry; and falls to
.00 for teachers adopting the more traditional,
formal approach. (The numbers of observations are
as follows. Informal approach: 13 teachers, 364
students. Formal approach: 25 teachers, 719 students.)
This makes good sense since the informal method is
global with respect to the curriculum, whereas the
formal method treats the subject areas as relatively
autonomous entities. Unfortunately the informal
teachers in this sample were a good deal less
effective than their formal counterparts in teaching
both Irish and English, 10 percent less effective in
some aspects of Irish. So the high correlation must

be thought of not in terms of transfer in some positive sense but rather in terms of a mutual, or at any rate a joint impoverishment of the two languages. Why this should be so is a question that cannot be pursued here.

3. Broadening the interpretation of the models

Transfer and interference correlations have all the problems associated with statistics computed from large-scale surveys, and a few others besides. The twin problems of multiple determination and interpretation loom very large. Alternative explanations for alleged transfers, such as the joint operation of larger influences on both variables, are not entirely brought under control by the use of residual gain scores or other partialling techniques. Similarly, while interference correlations can be readily found in the areas of resource allocation, they hardly ever provide evidence for interference in the cognitive and linguistic domain - even if this is often what they are meant to imply. Again, interference patterns in third level and late second level education are largely a reflection of the policy of specialization. All of these problems are made worse when the data have a cross-cultural dimension, since the cultural variable, more than any other, is one which would be expected to have multiple effects without necessarily implying transfer or interference between the variables affected.

Added to these problems is one which is specific to correlations: they do not take into account differences between the population means for the variables correlated. Suppose that strong interference existed for the national means of L1 and L2, and that longitudinal data showed L1 gradually improving as L2 disimproved - as data gathered in this country in recent years would suggest (Greaney 1978; McGee 1982). Such a pattern implies nothing at all about correlations observed at student, or teacher, or school level, but only about the correlation of national means over time. In this instance it might be said that national targets on L1 and L2 were adjusted, upwards in the first case, downwards in the second, without disturbing the tendency of students/teachers/schools doing well on the upwards adjusted goals of L1 to do well also on the downwards adjusted goals for L2.

Such considerations make problems both for alleged transfer effects and for alleged interference effects. We have just noted that interference can still be postulated beneath a surface-pattern which records

transfer. This means that in the absence of very good
longitudinal data the interference hypothesis becomes
virtually unfalsifiable. When refuted at one level,
it can be reformulated at a deeper level. In this
country an interference hypothesis was first formulated in terms of the time spent teaching L1 and
L2 in primary school (Macnamara 1966). Research since
then suggests that standards in L1 and L2 are changing
in opposite directions, as the interference hypothesis
would predict. L1 is improving and L2 is disimproving.
However, the time spend teaching L1 and L2 did not
greatly change in the meantime. This has not led
to any rejection of the interference hypothesis but
to a reformulation in terms of the quality of the
teaching, the teacher's perception of the relative importance of L1 and L2, and so on (McGee 1982). It
is clear that this retreat to higher levels of explanation can be carried on indefinitely, no matter
what data the educational researcher brings in. Of
course the same applies to the transfer hypothesis.
If you do not find evidence for it in one domain
you simply move camp and look for it elsewhere.

I do not believe that such considerations make
transfer and interference correlations useless. They
are still essential in quick overviews of the position
of the two languages in the educational system.
Moreover, in conjunction with other variables, such as
teaching style, or socioeconomic status, or the urban/
rural variable, they can provide a lot of insight into
the dynamics of bilingualism in the school system.
Even simpler statistics than the correlation coefficient
can be highly informative. A decomposition of
achievement variance will quickly show that L2 depends
on the teacher and the school in a way that L1 does not
(Egan 1982). For example, 70% of the variance on the
school leaving certificate at the end of second level
is between schools for the higher L2 paper, but only
20% for the higher L1 paper (Madaus, Kellaghan and
Rakow 1976). This suggests that motivational and
policy variables operating at school and teacher level
are crucial for L2 learning, while L1 seems quite
insensitive to effects of this sort. This, incidentally,
is a further reason for thinking of competence in L1
as a relatively constant quantity, and also a reason
for doubting that L1 could ever be 'interfered with' to
any significant degree. For if levels of competence in
L1 are circumscribed to such a degree by factors over
which schools and teachers have little control, then it
is all the less likely that small modifications of the

school programme, such as taking time from L1 for L2, are of critical importance.

4. Semantic enrichment

But even if correlations and other summary statistics can provide a lot of food for thought on the general relationship of L1 to L2 in the educational system, the fact remains that their usefulness declines rapidly as we move in to examine interlinguistic influences at closer quarters. The principal difficulty, I would suggest, is that they provide only the crudest of all models for the process of interlinguistic influence, addition and subtraction, thus suggesting that L1 and L2 are relatively closed systems, pushing and pulling each other around in ways which turn out to be mutually helpful or harmful, or helpful to one and harmful to the other. At the very least it seems essential to acknowledge the asymmetry which will generally characterize relationships between L1 and L2. Irish is a second language for almost all our students, and it is a weaker language in many other senses too. It is not needed in pragmatic terms because virtually everybody can now speak English. Accordingly, cultural and historical identity are the principal reasons given for attempting to retain it. Under these circumstances it seems quite inappropriate to formulate interlinguistic influence by means of additive models applied to reading scores.

How else might we conceive of the influence of L2 on L1? Lay thinking on this matter has been decidedly Whorfian. The value of the second language is typically expressed in terms of a certain unique 'Irishness' which is felt to be preserved in it because of its long association with the country's history. The origins of such ideas are in the romantic movement of the last century, and in particular in the theories of German nationalism proposed by Herder. As an integral part of the nationalist movement in this country, such beliefs provided the ideology for the movement to revive Irish. Unfortunately, from an empirical point of view it is very difficult to demonstrate the value of cultural or personal identity of this variety. It is true that there is a well-articulated theory of personality development, associated with the work of Erik Erikson, which makes use of the concept of identity, and indeed this notion is now quite central in the psychology of adolescence. When one focuses on linguistic matters, however, the question of cultural identity becomes far more difficult to pin down.

On closer analysis, it becomes less and less obvious that different languages embody radically different ways of looking at the world. The work of Quine (1960) on cross cultural translation draws attention not so much to the phenomenon of cultural relativism but to our weakness, our 'dramatic propensity' as Quine calls it, for attributing flowery thoughts to those whom we feel entitled to regard as 'natives', 'peasants', 'characters', or whatever. As Quine has long argued, eccentric translation from unfamiliar languages, intended to capture the 'colour' of the original, generally says more about the translator than it does about the speaker. At the risk of adopting a paternalistic, or even a colonial attitude, we must assume that the native's Ll is as uncolourful for the native as our own Ll is for us. This viewpoint is strengthened by the experience of contemporary cognitive psychology, where it is shown that vastly different representational systems can still be empirically indistinguishable. In practice we will find only an aesthetic or a dramatic reason, not an empirical one, for preferring one to another.

5. Metalinguistic awareness

It seems unlikely, therefore, that a compelling empirical account can ever be given of the contribution of L2 to Ll considered as a semantic system - even if we cannot dispute the experiential evidence that such contributions do occur. To conclude the paper, I would like to suggest reasons for thinking that metalinguistic awareness, the awareness of language as language, as a unique system of naming and communicating, is a far more promising area for the application of empirical models of inter-linguistic influence. It can hardly be doubted, of course, that some additional awareness of language as such will be gained even by very minimal levels of acquaintance with L2. The question is whether the additional awareness is a fairly trivial by-product of learning L2, or whether it represents a cognitive development which should be valued for its own sake.

In the first place, it will be clear that meta-linguistic awareness is not an optional appendage of language but an essential part of it. The transformational movement makes it clear that knowledge of language is as much a part of linguistic performance as knowledge of the world. The same point was evident a lot earlier in the clinical accounts and personal reminiscences of the many people who had to struggle to achieve basic linguistic competences

denied them through illness or accident. When Helen
Keller let her mug fall on the famous day when she understood the word 'water' for the first time, it was not
the fact that the word named the thing which had stunned
her - she had known that a long time - but the fact, as
she now realized, that everything has a name, and must
have one once you realize what kind of operation naming,
as opposed to signalling, really is (Keller 1903/58,
p. 26). Without an understanding of language as
language, as a unique system for naming and making
contents of all kinds present in consciousness, there
can be no real use of language at all.

In placing an emphasis on metalinguistic awareness,
therefore, an L2 programme need not take us away from
language but can take us to a deeper understanding of
its essence. This is doubly true in the case of L2
programmes for children, since children already use
a kind of language which cultivates a high degree of
metalinguistic awareness by means of word-play,
mimicry, singing, rhyming, and riddling (Opie and
Opie 1959). Indeed the dictates of child-centred
education would of themselves require us to place a
greater emphasis on metalinguistics in any case, even
if there were no other reasons for doing so.

Further reasons are to be found in the literature and the literary criticism of our century. There
one finds a great concern.with the nature of language
and poetry; and our ideas about both, particularly
about the poetry of ancient times, have been revo-
lutionised by the study of oral cultures still sur-
viving in southern and eastern Europe (Parry 1971).
In the literature of our times, also, one finds a
distinctive preoccupation with language as language.
And if, as happens in Ireland, L2 is blessed with a
large corpus of folklore, the metalinguistic approach
is appropriate since oral literature, like children's
speech, also maintains a high level of metalinguistic
awareness.

The metalinguistic approach would also be in
keeping with the widespread unease which is felt with
the capacity of the dominant languages to absorb
lesser languages, and with the growing trend towards
multiculturalism in education. Fishman (1982) notes
that Whorf's thesis about the semantic distinctiveness
of languages was closely linked with another which
may be more defensible in the long run: the thesis
that respect for minority cultures is valuable in
itself and can contribute eventually to world peace.

In line with this thinking the teaching of L2 can serve also as an introduction to cultural relativism and a component in a more general programme to break down the grosser forms of ethnocentrism.

Another useful feature of the metalinguistic model is that it highlights the gains to L1 which can occur at very low levels of L2 - the alleged value of speaking 'the few words' of L2. Admittedly any credible L2 programme must aim for, and achieve good levels of competence in the long term. Nonetheless, in certain important areas, such as the education of the handicapped and the disadvantaged, there has been a tendency to abandon L2 programmes, usually in the belief that they could not be carried forward to the point where they conferred any cognitive advantage on the pupils. The metalinguistic model, on the other hand, in conjunction with the values espoused by the multiculturalist movement, will suggest that the threshold for cognitive gains from second language learning can be moved back to the very beginnings of L2.

The final reason for switching attention from semantics to metalinguistic awareness is that it is far more amenable to empirical study. The various forms of cultural and linguistic 'decentration' which might be sought in an L2 programme can be readily tested for. So also can the metalinguistic skills which L2 may bring. In a study conducted here in Dublin, Cummins (1978) showed that fluency in L2 was associated with superiority in handling the distinction between meaning and reference, between analytic and synthetic sentences, and other distinctions made in the philosophy of language. In other words, there is evidence that the bilingual has a more reflective attitude towards language.

In exploring the characteristics of this re-flectiveness I suspect that we will be putting our-selves in a better position to appreciate the distinctive features of the corpus of oral literature which is available to us in our L2, while at the same time aligning ourselves more closely with important developments in contemporary literature, with the world-view of the children we are teaching, and with the intuitive theories of bilingualism which are held by their parents.

BIBLIOGRAPHY

Cummins, J. (1978), 'Bilingualism and the development of
metalinguistic awareness', Journal of Cross-Cultural
Psychology 9, pp. 131-149.
Egan, O. (1982), 'Informal teaching in the primary
school: Effects on pupil achievement'. Irish
Journal of Education 16, pp. 16-26.
Fishman, J. (1982), 'Whorfianism of the third kind:
Ethnolinguistic diversity as a worldwide societal
asset', Language in Society 11, pp. 1-14.
Greaney, V. (1978), 'Trends in attainment in Irish
from 1973 to 1977', Irish Journal of Education
12, pp. 22-35.
Keller, H. (1903/1958), The story of my life, London:
Hodder & Stoughton.
Macnamara, J. (1966), Bilingualism and primary education,
Edinburgh: Edinburgh University Press.
Madaus, G., T. Kellaghan and E. Rakow (1976), 'School
and class differences on the Leaving Certificate
Examination', Irish Journal of Education 10, pp. 41-50.
McGee, P. (1982), 'Trends in reading achievement in
Dublin over a ten-year period', Oideas 26, pp. 73-81.
Opie, I. and P. Opie (1959), The language and lore of school-
children, Oxford: Clarendon Press.
Parry, M. (ed.) (1971), The making of Homeric verse,
London: Oxford.
Quine, W.V.O. (1960), Word and object, Cambridge, Mass.:
MIT Press.

A SOCIO-CULTURAL MODEL OF COMMUNICATION: PARAMETERS THAT DEFINE IT.

Stathis Efstathiadis
Aristotle University
Thessaloniki

1   Language has been variously defined, though most
definitions agree that it is the most complex and highly
developed instrument available to man for inter-personal
communication. Simple and straightforward enough though
this definition may sound, it involves a number of
notions which are far from being universally understood
or agreed upon. 'Communication', for instance, can be
defined as the deliberate transmission of factual (and
other types of) information by means of some well-
established system of conventions [1], a definition
which in itself introduces additional complications.
Similarly with the term 'inter-personal communication',
which presupposes - among other things - both knowledge
of the conventions, the code used (of language, in our
case) and the ability to make functional use of such
a code, i.e. for purposeful communication. The word
'functional' makes it necessary to at least mention
some of a wide variety of functions which language
is used to perform and which all depend on the presence
of one or more of the variables on which the participants in the communicative event focus their interest
and attention. The functions listed below, then, are
only indicative of this wide range: the social function,
the descriptive, the narrative, the expressive, the
poetic/aesthetic, the emotive, the contextual, the
environmental, the metalinguistic, the referential, the
phatic, the informative; the function of suasion, the
function of appeal   etc. [2]. An utterance may have
more than one function: Fetch me that book, for instance,
has both a 'referential' and a 'directive' function: the
utterance asserts the book's existence, names the object,
and directs the hearer to do something with/to it. It
is obvious both that there are various combinatorial
possibilities of such functions and that there exist
certain restrictions as to which function can co-exist
with which in situated discourse. To take a negative
example: the 'phatic' and the 'informative' functions
are mutually exclusive in the same communicative event.
From what has been said so far it should be clear that
the above (and many other) language functions as well
as the purposes that they serve during communication
may be intentional or unintentional, conscious or
unconscious, ultimately accomplished or not, etc.

2 At this point it would be in order to try and clarify in a rather crude and oversimplified way some of the much-used terms relevant to this discussion.

2.1 Let us take first Chomsky's distinction between competence and performance(3). For Chomsky: competence is the tacit, non-conscious knowledge of the structure of the language, which knowledge is expressed (indirectly) through the use of the language by an ideal speaker-hearer without any extra-linguistic or para-linguistic interference; clearly, competence is associated with the language-system, with that which is grammatically well-structured; in other words, with grammaticality, a purely linguistic term; whereas performance is in fact primarily concerned with everything which is involved in the process of encoding and decoding of language messages; thus, the notion of performance relates to what is socio-culturally acceptable.

2.2 Hymes, on the other hand, goes to great pains discussing what he calls communicative competence, in particular the parameters that determine the language user's ability for communication. He lists four such parameters(4):

a. the grammatical: whether (and to what degree) something is formally possible;
b. the psycholinguistic: whether (and to what degree) something is feasible in view of the available means of implementation;
c. the socio-cultural: whether (and to what degree) something is appropriate in the context where it will be used and evaluated; and finally,
d. the 'pragmatic': whether (and to what degree and with what frequency) something is actualised and what its actualisation entails.

To take an example from language use: a sentence may be (a) formally ill-formed, (b) inelegant, (c) impolite, and (d) infrequent.

2.3 Lyons also discusses the notion of 'communicative competence', which he defines as a person's knowledge of and ability to use all the semiotic systems available to him as a member of a given socio-cultural community'(5). This definition, related to Hymes's thesis as it is, makes it clear that mere knowledge of the language-system (i.e. Chomsky's 'competence') is but one of the components that make up ability for communication and that other, perhaps less rigorously definable, types of knowledge are also necessary(6).

2.4 I will not spend any more time on the theoretical
background relevant to this discussion. I will only use
an example which will hopefully serve to clarify some of
the complexities introduced in the presentation so far.
When a normal child learns his language, he acquires
knowledge not only of sentences constructed in accordance
with the rules of grammar, but primarily of sentences
which are contextually appropriate. In other words, the
child learns what he can or must say, to whom, in what
setting, at what time, in what way, and for what reason
to say it; above all, the child learns when to speak
and when to remain silent. In brief, he learns to
participate in full communicative events. This implies,
among other things, ability to continuously interpret
and evaluate the reactions of the other language users,
as well as possibility to re-orient, modify, or adjust
accordingly his general attitude during discourse, and
even to switch to a code different from the one he has
been using on a particular occasion; an illuminating
instance of such code-switching would be the language
used by a child when he talks with his mother at home
as compared to the language the same child uses when
talking with his teacher in class: the two 'languages'
would be different on a number of counts.

To sum up what has been said so far: the construction of a broader theory of communicative competence is justified to the extent to which such a
theory is capable of showing the way in which what
is possible, feasible and appropriate can be co-
examined and combined so that the linguistic behaviour
produced, interpreted and evaluated is not just ideal
linguistic knowledge, but rather actually occurring
social language behaviour.

3 At this point it would be useful to concern
ourselves briefly, almost epigrammatically, with the
variable factors that make up a model of (inter-personal
or other kinds of) communication. A number of such
models have been synthesised so far; to a lesser or
greater degree they all make use of the same parameters; they differ mainly in the aims that the model
is to serve. The schematic representation that follows
is in fact a modification and an expansion of Lyon's
'simple model of communication' [7].

As can be seen from the diagram, the intended
M(essage), which has a topic and a comment, originates
in the S(ource); it is fed as input to a T(ransmitter),

A Model of Inter-personal Communication

SOURCE   TRANSMITTER

CODE X

Message:
- topic
- comment/
  content

Message
encoded
- signal

social
setting

Speaker/
Sender

Intention: COMMUNICATION

Transmitted
signal

Received
signal

(≠)

CHANNEL

Properties -
limitations

Mode of

message
transmission

Signal distorted
by 'noise'

failure in
communication?

Knowledge shared by participants in Communicative Event

RECEIVER

Signal
decoded

CODE X

DESTINATION

Message

- social
  setting
- function of
  message in it

Hearer/
Receiver

Effect: INFORMATION

where it is encoded - with the use of a particular C(ode) - into a $\underline{Si}$(gnal) with a particular shape, and as such it is transmitted through a particular $\underline{Ch}$(annel) in a particular $\underline{Mo}$(de) and reaches the $\underline{R}$(eceiver), where it is decoded - with the use of the same $\underline{C}$ as above - in the form of the original $\underline{M}$ or some other slightly or drastically modified $\underline{M}_i$[8]; it is in this shape that the $\underline{M}$ eventually reaches its $\underline{D}$(estination) to be used in some social setting. In the case that interests us here, i.e. of human communication, $\underline{S}$ and $\underline{T}$ are combined in the brain of the $\underline{Sp}$(eaker) (whose intention is to communicate something previously unknown to the $\underline{H}$(earer)), while $\underline{R}$ and $\underline{D}$ are combined in the brain of the $\underline{H}$ (on whom the effect of the $\underline{M}$ is informative).

3.1 Now it is obvious that if the message is to be successfully and unambiguously transmitted, interpreted[9], and evaluated, the participants in the communicative event (i.e. the speaker and the intended hearer) (a) should perform some 'work': detect the controlling features of the social situation, know what it is they want to accomplish in it, produce relevant language behaviours; and (b) should share some common knowledge; specifically, they should: (i) know as much as possible about each other's identity; among other things, this implies knowledge of each other's age, sex, race, family condition, social position, education, profession, interests, origin, characteristics of voice, style of speaking, etc. All these traits are of particular significance to the hearer as they tell him certain things about the speaker, thus helping him to identify and understand the latter more easily. The speaker should additionally make known to the hearer his intention to communicate with him; (ii) be able to make use of a common code (linguistic, paralinguistic, musical, etc.) in order for the message to be comprehensible; (iii) have knowledge of the channel being used (visual, auditory, tactile, etc.); (iv) know the mode of transmission of the message (phonetic, graphic, etc.); (v) share knowledge of the co-ordinates relating to the spatio-temporal setting of the communicative event, that is to say, knowledge of the space (home, office, church, etc.) and of the time (appropriate, inappropriate, timely, etc.) of the event; (vi) know the role relationships between the participants (teacher-student, boss-secretary, etc.) and also their status (Prime Minister, policeman, priest, etc.); (vii) estimate properly and not exceed the degree of formality between them[10]; (viii) be able to evaluate correctly the domain to which the communicative situation belongs (family:home, religion:church, education:school, etc.); (ix) have the ability to adjust the language being used according to the subject matter, to the attitude, and to the emotional involvement of the participants in the topic; for instance a sentence may be (phonologically and/or lexically) loaded with irony[11], sentimentality, scepticism, reservation, enthusiasm, contempt, etc.

3.2 The simplified model just discussed is not without flaws and weaknesses. In particular:

a. It ignores the fact that propositions, information, messages are not always or necessarily accessible after their storage in the hearer's memory.

b. It does not take into account the fact that during the process of communication the participants always have some knowledge of one another.

c. It takes for granted the reliability and sincerity of the participants; specifically, when the S passes a M to the H, the H either accepts or rejects the M and stores in his memory the fact that the S regards the content of the M as true. Additionally, when the S has successfully transmitted a M to the H, the S acts thereafter on the assumption not only that the H has accepted the M as true, but also that the H knows that the S knows that the H holds the M to be true[12].

3.3 It is evident that the parameters which are involved in the construction of a socio-linguistic model for inter-personal communication vary in degree and intensity and that every variation plays a definitive role both in the general operation of the model and in the fidelity and reliability of the messages transmitted. It is also obvious that such variations entail linguistic differentiations of a lesser or greater degree. It should be emphasised, however, that it is not so much these objectively observable linguistic differences (i.e. the formal exponents that materialise a function) that matter, but rather the attitude of the participants towards them, the functional role that is assigned these differences and the use that is made of them in the process of communication.

4 In conclusion, I would like to note emphatically that it is the linguist's job to discover, classify, describe, and (as far as this is possible) explain the elements, the structures, the processes, and the rules that each language user has available as a tool of communication; in other words, to construct the

grammar of the particular language he is concerned with.
This is a very interesting and useful intellectual
exercise in its own right. Nevertheless, when we see
things from a social and thus pragmatic and utilitarian
angle, we find that it is at least equally reasonable,
interesting and rewarding to study how, for what
reasons, and in what social circumstances the users
of a language make actual use of such a grammar.

NOTES

(1) See Lyons (1977), ch. 2; also Corder (1973), ch. 2.
(2) For a detailed treatment of the nature of such
    functions and of their linguistic correlates, see
    Council of Europe publications, esp. J. van Ek's
    work.
(3) See Chomsky (1965), p. 3f; cf also Saussure's terms
    langue and parole and the influence they have
    exercised on modern linguistics.
(4) In Pride and Holmes (1979), ch. 18, p. 281f.
(5) See Lyons (1977), ch. 14.2.
(6) It should be noted that Chomsky makes use of clearly
    linguistic data and criteria, whereas Hymes and Lyons
    approach the subject from a broader socio-linguistic
    angle.
(7) See Lyons (1977), ch. 2.2.
(8) The extent of the change effected on the M varies
    with the presence, nature, and intensity of factors
    like 'noise', redundancy, etc.
(9) The speaker's intended message is subjectively
    interpreted by the hearer; for example, a sentence like:
    It is raining, may receive a number of different inter-
    pretations which do not all and always reflect the
    speaker's intention. (Lyons (1977), ch. 14.2).
    Occasionally, though not frequently, the hearer may
    give the intended message a broader interpretation
    than that intended by the speaker. (Fillmore (1979),
    p. 7f).
(10) Joos (1962) recognises five such degrees: the frozen,
    the formal, the consultative, the casual, the intimate.
(11) For irony and the like to be put across, the relevant
    conventions for expressing such states of mind should
    be known to both participants.
(12) See Lyons (1977), ch. 2.2, pp. 39ff.

RELEVANT BIBLIOGRAPHY

Carroll, J.B. (1953), The study of language, London: Oxford University Press.
Chomsky, N. (1965), Aspects of the theory of syntax, Cambridge, Mass.: MIT Press.
Corder, S.P. (1973), Introducing applied linguistics, Harmondsworth: Penguin.
Dreitzel, H.P. (ed.) (1970), Recent sociology No. 2: Patterns of communicative bebahiour, London and New York: Macmillan.
Ferguson, C. (1966)), 'Sociolinguistically oriented language surveys', Linguistic Reporter 8.4, pp. 1-3.
Fillmore, C.J. (1979), 'A grammarian looks to sociolinguistics' in Pride (1979), p. 7f.
Fishman, J. (ed.) (1968), Readings in the sociology of language, The Hague: Mouton
Giglioli, P.P. (ed.) (1975), Language and social context, Harmondsworth: Penguin.
Joos, M. (1962), The five clocks, Publication of the Indiana University Research Center in Anthropology, Folklore and Linguistics, No. 22.
Labov, W. (1970), 'The study of language in its social context', Studium Generale 23.1, pp. 30-87.
Lyons, J. (ed.) (1970), New horizion in linguistics, Harmondsworth: Pelican.
Lyons, J. (1977), Semantics, Cambridge: Cambridge University Press.
Miller, G.A. (1968), The psychology of communication, Harmondsworth: Penguin.
Pride, J.B. (1979), Sociolinguistic aspects of language, learning and teaching, London: Oxford University Press.
Pride, J.B. and J. Holmes (eds.) (1979), Sociolinguistics, Harmondsworth: Penguin.
Saporta, S. (ed.) (1961), Psycholinguistics: a book of readings, New York: Holt, Rinehart and Winston.
Sapir, E. (1921), Language, New York: Harcourt, Brace and World.
Shuy, R.W. and R. Fasold (1972), 'Contemporary emphases in sociolinguistics', Monograph Series on Languages and Linguistics 24, Washington, D.C.: Georgetown University Press.
Weinreich, U. (1963), Languages in contact: Findings and problems, The Hague: Mouton.

LANGUAGE AND ETHNIC IDENTITY:
THE IRISH LANGUAGE IN THE
UNITED STATES[1]

Jeffrey L. Kallen
Trinity College
Dublin

A question which emerges from the comparative study
of language contact is whether or not an ethnic language
is necessary for cultural identity. This paper asserts
that language use is not essential to ethnic identity;
that a distinction must be made between what Eastman (to
appear) terms 'primordial' language identity, in which
a language may serve an associative function without
being the language of everyday use, and ordinary language
use within the total range of culturally marked
behaviours; and that minority languages are best understood within a materialist framework that takes account
of a group's position in the economic and ideological
order of the wider society.

At first, a discussion of the Irish language in
the United States seems to be a contradiction in terms.
Irish receives virtually no consideration in general
studies of language in America, nor does the language
figure in most published work on the history of the
Irish community. Thus Kloss (1977, p. 17) speaks of
'foreign language minorities (to which the Irish do
not belong)', while Fishman (1966) neither lists Irish
as one of the languages spoken in colonial times nor
discusses Irish at any time as an immigrant language.
Kloss (1977, p. 14) goes so far as to enumerate an
immigrant class of 'English plus Celtic', despite the
obvious linguistic differences between English and any
Celtic language. The Irish language in America is not
mentioned in works dealing with either the Irish-
American press or the ethnic press in general
(Buenker and Burckel 1977, Lubomyr and Wynar 1976,
McLoren 1973, Walsh 1968, Willigan 1934).

Irish receives no more consideration from most
discussions of Irish-American history. Glazer and
Moynihan (1970, p. 239) state that 'the peasants who
poured into America brought with them little by way of
an Irish culture', while McAvoy (1969, p. 3) says
that 'it can scarcely be said that they [Irish immigrants
of the late 1840s] brought with them much of their
Irish cultural tradition'. Hutson (1947, p. 23) assumes
that 'the Irish were practically all English-speaking'
in the U.S. O'Brien (1919, p. 259) and W.F. Adams

(1932, pp. 360-61) give only the most fragmentary references to Irish-speaking communities in the U.S.

Yet to assume that Irish was not spoken in America runs counter to all implications from the population distribution in Ireland during the 17th, 18th, and 19th centuries. Discussing poll tax reports, G.B. Adams (1983, p. 1) suggested that 82% of the Irish population in 1659 were Irish-speaking. De Fréine (1977, p. 80) estimates that as late as 1800, of a total population of five million people in Ireland, two million were monolingual speakers of Irish, one and one half million were bilingual, and another one and one half spoke only English. By 1828, according to Bliss (1977, p. 16), Irish was still the majority language in the west of Ireland, with English the language of only 10% of the population in the western province of Connaught. Even in 1861, following the establishment of primary education in English and the massive emigration of the late 1840s, the Census of Ireland shows a national average of 24.5% of the population speaking Irish, rising to 44.8% of the population of Connaught. By 1881, though the proportions in Connaught and Munster had dropped to 31.7% and 33.5% respectively, the national average, which is generally accepted as an underestimation, remained as high as 23.9%. (Central Statistics Office 1976, p. 2).

Such a distribution of Irish would not necessarily imply that large numbers of Irish speakers came to America, if it were the case that emigration did not affect the Irish-speaking districts: yet exactly the opposite is true. Schrier (1958, p. 4) states that the counties of Cork, Kerry, Tipperary, Limerick, Galway, and Mayo (all in Munster and Connaught) account for 'almost 48%' of all Irish emigration up to 1900. All of these counties had substantial Irish-speaking populations throughout this period (Ó Cuív 1969, [pp. 138-39]). Wall (1969, p. 87) describes the period of the most significant Irish emigration as follows:

> It has been estimated that one and a half million people died during the Famine and between 1846 and 1851 a million emigrated. It is not unreasonable to assume that a great proportion of these were Irish speakers. The poorest districts, from which the greatest flow of emigration has continued ever since, have been, in general, the districts which were predominantly Irish-speaking.

Though the Irish emigration from the famine of the late 1840s, is the best-known, Irish people had been coming to the North American colonies since the 17th century. According to Lockhart (1976, pp. 4-5), Irish indentured servants came to the colonies from 1619 or 1620 until the American Revolution, and, due to restrictions on emigration from England and Scotland, provided the main source of colonial labour in the late 17th century. Of the total Irish colonial immigration, Lockhart (1976, p. 28) estimates that 10% were 'men of substance', mostly Protestant, while the great majority, largely Catholic, were 'relatively poor people'. In addition to indentured servitude, trans-portation accounted for a sizeable number of Irish immigrants to the colonies: Lockhart (1976, pp. 90, 96) cites the estimate that between 1703 and 1776, at least 10,000 people, a 'disproportion' of whom were Catholic, were deported as felons from Ireland to the North American colonies.

It is impossible to estimate accurately the proportion of the population in the colonies which came from Ireland. The American Council of Learned Societies (ACLS) report (1932, p. 232ff) estimated that in 1790 the population of the United States was 6.34% Irish, ranging from 12.57% in Maryland to 1.63% in Connecticut (ACLS 1932, p. 251). Despite such a scanty Irish contribution, the report notes that if the immigration rate for the Catholic Irish had been as high as that of the 'Scotch Irish' (i.e., Ulster Protestant), the total Irish contribution to the American population of 1790 would have been 30.24% (ACLS 1932, p. 264).

O'Brien (1919, pp. 134-35) similarly estimates that the Irish population in the United States at the time of the Revolution was 37.8%. Like the ACLS report, O'Brien bases his estimates on a survey of names in colonial census records, but unlike the ACLS report, O'Brien attempts to extrapolate data concerning Irish people who did not have dis-tinctively Irish names in official records. O'Brien (1919, pp. 122, 125) points out that many Irish families, either in Ireland or on coming to America, adopted English names or translated Irish names into English. Thus, for example, the Irish name Kirwan (from Irish cíor bhán - white comb) could be assumed to be translated into the English name Whitcomb (p. 125).

Criticising colonial census records, O'Brien (1919, pp. 376-77) points out that although the census of 1790 showed only 37 people named O'Brien in the state of Massachusetts, he counted 83 soldiers by that name in the Massachusetts muster roles for the revolutionary army. In a similar vein, Willigan (1934, p. 76) estimates that a third of the colonial army was 'of Irish extraction'.

By the 19th century, census records of immigration provide a more reliable picture of the Irish-American population. Table I shows the European immigration and its three major contributing groups from 1820 to 1845, according to the U.S. census (1960, p. 57). Note that Great Britain is given as a single category in census figures, but the statistics for the foreign-born population which separate England from Scotland and Wales (Table II) suggest that the Scots and Welsh contributions to the totals from Great Britain were considerable.

TABLE I

Immigrants to the United States 1820-1845

Year	Total European	Ireland	Ireland % of total European	Great Britain	Germany
1820	8385	3614	43	2410	968
1825	10,199	4888	48	2095	450
1830	7217	2721	38	1153	1976
1835	41,987	20,927	50	8970	8311
1840	80,126	39,430	49	2613	29,704
1845	109,301	44,821	41	19,210	34,355

TABLE II

Foreign Born Population 1850-1880 (U.S. Census 1960, p.66)

Year	Total European	Ireland	Ireland % of total European	England	Germany
1850	2,031,867	961,719	47	278,675	583,774
1860	3,805,701	1,611,304	42	483,494	1,276,075
1870	4,936,618	1,855,827	38	555,046	1,690,533
1880	5,744,311	1,854,571	33	664,160	1,966,742

The mid-19th century, then, represents a turning
point in the proportion of the Irish population in the
United States. From 1846 to 1851, 814,697 Irish people
immigrated to the U.S., representing 52% of the total
European immigration from that span of time. Yet by
1855, Irish immigration represented only 26% of the
European total, falling off to around 20% by the end
of the century (U.S. Census 1960, p. 57). From 1820
to 1854, the Irish constitute the largest group of
immigrants from any one country listed by the Census
in nearly every year's reckoning. Only by combining
Ireland with Great Britain and by discounting the
Celtic element throughout this anomalous grouping
can Kloss (1977, p. 11) state that 'in 1850 the
Germans were the only important immigrant group'.

On a statistical basis, given both the large
proportion and number of Irish people emigrating to
the United States at a time when Irish was still
the vernacular language in much of Ireland, as well
as the attraction of emigration to the poorer,
Catholic majority which provided the greatest
proportion of Irish speakers in Ireland, it is
implausible to suggest that Irish speakers did not
come to the U.S. in large numbers. Two questions
remain: what traces are there of American Irish, and
why did the language evidently vanish so completely.

Most evidence concerning the use of Irish in
the colonies is anecdotal or circumstantial. O'Brien
(1919, pp. 159-60) states that many advertisements for
runaway Irish servants include the words 'speaks
English', presumably implying that other Irish
servants were not expected to be English-speaking.
Lockhart (1976, p. 78) notes that these advertisements, while not referring to religion, often use
the phrase 'native Irish', and rely on a distinction
made about Irish servants concerning their ability
or lack of fluency in English. Mac Aonghusa (1979,
p.14) notes the records of the witchcraft trial of
Anne Glover in Massachusetts in 1688, in which it is
stated that the defendant 'could have no answers ...
but in the Irish which was her native language'.

From the 19th century, there are numerous
anecdotal references to Irish speakers in various
parts of the U.S.: priests in Lowell, Massachusetts
officiated in Irish in the 1830s (De Fréine 1966,
pp. 126-27, Mac Aonghusa 1979, p. 17); Israel Rupp,
as cited by O'Brien (1919, p. 259) reported that
among some of the Pennsylvania Irish in 1845, 'the
greater proportion of them are Catholics and have
priests officiating in the Irish language'; groups
of Irish speakers were reported in Scituate,
Massachusetts between 1847 and 1876 (Mac Aonghusa
1979, p. 19); Mac Aonghusa (p. 19) also notes Jeremiah
O'Donovan's reminiscence of meeting and talking in
Irish with an Irish speaker in Boston. Beaver Island
in Lake Michigan, says Mac Aonghusa (pp. 19-20), had

an Irish population and a priest who, from 1866 to 1889, did most of his work in Irish, while the island, he states, still has residents who understand the language and a Céad Míle Fáilte (Ir. 'Hundred Thousand Welcomes') sign on the docks. De Fréine (1966, pp. 126-27) asserts, too, that 'Irish was still spoken extensively in Portland, Maine at the beginning of the twentieth century'.

It is in documenting Irish in written literature that the trail of the language in America is lost. Under the indentured servitude system, Irish servants were bonded as individuals to owners for a fixed period, rather than immigrating in families, clans, or communities. As with African slaves, this social division rooted in the Irish economic relationship to capital broke up, from the colonial period, the sort of community which would be liable to maintain a minority language. Aside from Maitias Ó Conmhidhe's unfinished English-Irish dictionary project, begun in 1812 and continued until his death in 1842, the only American work in Irish up to 1835 that I am aware of is Donald MacIntosh's A Collection of Gaelic Proverbs and Familiar Phrases; Accompanied with an English Translation; the Way to Wealth by Dr. Franklin, Translated into Gaelic, which, according to Willigan (1934) was published in either 1789 (p. 215) or 1783 (p. 277).

American writing in Irish does not emerge, as far as I know, until 1857, but even then not in earnest until 1873, a generation at least since the bulk of Irish immigration. According to Mac Aonghusa (1979, p. 20) the Irish-American magazine contained an occasional Irish column from 1857, but it is not until the foundation of the Philo-Celtic Society of Boston in 1873 that a true Irish-language preservation or maintenance effort can be said to have started. The actions of this society, and of those like it in Philadelphia and elsewhere, included language classes, publication in Irish, traditional music and dance events, and efforts to introduce Irish language and history instruction into Catholic schools.

This language movement covered a variety of social domains: though An Gaodhal (1881-1904), possibly the only regular Irish-language periodical of such scope published in the U.S., has been described by Mac Aonghusa (1979, p. 25) as being for workers and not for the erudite, the Ancient Order of Hibernians was responsible in 1895 for the establishment of a Chair of Celtic Studies in the Catholic University of America. Space limitations preclude a full discussion

of the scope of Irish language usage in America, a usage
which includes private journals and manuscripts, various
community organisations and nationalist political
activity, and connections to traditional music and song,
yet as the wide-ranging discussion in Ó hAnnracháin
(1979) shows, it is simply not accurate to state that
Irish was not spoken or written in the United States.
(Because of its rather different social characteristics,
I ignore here the usage of Irish in contemporary
America, for which there is ample evidence, though,
again, most of it is anecdotal.)

The later 19th century provides a key to the
position of Irish in the U.S., both in fact and in
historiography. Having come in large numbers to a
United States which was on the brink of rapid economic
expansion, the Irish-American community was in a prime
position for integration into the dominant American
economic structure. The expansion of the economy and
the relative shortage of labour in the industrial
north enabled the Irish to rise from their previous
position as the most proletarian white ethnic group
to form an emerging working middle class. Particularly
in the 1860s and 70s, the Irish formed the largest
and formerly poorest group for whom the American
Dream of economic and political opportunity seemed to
be working. The concentration of Irish communities in
cities, including relatively new ones such as Chicago,
enabled the Irish population to obtain a degree of
political power which had previously been unthinkable.
This political and economic power was unobtainable for
a landless group lacking capital through any language
other than English.

By the time of the industrial expansion of the
late 19th century, the Irish community had started to
differentiate into a truly middle or upper middle class
and a 'solid' working class. This industrial expansion
required a much larger work force than that already
in America, yet Western European immigration yielded
to immigration from Eastern and Southern Europe (and
to a lesser degree Asia) - creating a new identifiable
proletariat which was considerably more removed from
English than Irish immigrants had ever been.

Competition between the Irish working class and
the newly arrived immigrants of the late 19th century
was a force which encouraged the interpretation of the
Irish as being in some crucial sense truly American -
the Irish were 'at the head of the queue' in
opposition to new arrivals, and the development of
Irish power structures in politics and business enabled
the synthesis of Irish ethnicity (now excluding language)
with the dominant American cultural ideology. Ironically,
it was just the power which this new position granted

that enabled the development of the diminutive Irish-language maintenance movement in the U.S.

Quite clearly, however, within the American context, the loss of Irish has not resulted in a loss of ethnic identity. Much of the history of the rise of the Irish community involves its self-awareness in opposition to a more dominant, less 'ethnic' (in ideological terms) culture derived from England. The Irish policital machines of the 19th and 20th centuries, for example, did not require Irish for their strength, but they did require ethnic cohesion within the American class structure. The Irish community has maintained, particularly since the acquisition of power in the later 19th century, a host of ethnic institutions: the Ancient Order of Hibernians, the Friendly Sons of St. Patrick, Comhaltas Ceoltóirí Éireann, etc., and has maintained or revived musical and dance traditions in many communities.

Irish ethnicity is also maintained more generally in American culture, at times achieving a syncretism with the dominant culture. St. Patrick's Day, for example, is the only specifically national festival which has been absorbed into the national culture, yet this absorption has not diminished its ethnic character: rather, all Americans may become Irish for a day. Phrases such as 'an Irish temper' or 'luck of the Irish' refer to folk conceptions of ethnicity for Irish-Americans which maintain identity without reference to language. The connection between the United States and the nationalist movement in Northern Ireland could not be continued without a strong ethnic American interest in the politics of the home country. (One can, by comparison, hardly imagine ethnic German-Americans taking a strong interest in contemporary German politics).

I concur, then, with Eastman (to appear), who states that 'when we stop using the language of our ethnic group, only the language use aspect of our ethnicity changes; the primoridal sense of who we are and what group we think we belong to for the remainder remains intact'. It has not only been possible for the Irish community in the United States essentially to lose Irish as a vernacular tongue, but for the ideological history of the Irish community essentially to write Irish out of the picture altogether; nevertheless, Irish ethnicity has not been discarded in the process. Rather, ethnicity has manifested itself in the behaviours which are directly relevant to the status of the immigrant group within the wider community: by organisation for economic and political power, and by other cultural means (religion, music, folklore, public festivals, etc.) which serve both to differentiate the Irish community and to incorporate it into the basic ethnic charter of the United States. The only way in which Irish-Americans could have achieved this backdated primordial American-ness (as opposed to 'ethnicity') was, under the economic circumstances, to disallow the status of being speakers of a language other than English.

This paper has concentrated on arguably the most neglected aspects of the position of Irish in the United States. A full account would need, especially, to take cognisance of the decline of Irish in Ireland during the period in question, including both the decline in the number of speakers and the lack of educational opportunities through Irish. Nevertheless, I think it possible to suggest a general model for the study of minority (and particularly immigrant) languages based on the preceding discussion.

First, an immigrant language should be examined in its international context, not simply in terms of its history in the target country. In examining Irish, both the history of the language in Ireland and its status relative to English in Ireland and Great Britain have had direct bearing on its development in the United States.

Secondly, the position of immigrant groups within the matrix of relations of production in the target country must be considered in understanding language sociology. Not only numbers of speakers or the presence of 'quality language maintenance' as seen in literature, education, or organised religion determine the fate of an immigrant language; the social position of the language group in a dynamic economic structure is crucial. If, for example, the Irish famine emigration had occurred during a contraction of the American economy and the demand for labour, or, conversely, had the first Irish speakers come to the U.S. not as indentured servants and unskilled labourers but as merchants from an independent Irish-speaking nation, the history of Irish in the Irish community might have turned out quite differently.

Thirdly, I see no reason to give language primacy over other forms of ethnic behaviour. Where a minority language becomes essential to the development of a group's productive relations in society, it may remain as a minority language; otherwise it may not. Nevertheless, other ethnic markers may be maintained to fulfil any necessary functions.

Finally, and perhaps most importantly, the historiography of Irish in the United States illustrates the interactions among the class structure of a society, its ideology, and the scholarship which is one of its cultural products. American economic development has necessitated an ideology which is both monistic and pluralist: monistic in that non-American national aims have always had to be subordinated to American nationalism and in that there is an identifiable English-language culture associated with power and prestige, yet pluralist in that there has always been a tension between this dominant culture and a multitude of others[2]. In the case of Irish-American culture, we have seen a marriage of a continuing Irish ethnic identity with a more general American ethnicity in which English represents the 'unmarked' case. This marriage has been accomplished by change in the Irish economic status attendant on American economic development, by the loss of the ethnic language - giving the Irish equal claims to prior dominance with the English - and by the maintenance of other ethnic behaviours which interacted positively with the economic actions of the community. The supposed 'lack' of an Irish language historically in the United States can, further, be seen not as a fact in evidence, but as a counterfactual reflection of the more general American cultural ideology.

NOTES

1. This paper concerns only the position of Irish in the United States of America and the British colonies which subsequently formed the U.S. Developments in Canada represent a very different picture from the one presented here.

2. Though disagreeing with its Cold War ideology, I refer in this connection to H.M. Kallen (1956) for a historical discussion of American pluralism.

REFERENCES

Adams, G.B. (1983), 'Linguistic cross-links in phonology
    and grammar', Teanga: Journal of the Irish
    Association for Applied Linguistics 3, pp. 1-11.
Adams, W.F. (1932), Ireland and Irish emigration to the
    New World, New Haven: Yale University Press.
American Council of Learned Societies (1932), 'Report
    of the committee on linguistic and national stocks
    in the population of the United States,' in Howard
    Barker and Maurice Hansen (eds.), Annual Report of
    the American Historical Association: 1931, Vol. 1,
    Washington D.C.: U.S. Government Printing Office.
Bliss, A.J. (1977), 'The emergence of Modern English
    dialects in Ireland', in Ó Muirithe (ed.) (1977),
    pp. 7-19.
Buenker, J.D. and N.C. Burckel (1977), Immigration
    and ethnicity: A guide to information sources,
    Detroit: Gale Research Company.
Census, U.S. Bureau of the (1960), A statistical
    abstract supplement: Historical statistics of
    the United States: Colonial times to 1957,
    Washington D.C.: U.S. Department of Commerce,
    U.S. Bureau of the Census.
Central Statistics Office (1976), Daonáireamh na
    hÉireann: 1971: Imleabhar VIII An Ghaeilge:
    Census of Population of Ireland: 1971:
    Volume VIII, Dublin: The Stationery Office.
De Fréine, S. (1977), 'The dominance of the English
    language in the nineteenth century', in
    Ó Muirithe (ed.) (1977), pp. 71-87.
De Fréine, S. (1966), The great silence, Dublin:
    Foilseacháin Náisiúnta Teoranta.
Eastman, C. (to appear), 'Language, ethnic identity,
    and change', in John Edwards (ed.) Linguistic
    minorities, pluralism, assimilation, and
    multiculturalism, New York and London:
    Academic Press.
Fishman, J. (1966), Language loyalty in the United
    States, The Hague: Mouton.
Glazer, N. and D.P. Moynihan (1970), Beyond the
    melting pot, Cambridge, Mass.: MIT Press.
Hutson, A.E. (1947), 'Gaelic loan-words in American',
    American Speech 22, pp. 18-23.
Kallen, H.M. (1956), Cultural pluralism and the American
    idea, Philadelphia: University of Pennsylvania Press.
Kloss, H. (1977), The American bilingual tradition,
    Rowley: Newbury House Publishers.
Lockhart, A. (1976), Some aspects of emigration from
    Ireland to the North American Colonies between
    1660 and 1775, New York: Arno Press.
Lubomyr, R.W. and A.T. Wynar (1976), Encyclopedic
    dictionary of ethnic newspapers and periodicals
    in the United States, 2nd ed. Littleton,
    Colorado: Libraries Unlimited.

Mac Aonghusa, P., (1979), 'An Ghaeilge i Meiriceá', in
Ó hAnnracháin (ed.) (1979), pp. 13-30.
McAvoy, T.T. (1969), A history of the Catholic Church in
the United States, South Bend: University of Notre
Dame Press.
McLoren, D. (1973), Ontario ethno-cultural newspapers
1835-1972, Toronto: University of Toronto Press.
O'Brien, M.J. (1919), A hidden phase of American history:
Ireland's part in America's struggle for liberty,
New York: Dodd, Mead, and Co.
Ó Cuív, B. (ed.) (1969), A view of the Irish language,
Dublin: Stationery Office.
Ó hAnnracháin, S. (ed.) (1979), Go Meiriceá siar: Na Gaeil
agus Meiriceá: Cnuasach aistí, An Clóchomar Tta.
Ó Muirithe, D. (ed.) (1977), The English language in
Ireland, Dublin and Cork: The Mercier Press.
Schrier, A. (1958), Ireland: And the American emigration
1850-1900, Minneapolis: University of Minnesota Press.
Wall, M., (1969), 'The decline of the Irish language',
in Ó Cuív (1969), pp. 81-91.
Walsh, F.R. (1968), 'The Boston Pilot: A newspaper for the
Irish immigrant, 1829-1908', unpublished Ph.D.
dissertation, Boston University.
Willigan, W.L. (1934), 'A history of the Irish-American
press from 1691 to 1835', unpublished Ph.D.
dissertation, Fordham University.

A PRAGMATIC ACCOUNT OF REFERENCE
IN ENGLISH AND POLISH

Barbara Kryk
Adam Mickiewicz
University
Poznan

Words or phrases of the language are not explicitly
or uniformly marked for the feature that concerns
us. Thus, there can be considerable scope for
misidentification when trying to establish how
that feature is conveyed. (Rundle 1979, p. 83)

Let this quotation serve as the starting point of
the present discussion concerning reference. Although
the notion has been disputed by philosophers and
linguists ever since, many relevant issues still remain
unresolved. There has been no common consent as to
whether reference should be approached as a philosophical
concept, thus contributing to a theory of truth, or
rather as a pragmatic notion having to do with speaker's
choices and intentions. Controversies have arisen even
among the advocates of the same approach. On the one
hand, reference has traditionally been employed by
philosophers in their discussions of truth values of
sentences (to mention only Frege 1952; Quine 1960;
Russell 1905; Strawson 1970), whereas Davidson (1980,
p. 140) claims that the notion should be excluded
from the theory of truth since it plays no essential
role in actually explaining the relation between
language and reality. On the other hand, linguists
realize the undeniable relevance of the concept of
reference to the analysis of language. The referential
potential of expressions is interrelated with such
notions as deixis, definiteness, spatio-temporal
locations, not to mention presupposition, entailment,
and other sentential relations. Last, but not least,
the processes of pronominalization and reflexivization
would have to be abandoned, if it were not for the
related concept of coreferentiality.

Being indispensable to linguistics, reference
nonetheless has been subject to varying interpretations.
As a result of on-going disputes it cropped up as a
pragmatic, utterance-dependent notion (cf. Katz 1977;
Lyons 1977; Quine 1960), but even being transferred to
the field of pragmatics, the referential theory of
meaning is still supposed to comprise some context-
independent referential expressions, e.g. proper names
(cf. Fodor 1977).

Thus the issue at stake is far from clear. The fuzziness of the concept of reference is still with us and, as will be shown below, it remains difficult to systematize. The present remarks aim to elucidate the problems which arise with referential expressions such as proper names, definite descriptions, NPs with demonstratives, etc. in contexts which might lead to cancellation of reference. Although it may be taken for granted that proper names never lose their referentiality, can this assumption be made for fictitious characters or indefinite NPs, or the relevant expressions used in identity statements, opaque contexts or Reported Speech? The analysis carried out below will examine these instances so as to suggest a systematic approach to various occurrences of reference. The employment of semantic features such as referentiality, definiteness and spatio-temporal variables will introduce some formalization into the referential characteristics of the expressions in question. The data from English to Polish will demonstrate that the present remarks might be of a more universal nature which would be worth testing on a larger cross-linguistic scale.

1.   If one approaches the issue pragmatically the referential status of expressions should pose no problems at all. If we take it, after Thrane 1980 and others, that an expression is referential solely by virtue of its form, then the form will secure its referential potential and the context will assign the referent to the expression. It is obvious that it is the speaker who selects particular expressions in accordance with his intentions and his knowledge of extra-linguistic reality. Hence, it would be against any principles of discourse to talk about referents whose existence is questionable or unknown to the speaker (cf. Gricean Cooperative Principle, 1975).

Consequently, if we utter under normal circumstances sentences like 1-4, it is taken for granted that the entities mentioned exist, i.e. the relation of reference between the name of the object and the object itself is thus secured. Consider the following examples which contain the relevant types of referential expressions, i.e. proper names, definite descriptions, NPs with demonstratives or combinations thereof:

1.   Pope John Paul II has visited Poland twice.
1'. Papież Jan Paweł II odwiedził Polskę dwukrotnie.
2.   Mary Smith is my best friend.
2'. Marysia Kowalska jest moją najlepszą przyjaciółką.
3.   The tall man in glasses refused to pay the bill.
3'. (Ten) wysoki człowiek w okularach odmówił
     zapłacenia rachunku.

4. This linguistic paper is good for nothing.
4'. Ten referat językoznawczy jest do niczego.

That these sentences all contain referring NPs as their
subjects can hardly be questioned. However, the NPs
do differ as regards the kind of their referential
potential. It was traditionally claimed that proper
names are endowed with unique reference, since they
designate unique objects (cf. Russell 1905). This
viewpoint was later abandoned in virtue of the fact
that unique reference of a proper name is in most
cases context-dependent (cf. Linsky 1970, p. 77;
Lyons 1977, p. 184); Quine 1960, p. 130). This
turns out to be the case in example 2, which can be
commented on in the following manner:

2. A: Mary Smith is my best friend.
   B: Which Mary Smith do you mean? The redhead
      typist or the blond teacher?
2'. A: Marysia Kowalska jest moją najlepszą
       przyjaciółką.
    B: Którą Marysię Kowalską masz na myśli?
       Tę rudą maszynistkę czy blond nauczycielkę?

Hence, it has been agreed that while proper names
lack unique reference, it is only definite descriptions
or names signifying an idiosyncratic attribute that
retain it, as is the case in example 1, with Pope
John Paul II as its subject.[1] If a question of the
which-do-you-mean kind were attached to it, an odd
structure would result. Compare Strawson's comment
(1970) on such expressions to the effect that uniquely
referring titles have a tendency to grow capital
letters and to be treated in written English as proper
names.[2]

If proper names lack unique reference both in
English and in Polish, it is even more true of definite
descriptions and NPs with pronouns like demonstratives
(cf. 3-4). At this point a counter-argument could be
raised concerning the contextually-conditioned
characteristics of the relevant NPs, i.e. the tall man
in glasses and this linguistic paper, which make the
possibility of their non-uniquely referring uses very
unlikely. And this is, indeed, most often the case.
But what if we were dealing with a situation in which
two tall men wearing glasses or a few linguistic papers
were involved? Then the comment Which man/paper do you
mean? would not be out of place.

115

The point here is that only in example 1 is the unique reference not contextually conditioned, the Pope having one and the same referent regardless of the spatio-temporal variables. This is by no means true of the remaining examples. These distinct types of reference should therefore be defined in a formal manner, so that each referential expression would obtain only one unambiguous semantic reading as, say, uniquely or instantaneously referring. It would be both in accordance with discourse principles and psychologically real to postulate a set of features that are ascribed to an NP by the speaker before he uses it referentially.

This is how the above-mentioned instances of reference are to be approached. The pragmatic waste-basket allows us to take into account speaker's choices and intentions on his construal of particular propositions. On the basis of examples 1⁻4, we will be able to discriminate between two kinds of reference: unique (represented by 1), and instantaneous, exemplified by 2-4. Consequently, the corresponding NPs would be ascribed the following features:

5. NP_i NP_j

+REFERENTIAL   +REFERENTIAL
+DEFINITE   +DEFINITE
TIME/PLACE   ∝TIME/∫ PLACE

Note that the features employed here denote semantic primitives relevant to the use of NPs. Once the speaker decides that the NP he will be using does have a referent (hence the feature [+REFERENTIAL]), he will select a definite entity (the feature [+DEFINITE]) and finally make a choice concerning uniqueness. This calls for a decision whether the relevant NP would refer to one and the same entity under all spatio-temporal circumstances (i.e. ⌈T/P) or, as in case of non-unique (instantaneous) reference, only at a particular time and place (i.e. ∝T/ P).

One may question at this point the relevance of the feature [+DEFINITE] to the present analysis. As will be shown below, it is in fact essential, since indefinite NPs are by no means deprived of referential readings in some contexts. And, surprisingly, the opposite situation holds true as well, i.e. definite NPs can lose their referential characteristics. And it is to this problem that our discussion will next turn.

2.   It has already been mentioned that apart from proper names, which were considered paradigm examples for a referential theory of meaning, definite descriptions and NPs preceded by the definite article or a demonstrative pronoun were also labelled referential expressions due to their form. Does this imply that definiteness is the necessary condition for an NP to function referentially? It is worth examining at this point if the occurrence of the

indefinite article and pronouns like <u>some</u> would deprive
an NP of its referential reading. Consider the
following examples:

    6. I must telephone a plumber tomorrow.
    6'. Muszę zadzwonić jutro do hydraulika.
    7. A Mr. Brown has also signed this petition.
    7'. Jakiś pan Brown też podpisał tę petycję.
    8. Some children have destroyed our flower beds.
    8'. Jakieś dzieci zniszczyły nasze grządki z kwiatami.

At a first glance the indefinite NPs in these
sentences will be taken as non-referring.[3] This seems to
be the case in the above examples, since they can be
commented on by <u>Which plumber/Mr. Brown/children do you
mean?</u> (in Polish: <u>Którego hydraulika/pana Browna/które
dzieci masz na myśli?</u>). Note also that the markers of
indefiniteness are even more uniform in Polish than
they are in English - i.e. <u>jakiś</u> corresponds both to
<u>a</u> and <u>some</u>. The point here is that if the speaker,
while mentioning under normal circumstances a plumber
or a Mr. Brown, had a particular person in mind, he
would probably signal it by a more explicit indication
of reference (i.e. definite description). It follows
then that the non-referential reading would be the
so-called 'preferred interpretation', to use Wilson's
(1975) term, of the sentences in question.

Having given priority to that reading we cannot,
however, exclude another use of indefinite NPs, namely
such that the speaker has some knowledge of the
identity of the person mentioned. Consider the
following continuations of 6-8:

    6. I must telephone a plumber; there is one
        living next door.
    6'. Muszę zadzwonić do hydraulika: mieszka tu
        taki jeden obok.
    7. A Mr. Brown has also signed this petition;
        I could tell from his signature that it was
        Neil Brown.
    7'. Jakiś pan Brown też podpisał tę petycję;
        mogłam stwierdzić na podstawie podpisu, że
        to był Neil Brown.
    8. Some children have destroyed our flower beds;
        I saw little Jimmy running away.
    8'. Jakieś dzieci zniszczyły nasze grządki z
        kwiatami; widziałam jak mały Jimmy uciekał.

Such a type of reference will be labelled after
Rundle (1979) covert reference, since it is not
explicitly marked by linguistic means but still
entails speaker's knowledge of the referent's
identity. Covert reference will thereby have to be
distinguished, on the one hand, from identifying

reference (where the referent is explicitly marked as identifiable by the speaker) and, on the other hand, from non-referential uses of definite descriptions (where the speaker has no idea as to the referent's identity). It is possible to think of an example incorporating all three readings, cf.:

9. She wants to marry a millionairs.
    a) you know, that elderly estate agent.
    b) I know she met one in Saudi Arabia.
    c) that is her fancy, so if she meets one,
       she will do it!
9'. Ona chce poślubić milionera.
    a) wiesz, tego starego agenta od nieruchomości.
    b) wiem, że poznała jakiegoś w Arabii Saudyjskiej.
    c) to jej kaprys, więc jeśli jakiegoś pozna,
       zrobi to!

In order to distinguish covert and $\emptyset$ (or non-identifying) reference from its unique and instantaneous uses, an NP will have to be marked according to the previously adopted convention in the following way:

10. NP_k NP_1

    +REFERENTIAL   -REFERENTIAL
    -DEFINITE   -DEFINITE
    $\emptyset$TIME/ PLACE   TIME/ PLACE

Note that for the time being only indefinite NPs have been subsumed under the label of non-identifying reference. The question whether this properly applies at all to definite NPs will be answered in the following section.

3. One may wonder how such ex-definitione referential entities as proper names or definite NPs can be used non-referentially. It was Kripke who tried to give some insight into the link between a proper name and its referent in terms of the notion of rigid designation (1972). Thus a designating term is called rigid if it designates the same individual in every possible world. However, if a name loses its referring function it is no longer a name. But consider the following:

11. Mr Pickwick had numerous adventures with
     his friends.
11'. Pan Pickwick miał liczne przygody ze swoimi
     przyjaciółmi.
12. Apollo was very well built.
12'. Apollo był bardzo dobrze zbudowany.

While uttering propositions with these types of NP the
speaker does not refer to any elements of extra-linguistic
reality, since our world does not contain referents of
either Mr. Pickwick or Apollo. But they do exist in
other possible worlds of fiction and mythology,
respectively. So either the present names are not names
by Kripke's standards or still another type of reference
is involved. Within the adopted pragmatic framework
it seems plausible to include this instance of reference
(call it conventional) in our model. Note that the
solution goes back to Frege (1952) who assigned conventional denotation to fictitious characters. Moreover,
some independent evidence supporting this approach can
be found if our examples are compared to statements about
non-existent objects whose existence is, moreover, denied,
as in:

> 13.   The golden mountain does not exist.
> 13'. Złota góra nie istnieje.

In connection with such sentences Linsky (1970, p. 85)
observed that fictitious characters are to be distinguished
from NPs like these, (e.g. the golden mountain, the round
square), since although it makes perfectly good sense to
ask whether Mr. Pickwick ran a bookstore, it makes no
sense to ask if the golden mountain is in California.
Thus, expressions of this type will be assigned Ø
reference and our stock of context-dependent uses of
referential expressions will be enlarged to the
following:

> 14.   NP$_m$ NP$_n$
>
>   -REFERENTIAL   +REFERENTIAL
>   ±DEFINITE   +DEFINITE
>   ₀TIME/ PLACE   ₗTIME/PLACE

Note that the previously discussed Ø (or non-identifying)
reference is exemplified by both [±DEFINITE] NPs. As to
conventional reference, it encompasses definite expressions
denoting unique entities (indeed, there was only one Mr.
Pickwick, Apollo, etc).

However, a problem arises with such uses as:

> 15.   He is a real Apollo.
> 15'. On jest prawdziwym Apollo.

These pertain to what I called elsewhere (Kryk 1983)
secondary extensions of proper names employed to
transfer the characteristics of their original
bearers to some other objects. Hence they lose their
name-like properties and become common nouns in a
process labelled by Zabrocki (1980) secondary
appellativization. If, however, these marginal instances are put aside due to their limited distribution, we are left with a group of proper names
sharing their semantic characteristics with those of
uniquely identifying reference (e.g. Pope John Paul II).

4. Another issue to be tackled here concerns the referentiality of NPs under the scope of world-creating predicates. On the one hand, the analysis will comprise verbs like <u>think</u>, <u>believe</u>, <u>assume</u>, etc. and modals like <u>possible</u>, which lead to what are often labelled opaque contexts. On the other hand, the properties of referential expressions will be examined when they occur in Reported Speech, which is supposed to deprive NPs of their referring function.

Consider the following examples:

16. Mark thought that the director of the Institute must have been ill.
16'. Marek myślał, że dyrektor Instytutu musi być chory.
17. Charles believed that Mr. Black was the editor-in-chief of 'Newsweek'.
17'. Karol wierzył/sądził, że pan Black jest redaktorem naczelnym 'Newsweeka'.
18. It is possible that Betty is pregnant.
18'. Możliwe, że Betty jest w ciąży.

According to Frege (1952, p. 68), names occurring under the scope of such predicates would shift their reference from objects to their senses, hence they will lose their referential capacity. Indeed, it seems to be psychologically real that while quoting someone's opinions we are normally dissociated from the commitment as to the existence of referents, truth values of propositions, etc. In fact, it might be the case that the speaker is able to suspend the referential capacity of the relevant NPs, cf.:

16a. Mark thought that the director of the Institute must have been ill since no-one welcomed him on his arrival; he didn't realize that we've got no director at present.
16a'. Marek myślał, że dyrektor Instytutu musi być chory, skoro nikt nie powitał go w momencie przyjazdu; nie zdawał sobie sprawy, żeobecnie nie mamy żadnego dyrektora.
17a. Charles believed that Mr. Black was the editor-in-chief of 'Newsweek'; he must have misheard the name, as there is no Mr. Black on the editorial board.
17a'. Karol wierzył, że pan Black jest redaktorem naczelnym 'Newsweeka'; musiał źle usłyszeć nazwisko, ponieważ nie ma żadnego pana Blacka w Komitecie Redakcyjnym.
18a. It is possible that Betty is pregnant ... but maybe it is her sister; I just saw their family buying a pram.

18a'. Możliwe, że Betty jest w ciąży ... ale może
to jej siostra; po prostu widziałam jak ich
rodzina kupowała wózek dziecinny.

Note that although Sequence of Tenses is irrelevant
to Polish data, suspension of reference works
analogously to English due to the above-mentioned
pragmatic factors which seemed to be shared by both
languages in question.

However, referential readings of the NPs under
discussion can be retained so that there are numerous
examples of sentences allowing a two-fold interpretation, cf.:

19. He thought that the child's teacher was
going to call.
19'. Myślał, że nauczyciel dziecka zadzwoni.

where the child's teacher may but does not have to
have a referent known to the speaker. Hence, while
opaque contexts allow two distinct interpretations
as to the referentiality of NPs, it is worth
bearing in mind that it is not the verb or the modal
which are responsible for either of the readings,
but first the speaker must decide the use of the NP
and the correct construal of the modal, and other
qualifications will then fall into place. Furthermore,
it is because we can in this way bring about a
different reading of the sentence overall - which may
affect truth - that we are entitled to distinguish
uses of definite descriptions that differ semantically
and not merely psychologically (Rundle 1979, p. 167).

Despite this general tendency, some expressions
never lose their referential properties, not even in
opaque contexts. This holds true for both English
and Polish NPs used deictically, cf..

20. Mary thought that that book was very good.
20'. Marysia sądziła, że ta książka jest bardzo
dobra.

With the capability for a two-fold interpretation,
opaque contexts will be left out from our systematization
and the analysis will turn to the referential characteristics of NPs in Reported Speech. Again, it might
be suspected that quotations will diminish the speaker's
responsibility for what he is reporting and the non-
referential reading of NPs should then prevail. But
consider the following:

21. *Mark said that the director of the Institute
must have been ill since no-one welcomed him
on his arrival; but he didn't realize that
we've got no director at present.
21'. *Marek powiedział, że dyrektor Instytutu musi
być chory, skoro nikt nie powitał, go w
momencie przyjazdu; ale nie zdawał sobie
sprawy, że obecnie nie mamy żadnego dyrektora.

The continuations of sentences in oratio obliqua which
tend to suspend or cancel the referential identity
of the NP sound odd - and this is for various reasons.
Firstly, it is the speaker/reporter who bears the
responsibility for the correct use of a referential
expression (if he did not know the referent's identity
he could use direct quotes or elucidate the issue by
asking a relevant question). Secondly, apart from
pragmatic reasons, there are two linguistic ones.
It is expressions with this/that which can never have
their referentiality suspended and there are some
established names of persons and things whose
referentiality is always secured by language (recall
our example with the Pope). To conclude, the
referential quality of nominal expressions is speaker-
relative both in opaque and reported contexts in the
sense that he bears the responsibility for selection of
the expression and the contexts in which it occurs.
Apart from a few linguistic factors like deixis (marked
by demonstratives) as well as uniqueness employing some
conventionally accepted names, it is always the speaker
who decides about the referring or non-referring
reading of an NP.

To wind up the discussion on Reported Speech, it
has to be emphasized that it is not only the remote-
ness of the action that is signalled by linguistic
means to create a distance between the speaker and
the reported facts. The same holds true for
referential expressions, whenever the speaker wants
to be detached from a referent's identity of which
he is not sure or even has no knowledge, as in the
following examples:

22. Charles believed that a/some Mr. Black
was the editor-in-chief of 'Newsweek'.
22'. Karol wierzył, że jakiś pan Black jest
redaktorem naczelnym 'Newsweeka'.

5.   The final problem concerning reference to be dealt
with here is that of identity statements. How far one
can go in substituting different names referring
to the same entity has been the subject of heated disputes, particularly in philosophical writings. Frege
(1952) assumed that proper names have a twofold
structure; they express their sense, simultaneously
designating their reference. He did not, however,
realize that the build-up of NPs is far from
symmetrical. Thus his example of. the evening star
vs. the morning star constitutes a case where
identity of reference does not equal identity of
sense.

        Innumerable analyses of similar examples
(Tully vs. Cicero or Walter Scott vs. the author of
'Waverly') have occupied almost all linguistically-
oriented philosophers and philosophically-oriented
linguists. Various conclusions were reached, but
the most convincing standpoint was taken by Rundle
in his Principle of Extensionality for Referential
Terms (1979, p. 148).[4]

        Be that as it may, consider the falsity of the
following inferences from identity statements:

        23.   The morning star rises in the morning.
              The morning star = the evening star.
              *The evening star rises in the morning.
        23'. Gwiazda poranna wschodzi rano.
              Gwiazda poranna = Gwiazda wieczorna.
              *Gwiazda wieczorna wschodzi rano.
        24.   Prof. Fisiak is president of LSE.
              I'd like to be president of LSE. ≠
              I'd like to be Prof. Fisiak.
        24'. Profesor Fisiak jest przewodniczącym LSE.
              Chciałabym być przewodniczącym LSE. ≠
              Chciałabym być profesorem Fisiakiem.

        Consequently, identity statements should also
be approached pragmatically, as context-dependent
constructs, and the morning star vs. the evening
star, being by no means identical but referring to the
same object, are simply two different uses of the
same name. A more thorough analysis of this issue
would be beyond the scope of this presentation;
however, it has been shown that pragmatics can
encompass even such highly philosophical matters
as identity theories. This constitutes another

piece of evidence supporting our claim that reference is an entirely context- and speaker-dependent notion.

6. The present study has been an attempt to systematize some observations on referential expressions in simple and embedded sentences. Both the English and Polish data have revealed the speaker-relative characteristics of the concept of reference which can be further systematized with NPs in simple sentences. Hence, semantic variables such as referentiality, definiteness and time/place indications, while combined accordingly by the speaker in his contextually determined choice of NP, help to define distinct types of reference: unique, identifying (instantaneous), covert, conventional and non-identifying.

In the case of referential NPs under the scope of modals and world-creating predicates, the referential and non-referential readings are highly speaker-relative in both English and Polish. Consequently reference seems to be even more context- and speaker-dependent under these predicates, which is also the case with identity statements.

It is my conjecture that reference, constituting a link between language and extra-linguistic reality, has an analogous status in other natural languages and is constantly adjusted to the discourse situation by language users. Some evidence to this effect has been supplied by the present analysis, but it would need a more profound cross-linguistic study to confirm my assumptions on a larger scale and thus produce some significant generalizations concerning reference.

NOTES

1. However, it was noticed by Linsky (1970, p. 76) that even if we say the oldest American university and it is a matter of fact that the oldest American university is Harvard, nothing prevents one from referring to another school (by mistake or jest) with these words. But, jests aside, it can be assumed that certain definite descriptions and proper names (or combinations thereof) represent unique reference (which is the case in the example with the Pope).

2.   Cf. also Lyons's comment on Strawson's
statement (Lyons 1977 , p. 181).

3.   Compare Rundle's observation concerning the
referential potential of indefinite NPs   (1979, p. 86):

> ... the failure of the indefinite description
> to definitely pick out or identify a person or
> thing from others of the kind in question stands
> in the way of its classification as a potential
> referring expression.

4.   The Principle of Extensionality for Referential
Terms was formulated as follows:

> If a and b are one and the same, then whatever
> is true of a, is true of b. Accordingly, if
> substitution of b for a results in a change
> in truth value, then either the reference of
> the names if different, or the names cannot
> function referentially in the context under
> consideration.

(Rundle 1979, p. 148)

REFERENCES

Caton, Ch.E. (ed.) (1970), Philosophy and ordinary language, Urbana: University of Illinois Press.
Cole, P. and J. Morgan, (eds.) (1975), Syntax and semantics 3, New York: Academic Press.
Davidson, D. (1980), 'Reality without reference', in Platts (ed.) (1980), pp. 131-140.
Davidson, D. and G. Harman, (eds.), (1972), Semantics of natural language, Dordrecht: Reidel.
Fodor, J.D. (1977), Semantics: theories of meaning in generative grammar, New York: Crowell.
Frege, G. (1952), 'On sense and reference', in Geach and Black (eds.) (1952), pp. 56-78.
Geach, P. and M. Black (eds.) (1952), The philosophical writings of Gottlob Frege, Oxford: Blackwell.
Grice, H.P. (1975), 'Logic and conversation', in Cole and Morgan (eds.) (1975), pp. 41-58.
Katz, J.J. (1977), Propositional structure and illocutionary force, New York: Crowell.
Kripke, S.A. (1972), 'Naming and necessity', in Davidson and Harman (eds.) (1972), pp. 253-355.
Kryk, B. (1983), 'How do proper names refer? Some contrastive evidence from English and Polish', Papers and Studies in Contrastive Linguistics 16, pp. 61-72.
Linsky, L. (1970), 'Reference and referents', in Caton (ed.) (1970), pp. 74-89.
Lyons, J. (1977), Semantics, Vol. 1, Cambridge: Cambridge University Press.
Platts, M. (ed.) (1980), Reference, truth and reality, London: Routledge & Kegan Paul.
Quine, W.O. (1960), Word and object, Cambridge, Mass.: The MIT Press.
Rundle, B. (1979), Grammar in philosophy, Oxford: Clarendon Press.
Russell, B. (1905), 'On denoting', Mind 14, pp. 479-493.
Strawson, P.F. (1970), 'On referring', in Caton (ed.) (1970), pp. 162-193.
Thrane, T. (1980), Referential-semantic analysis, Cambridge: Cambridge University Press.
Wilson, D. (1975), Presupposition and non-truth-conditional semantics, New York: Academic Press.
Zabrocki, L. (1980), U podstaw struktury i rozwoju języka, Warszawa: PWN.

FOSSILIZATION, PIDGINIZATION AND THE MONITOR

Marquette Lowther
University of Texas
at Austin

In the field of secondary language acquisition (SLA),
a variety of ideas and questions compete for the
attention of those involved in research and study.
Questions regarding critical periods, sensitive periods,
the effects of hemispheric lateralization and age
continue to be under investigation. These competing
ideas are often difficult to compare in any significant
or enlightening way. Each idea approaches the issue
of SLA from a different perspective. This variation
in perspective and focus yields results which ought
not be compared across the board. Most of the possible
comparisons lie in the areas of implication and
inference. This paper will focus on two current
theories of SLA - the Pidginization Hypothesis and
Monitor Theory - and their relationships to
fossilization. Pidginization appears to explain
the acquisition process, while Monitor Theory accounts
for some of the differences between learned knowledge
and performance. The understanding of this distinction may indicate means for countering
fossilization.

Fossilization, as presented in much of the
literature, is understood to be the inability of
a person to attain native-like ability in the
target language (TL).

Fossilizable linguistic phenomena are linguistic
items, rules, and subsystems which speakers of a
particular NL will tend to keep in their IL
relative to a particular TL no matter what the
age of the learner or amount of explanation and
instruction he receives in the TL. (Selinker 1978,
pp. 118, 119)[1]

Fossilization is generally thought of as an undesirable
occurrence in the course of SLA. However, Vigil and
Oller (1976) point out that fossilization can be a
positive factor as well. Correct (i.e., native-
like) forms may fossilize as well as incorrect (i.e.,
non-native-like) forms. Fossilization, then, is the
cessation of change in a given target form or
structure in the grammar of the student[2].

One false inference that may be drawn from such a definition is that fossilization is a unitary process or occurrence (i.e., all components of the language cease to develop at the same point in time). On the contrary, different aspects of the developing language system may fossilize at different points in time and level. This recognition of various points of fossilization allows for some things to fossilize in their correct (i.e., native-like) form while other parts of the grammar are still developing.

Some controversy exists over the permanence of fossilization. Selinker and Lamendella (1978) contend that fossilization is permanent, and any halt in progress which is not permanent is labelled stabilization. Others do not make this distinction in their discussions of fossilization. As it is virtually impossible to determine the permanence of a halt in progress, the term fossilization will be used in this paper to refer to any halt in progress. As such, the term defossilization will be used to denote resumed development following a period of no movement. Whatever the cause for the initial fossilization, anything which removes, alters or overpowers that cause may be capable of initiating defossilization. The task of the researcher is to discover the source or sources of fossilization in order to help the student defossilize, if defossilization is indeed possible, or to prevent fossilization in the first place.

Many possible sources for fossilization have been proposed. Seliger (1978) views fossilization as the result of the maturational process of intra-hemispheric localization of function in the brain. Corder (1978) indicates that communicative need determines the level at which the TL will be fossilized. Nida (1971) sees fossilization as a result of the level of mutual adjustment necessary for communication which is established by the student and those with whom he/she interacts. Vigil and Oller (1976) propose a threshold level of corrective feedback as the determining factor in fossilization. Others look to affective variables to be the source. Schumann (1978d) proposes social and psychological distance to explain fossilization.

In his Pidginization Hypothesis, Schumann (1978d) has drawn a connection between the development of pidgins and creoles, and the development of a student's TL grammar. He argues that the first step in normal SLA is the simplification[3] of TL structures. This simplification has been studied most often in the syntax and morphology of the language. As the student progresses, he/she will complexify his/her TL grammar; and in so doing, he/she will more closely approach the grammar of the native speaker[4].

The term **simplification** must be interpreted carefully. **Simplification** does not mean **simple** in a straightforward sense. The terms **simplification** and **reduction** refer to the relationships between the forms and the functions of structures in the student's interlanguage. When a student uses a pre-verbal negator in all negations, he/she is using one form to perform a variety of functions. As the student's grammar complexifies, different forms of negation will be distinguished and acquired. As this happens, the earlier form will become increasingly restricted in its usage. A student's individual interlanguage rules are not necessarily less complex than those of a native speaker, but most individual rules in the student's interlanguage cover a greater amount of territory than do the individual rules in the TL or native language.

People who are involved with students endeavouring to perform in a secondary language are aware that at some point progress seems to cease. Schumann (1978a) indicates that it is the process of complexification which ceases. He then posits two causes for this halt: social and psychological distance. These two factors create an insurmountable barrier to further complexification of the grammar. Unless they are reduced, removed or overpowered, the student cannot progress any further in the SLA process.

> When we examine social factors that affect secondary language learning we look at variables which involve the relationship between two social groups who are in a contact situation, but who speak different languages. (Schumann 1978c: 163)

These variables may actually exist, or they may only exist in the minds of those involved. The reality of the situation is not as important as the perception of the situation.

Schumann (1978d) divides the social distance variable into several factors which interrelate and either encourage or inhibit language acquisition. In order to simplify matters, his factors have been collapsed into just two: 1) the power relationship between the cultures in contact, 2) the identification of the student with the target culture. The first category covers the political and social relationships between the two cultures involved. Schumann predicts that being dominated by another culture will inhibit the student's adjustment to that culture. The power struggle may take precedence over language acquisition.

The second category refers to the way the student adjusts to the new culture. Several options are available (e.g., assimilation, acculturation and preservation). Other factors may influence the student's choice of coping strategy. The size and cohesiveness of the student's native culture group within the target culture situation, the degree of difference (actual or perceived) between the two cultures involved, the student's intentions in the target culture situation, as well as other factors can act to influence the student's response to the target culture and language.

Psychological distance involves the individual student and how he/she operates. The factors categorized under this heading are diverse in nature. They range from biological limitations to instructional factors and on to attitude and motivation. Personality characteristics are included as well. The focus is on the individual and how he/she reacts to the TL and the target culture.

Schumann (1978d) implies that psychological distance is more powerful than social distance. Students who overcome negative social variables do so because of the positive affect of psychological variables. To a lesser extent, the opposite situation (i.e. positive social variables overcoming negative psychological variables) is also possible. In addition, the individual variables are not as important as the relationships between the variables. These interrelationships determine the level at which the student will fossilize. Pidginization describes the process of SLA and development; whereas fossilization describes or defines the finished product (i.e., the language used by the student once he/she has ceased to progress).

Why is it that some students perform very well in language classrooms and yet are unable to communicate when placed in the target culture? Others perform less well in the classroom and yet communicate with relative ease in the target culture. Still other students make certain errors quite consistently in their speech yet are able to produce virtually error-free writing. Often, they are also able to correct oral errors they make, once such errors are brought to their attention. What causes this variation in performance? Krashen supplies a possible answer to this question with his theory of the Monitor.

Krashen (1977b) draws a distinction between acquisition and learning. Acquisition is the unconscious absorption of the TL. Learning involves the conscious isolation and recognition of the rules of the TL. This distinction is the basis for differences in performance within the individual and across groups. Acquired knowledge initiates utterances, and learned knowledge acts to filter out or alter ungrammatical forms. Students may be able to consciously monitor their own output prior to its actual performance.

Acquisition is related to informal learning environments, yet Krashen emphasizes the value of formal classroom instruction. Communication seems to be the key to acquiring language. Krashen (1980) argues that students will take what they need from the input available to them, and acquire the language structures for which they are ready. This is his i + 1 hypothesis. Ideally, the teacher would know both the current level of the student, and the next level to be acquired in the developmental sequence. With this knowledge, the teacher would be able to provide the student with a rich source of +1 input from which to draw. Since language teachers do not live in an ideal world, they are not able to present such precise input to their students. Krashen suggests that the instructor provide input which is both rich in content and varied in structure. This may succeed in providing the student with the appropriate +1 input, in addition to the input which is not yet appropriate to his/her needs. The content of the input is important, because it is the means by which the student becomes interested and involved in communicating in the TL. Since communication seems to be the key to acquisition, and since acquisition is the goal, it follows that the content is a useful component to manipulate in an effort to encourage communication.

Learning, on the other hand, is most often connected
with formal instruction. However, situations which
appear to be informal may contribute to learning rather
than, or in addition to acquisition. Students themselves are capable of creating a characteristically
formal environment by isolating rules and either
requesting feedback or checking their own work for
errors. In much the same way, formal environments may
act as informal environments for the student who is
particularly interested in language and grammar in
and of themselves.

Krashen and Seliger (1975) posit two features
to distinguish formal situations from informal situations:
1) isolation of rules, 2) feedback. These two features
are rather flexible in actual application. Both can
be provided in a number of ways including an instructor
or the student him-/herself. Neither rule isolation
nor feedback necessitates or excludes either
acquisition or learning. Rather their presence may
increase the tendency for learning to occur and may
lessen the likelihood of acquisition occurring.

Lamendella (1977) and others contend that learning
may inhibit the acquisition process. If this is so,
it follows that learning ought to be discouraged in
order for acquisition to be encouraged. Krashen and
Seliger (1975) are not in agreement with this.
Although they would agree that acquisition is the
primary goal, learning is not seen as being necessarily
inhibitory.

After distinguishing between acquisition and
learning, Krashen (1977b) draws the two into a
working relationship via the Monitor. He suggests
that learned knowledge acts as a filter for acquired
knowledge. Utterances (oral and written) are
initiated by acquired knowledge or by the student's
native language. The result of this initiation may
then be matched against what is consciously known
about the TL (i.e. learned knowledge). This body of
conscious knowledge if known as the Monitor because
of its function in monitoring production. As the
Monitor is used, the initiated utterance is altered
to resolve any incongruencies between it and the
learned knowledge before the utterance is produced.
The Monitor may also act to check utterances after
production and thus stimulate self-correction.

Schumann (1978c) acknowledges the Monitor, and
uses it as one factor of psychological distance. It
is located in this category because of individual

132

variation in the use of the Monitor. Krashen (1978)
distinguishes three types of Monitor users: 1) overusers,
2) underusers, 3) moderate users. These different
styles of use operate to influence language production.
Underusers are those students who make few, if any,
self-corrections. They tend to be quite fluent in
their use of the TL, yet they lack high levels of
grammatical accuracy. Overusers, on the other hand,
attempt to monitor every utterance they produce in
the TL. They go so far as to monitor even those
structures which they have already acquired. This
results in grammatically accurate, but hesitant
productions. Overuse may also serve to limit the amount
of production attempted, as overusers tend to prefer
to remain silent rather than to make errors. The
third type of Monitor users, the moderate users, are
those who have managed to reach a happy medium between
overuse and underuse. They appear to be able to
monitor their production when it is appropriate and
beneficial to do so, and yet are able to produce
unmonitored language in more casual circumstances.

The major problem with the use of the Monitor
(and learned knowledge) is the ability to use the
Monitor effectively. Research indicates that the
Monitor is only effective in artificial, highly
focused situations which allow enough time for the
Monitor to be called into action. Schumann (1978b)
and Krashen[5] himself do not believe that learned
knowledge can transfer directly to acquired knowledge.
The two are separate bodies of knowledge related only
through the use of the Monitor.

Nevertheless, learning can be of direct and
immediate use to the student in a number of ways.
An obvious value is that it allows the student to
begin production in the TL almost immediately.
Utterances may be initiated in the native language
and then translated into the TL by the Monitor.

Another direct value of the Monitor is that
of editing written work[6]. Students studying in a
secondary language situation may be able to edit their
own written work by consciously using their learned
knowledge of the TL. Students could develop check-
lists of errors which they commonly make, and which
they are able to correct with their Monitor and use
these lists as editing prompters.

Indirect benefits may also be obtained from
learned knowledge. Although learned knowledge does
not transfer directly to acquired knowledge, it may
be possible for learning to facilitate acquisition[7].
One method of facilitation is that of self-stimulation[8].
The student, using learned knowledge as a monitor to

produce utterances beyond his/her acquired abilities,
is able to produce his/her own input. At some stage,
this input will contain those structures which the
student is ready to acquire. By producing these
utterances, the student will provide the input necessary
for their acquisition.

Early production, as enabled by monitoring, may
invite input. This involves patterns of discourse.
Hatch (1978a, p. 408) presents the first rule of
conversation as 'say something relevant'. When this
is not possible due to linguistic limitations, it may
be reduced to 'say something' (Hatch 1978a, p. 409).
The student is enabled to say something, or even to
say something relevant, by using his/her learned
knowledge. By getting into a conversation, and then
being able to maintain the conversation through a
variety of discourse techniques, the student is
making input available to him-/herself. This input
will probably be of great use and value to the
student because the focus is on communication, not
language. Much recent research indicates that the
communicative nature of input allows for and
encourages acquisition. By focusing the attention on
communication and away from the language itself,
acquisition is free to occur.

Other factors which may allow learning to facilitate acquisition relate to Schumann's psychological
distance variable. Students often have expectations
regarding language learning situations. Many expect
a certain amount of memorization, rule isolation and
corrective feedback to be part of language learning.
Not having these expectations fulfilled may cause
some anxiety or even rebellion on the part of the
student. Such tension could inhibit acquisition.

Learning also might be useful in reducing
anxiety in the terrified or unbelieving student. Some
people do not believe that they have the capabilities
required to learn/acquire language. By teaching them
basic rules and vocabulary which they can consciously
manipulate, they may be eased out of some of their
fears. If they once believe that they are able to
communicate something in the TL, they may be able to
acquire some of the TL.

If Monitor Theory is an accurate and valid
representation of the knowledge that language learners
possess, then it may be possible to aid students in
improving their TL production by training them to
use the Monitor.

In the case of students who have fossilized some

feature or features of their TL grammar at some point other than native-like production, learning to successfully use the Monitor might enable them to perform language tasks which are beyond their acquired capabilities, and yet are important to the student. In this way, the Monitor might be useful in overcoming deficiencies in their fossilized form of the language.

The first step in learning to use the Monitor may be learning to recognize errors. Language students are often aware, in a general or vague way, that they have errors in their production. However, they often do not notice the particular errors that they make. Teaching them to recognize their own errors may be difficult, but not impossible if the student and the teacher are both patient and enduring. Just how this is accomplished is not clear. Carroll (1981) suggests that reinforcement can play a role in strengthening or controlling one's own responses.

Although the behaviourist view of language as a set of habits has been supplanted by the cognitivist view that language is more rational in nature, it does not follow that habit plays no role in language or language acquisition. Learning to tune into errors may become habit or habitual in nature. On the other hand, it may be more like a learning strategy[10], composed of two parts: 1) recognizing the error, 2) using the Monitor to correct the error. Error correction via the Monitor could be taught as a language learning and production strategy. When knowing when to use the Monitor is viewed as a strategy, it is plausible to remove its use from the realm of linguistic processes. It is more logical or mathematical in nature, than it is linguistic. Language is creative and infinite; whereas the Monitor is static and finite.

Habit formation and learning strategies are both mental processes which may be involved in language acquisition and production in some way. As such, they are areas which need to be investigated further. They are of particular interest when they are thought of in connection with the fossilized student. Perhaps they will provide some insight into overcoming unwanted fossilization. The old cliché says that you can't teach an old dog new tricks. I hope that the use of the Monitor will invalidate this saying in regard to SLA.

NOTES

1. In this quote, NL stands for native language, IL for interlanguage, and TL for target language.

2. The term <u>student</u> as used here and throughout this paper refers to a person engaged in SLA or language learning. Because this paper deals with Krashen's distinction between acquisition and learning, I have chosen a more neutral term for clarity. The term <u>student</u>, as used in this paper does not imply a person necessarily involved in formal language study.

3. The criteria he uses for determining the simplicity or complexity of a given form are not given. The term <u>simplification</u> is accepted as indicating a lack of fullness in the function and form of the student's interlanguage grammar in comparison to both the TL and native language grammars.

4. Each successive complexification may not appear to be a closer approximation of the TL grammar; however, the overall direction of the complexifications will be towards a more native-like grammatical representation.

5. Personal communication, 15 May 1981.

6. I restrict this value to written work as it involves going back over the already produced utterances and then correcting them. Editing does not refer to any altering completed previous to production.

7. This does not mean that learning should or must precede acquisition.

8. Personal communication, Stephen Krashen, 15 May 1981.

9. Although Hatch presents these conversation rules in the context of child SLA, I believe that they may be applied to adult SLA as well. However, many discourse rules are culture specific, which might influence their use.

10. Suggested by Professor James W. Tollefson.

REFERENCES

Anderson, R.W. (1980), 'The role of creolization in
   Schumann's pidginization hypothesis', in S.D.
   Krashen and R.C. Scarcella (eds.), Issues in
   second language research, Rowley, Mass.: Newbury
   House Publishers, pp. 66-73.
Bialystok, E. (1978), 'A theoretical model of second
   language learning', Language Learning 28.1, pp. 69-83.
Brown, H.D. (1980), 'The optimal distance model of
   second language learning', TESOL Quarterly 14.2,
   pp. 157-164.
Carroll, J.B. (1981), 'Conscious and automatic processes
   in language learning', Canadian Modern Language
   Journal 37.3, pp. 462-474.
Corder, S.P. (1978), 'Language-learner language', in
   J.C. Richards (ed.), Understanding second and
   foreign language learning, Rowley, Mass.: Newbury
   House Publishers, pp. 71-92.
Hatch, E. (1978a), 'Discourse analysis and second
   language acquisition', in E. Hatch (ed.),
   Second language acquisition: A book of readings,
   Rowley, Mass.: Newbury House Publishers, pp. 401-435.
Hatch, E. (1978b), 'Discourse analysis, speech acts,
   and second language acquisition', in W.C. Ritchie
   (ed.), Second language acquisition research:
   Issues and implications, New York: Academic Press,
   pp. 127-136.
Krashen, S.D. (1979), 'A response to McLaughlin,
   "The Monitor Model: Some methodological
   considerations"', Language Learning 29.1, pp. 151-167.
Krashen, S.D. (1976), 'Formal and informal linguistic
   environments in language acquisition and language
   learning', TESOL Quarterly 10.2, pp. 157-168.
Krashen, S.D. (1978), 'Individual variation in the use
   of the Monitor', in W.C. Ritchie (ed.), Second
   language acquisition research: Issues and implications,
   New York: Academic Press, pp. 175-183.
Krashen S.D. (1977a), 'Some issues relating to the
   Monitor Model', On TESOL '77, pp. 144-158.
Krashen, S.D. (1977b), 'The Monitor Model for adult
   second language performance', in M. Burt, H.
   Dulay and M. Finocchiaro (eds.), Viewpoints on
   English as a second language, New York: Regents
   Publishing, pp. 152-161.
Krashen, S.D. (1980), 'The theoretical and practical
   relevance of simple codes in second language
   acquisition', in S.D. Krashen and R.C. Scarcella
   (eds.), Issues in second language research, Rowley,
   Mass.: Newbury House Publishers, pp. 7-18.
Krashen S.D., M.A. Long and R.C. Scarcella (1979),
   'Age, rate and eventual attainment in second
   language acquisition', TESOL Quarterly 13.4,
   pp. 573-582.

Krashen, S.D. and H.W. Seliger (1975), 'The essential contributions of formal instruction in adult second language learning', TESOL Quarterly 9.2, pp. 173-183.

Lamendella, J.T. (1977), 'General principles of neurofunctional organization and their manifestation in primary and nonprimary language acquisition', Language Learning. 27.1, pp. 155-196.

Lamendella, J.T. (1979), 'The neurofunctional basis of pattern practice', TESOL Quarterly 13.1, pp. 5-19.

Larsen-Freeman, D.E. (1978a), 'An explanation for the morpheme accuracy order of learners of English as a second language', in E. Hatch (ed.), Second language acquisition: A book of readings, Rowley, Mass.: Newbury House Publishers, pp. 371-379.

Larsen-Freeman,D .E. (1978b), 'Evidence of the need for a second language index of development', in W.C. Ritchie (ed.), Second language acquisition research: Issues and implications, New York: Academic Press, pp. 127-136.

McLaughlin, B. (1978), 'The Monitor Model: Some methodological considerations', Language Learning 28.2, pp. 309-331.

Nida, E.A. (1971), 'Sociopsychological problems in language mastery and retention', in P. Pimsleur and T. Quinn (eds.), The psychology of second language learning, Cambridge: Cambridge University Press, pp. 59-65.

Richards, J.C. (1978), 'Error analysis and second language strategies', in J.H. Schumann and N. Stenson (eds.), New frontiers in second language learning, Rowley, Mass.: Newbury House Publishers, pp. 32-53.

Schumann, F.M. and Schumann, J.H. (1977), 'Diary of a language learner: An introspective study of second language learning', in H.D. Brown, C.A. Yoma and R.H. Crymes (eds.), Teaching and learning: Trends in research and practice, Georgetown: TESOL, Georgetown University, pp. 241-249.

Schumann, J.H. (1978a), 'Implications of pidginization and creolization for the study of adult second language acquisition', in J.H. Schumann and N. Stenson (eds.), New Frontiers in second language learning, Rowley, Mass.: Newbury House Publishers, pp. 137-150.

Schumann, J.H. (1978b), 'Second language acquisition: The pidginization hypothesis', in E. Hatch (ed.), Second language acquisition: A book of readings, Rowley, Mass.: Newbury House Publishers, pp. 256-271.

Schumann, J.H. (1978c), 'Social and psychological factors in second language acquisition', in J.C. Richards (ed.), Understanding second and foreign language learning: Issues and approaches, Rowley, Mass.: Newbury House Publishers, pp. 163-177.

Schumann, J.H. (1978d), The pidginization process: A model for second language acquisition, Rowley, Mass.: Newbury House Publishers.

Schumann, J.H. (1978e), 'The relationship of pidginization, creolization and decreolization to second language acquisition', On TESOL '78, pp. 367-379.

Schumann, J.H. (1980), 'The acquisition of English relative clauses by second language learners', in S.D. Krashen and R.C. Scarcella (eds.), Issues in second language research, Rowley, Mass.: Newbury House Publishers, pp. 119-131.

Seliger, H.W. (1978), 'Implications of a multiple critical periods hypothesis for second language learning', in W.C. Ritchie (ed.), Second language acquisition research: Issues and implications, New York: Academic Press, pp. 11-19.

Seliger, H.W. (1979), 'On the nature and function of language rules in language teaching', TESOL Quarterly 13.3, pp. 359-368.

Selinker, L. (1978), 'Interlanguage', in J.H. Schumann and N. Stenson (eds.), New frontiers in second language learning, Rowley, Mass.: Newbury House Publishers, pp. 114-136.

Selinker, .L. (1971), 'The psychologically relevant data of second language learning', in P. Pimsleur and T. Quinn (eds.), The psychology of second language learning, Cambridge: Cambridge University Press, pp. 35-42.

Selinker, L. and J.T. Lamendella (1978), 'Fossilization in interlanguage learning', On TESOL '78, pp. 240-249.

Selinker, L. and J.T. Lamendella (1979), 'The role of extrinsic feedback in interlanguage fossilization: A discussion of "Rule fossilization: A tentative model"', Language Learning 29.2, pp. 363-375.

Stauble, A.M.E. (1980), 'Acculturation and second language acquisition', in S.D. Krashen and R.C. Scarcella (eds.), Issues in second language research, Rowley, Mass.: Newbury House Publishers, pp. 43-50.

Terrell, T., E. Gomez and J. Mariscal (1980), 'Can acquisition take place in the classroom?' in S.D. Krashen and R.C. Scarcella (eds.), Issues in second language research, Rowley, Mass.: Newbury House Publishers, pp. 155-161.

Vigil, N.A. and J.W. Oller (1976), 'Rule fossilization: A tentative model', Language Learning 26.2, pp. 281-295.

SOCIAL CONTEXT AND LANGUAGE USAGE:
IMPLICATIONS FOR CHILDREN WITH
IMPAIRED HEARING

Patrick McDonnell
University College
Dublin

Introduction

Children acquire the language of their environment
with remarkable ease and rapidity, even in the face of
dramatic handicaps (Lenneberg 1968). In addition, even
very young children develop an awareness of different
acts of language and that different linguistic forms are
appropriately used in different situations (Crystal 1976,
p. 55). In most countries school-going age normally
coincides with the time in children's lives when they have
mastered the principal grammatical structures of their
language. (McNeill 1970, p. 84).

Among the very few exceptions to these general rules
are children with profoundly or severely impaired hearing[1].
In the case of most of these children a conscious and
formal strategy is employed in enabling them to acquire
or develop a language. The implementation of this
strategy has been identified as the central task in
their schooling (The education of children who are
handicapped by impaired hearing, 1972, chap. 6). Unlike
the hearing child or the deaf child of parents who use
sign language, the majority of children with profound
hearing impairment are unlikely to have mastered the
basic grammar of any language, oral or sign, before they
enter school, usually a special school. The primary goal
of educational programmes in special schools is, therefore,
the establishment of a fluent system of communication which
in turn will provide the foundation upon which the
secondary language systems of reading and writing can then
be developed (Quigley and Kretschmer 1982, p. 10).

Despite the fact that individuals with impaired
hearing display the same range of intellectual abilities
as their hearing counterparts (Moores 1978; Vernon 1968),
numerous British, American and European studies agree
that they perform less well in tasks that involve
standard linguistic usage (Conrad 1977a; Kretschmer and
Kretschmer 1978; Morris 1978; Quigley and Kretschmer 1982).
The overall picture of the hearing impaired pupil's

achievement in school is one of very limited performance in oral communication and low levels of attainment in reading and writing. Conrad (1977a), for example, tested the reading ability of almost every 15 : 0 to 16 : 6 year old pupil with impaired hearing attending special schools in England and Wales. Of the total of 355 pupils, half failed to achieve a reading age of eight years. It is hardly surprising, therefore, that findings such as this have given rise to heated debate, particularly with regard to teaching methods currently employed in the schools.

The first section of this paper contains a brief account of the methods of communication that are employed in schools for pupils with impaired hearing. In the second section the use of oral communication techniques are critically examined in relation to the oral language and literacy achievements of pupils. The complex socio-linguistic environment of special schools is explored in the final section of the paper and areas of possible conflict are discussed. In conclusion, I would like, firstly, to consider briefly some implications for pupils of current schooling practices and secondly, to suggest a possible direction for the future.

Methods of Communication

Broadly speaking, methods of communication have traditionally fallen into three categories - oral, manual and combined methods. Oral communication involves communication between the hearing and the hearing impaired and among the hearing impaired themselves by means of speech and speechreading which are supplemented by amplified sound. Manual communication entails the use of a system of signs and gestures through which a language can be represented visually. A combined method of communication, or total communication as it is sometimes called, involves a combination of some or of all the elements of oral and manual communication.

There is a second issue involved here which is worth clarifying. While a system of signs can be devised to represent visually languages that are normally spoken, it is important to distinguish between signed English and, for example, American Sign Language. Native sign languages are now coming to be regarded as true languages with their own distinct grammatical structures (Lane and Grosjean 1980; Siple 1978; Wilbur 1979). American Sign Language therefore differs from

oral English both in its form - signs - and in its
structure. All over the world, however, schools employ
oral languages or signed versions of them as the basis
of their programmes. Nowhere is a native sign language
used as a vehicle of instruction (Tervoort 1978).

Since hardly any educationalists endorse an
exclusively manual method of communication (except
for children with multiple handicaps), in current
practice two approaches - oral and combined - are
employed in teaching children with impaired hearing.
There are, however, serious differences of opinion
as to which of these methods is the 'better'.
Research findings so far available suggest the
following conclusions:

(a)   It is universally believed that all children with
      impaired hearing should have the opportunity
      of developing speech skills. There is no
      opposition to the use of hearing aids, though
      there are differences of opinion as to what can
      be achieved through their use (Erber 1972; Plomp
      1978; Pollack 1964).

(b)   The view that exposure of young children to forms
      of manual communication hinders their acquisition
      of vocal, reading or written language skills is
      not warranted (Meadow 1968; Montgomery 1966;
      Moores 1978; Quigley 1969; Stuckless and Birch 1966).

(c)   Early exposure of children to some forms of manual
      communication has led to significant improvement
      in language and communication skills, including
      oral skills (Brasel and Quigley 1977; Prinz and
      Prinz 1979).

(d)   The introduction of the child to manual
      communication at an early stage does not, necessarily,
      eliminate reading and writing difficulties. The
      fact that the communication controversy persists,
      suggests that there may be no one 'best' method for
      all children (Kretschmer and Kretschmer 1978).

(e)   Attempts to define objective criteria that might
      be used in selecting oral or combined communication
      options have, so far, been unsuccessful (Ling, Ling
      and Pflaster 1977).

(f)   The term 'manual communication' is not always
      clearly defined in literature on the education of
      children with impaired hearing. It can be used
      to describe a native sign language, English in a
      signed form, or a linguistic system that incor-
      porates elements from both (Moores 1974; Wilbur 1979).

(g) Finally, over the last twenty years an increasing
amount of research has been conducted on this
issue. Until, however, many more studies have
been undertaken and much more evidence accumu-
lated, conclusions can be only tentative.

Oral Schooling and the Teaching of Language

In Ireland and in Britain the great majority of
children with impaired hearing are placed in schools
where the declared policy is one of oral communication
only. (The education of children who are handicapped
by impaired hearing, 1972; Henderson 1976). In
training colleges and on official courses for teachers
of the hearing impaired, oral communication techniques
are the only ones taught at length. The question
then arises as to how a strictly oral methodology can
remain tenable in view of the failure of so many
pupils to achieve adequate standard language skills.

Many oralists hold that the system which they
advocate ' ...has not as yet had a fair chance to
succeed' (Reeves 1976, p. 15). It has been argued
that there are '... few schools in which oral
communication inside and outside the classroom is
consistently maintained' (John and Howarth 1973,
p. 105). There is a shortage of teachers with
special training as well as a high turnover of
teachers with special qualifications (Reeves 1976). Early
diagnosis and assessment of hearing impairment is
neither universal nor efficient (Shah, Chandler and Dale
1978). Equipment is often outdated and servicing arrangements leave much to be desired (Reeves 1976). Morris
(1978), however, maintains that extremely low standards
have existed in special schools for decades and that
relative improvements in equipment, training or
personnel, parent guidance and assessment procedures
do not appear to have altered the situation.

A different explanation has been postulated by
Clark (1978). She argues that the failure of so many
pupils to develop fluent oral communication skills is
primarily due to the widespread use of an analytic[2]
approach in the teaching of language. This approach,
which emphasises repetitive drill procedures in the
teaching of syntax and practice on 'model' sentences,
is at odds, she believes, with the manner in which
children acquire a mother tongue. The focus on form
rather than content disrupts the normal functioning
of language in communication (Brennan 1975; Brown 1973).

Clark's argument implies that children with impaired
hearing go through the same stages of language development as their hearing counterparts, but at a delayed
rate. The children must be allowed to construct their
own sentences when they have something they really
want to communicate. No attempts must be made '... to
"get voice" before a child is ready to give it or to
"say a word" before a child has anything to say' (Clark
1978, p. 152). Very little progress is, therefore,
seen during the early years in terms of encoding
language.

There are two main difficulties in sustaining
the position outlined by Clark. The first is related
to the use of residual hearing. Children with a
severe or profound hearing loss must depend on
extremely limited and imperfect acoustic signals, and
on ambiguous visual cues for their linguistic output
(Conrad 1977b). In the light of restrictions of
this nature the capacity of children with profoundly
impaired hearing to utilize residual hearing for speech
discrimination is very circumscribed indeed (Erber 1972;
Plomp 1978).

The second difficulty relates to the children's
need to communicate with both adults and peers
before they have acquired sufficient mastery of an
auditory-vocal channel of communication. The fact
that children produce no oral output does not mean
that they have nothing to communicate. The achievement of relatively fluent oral communication between
hearing individuals and individuals with impaired
hearing is a formidable enough task. The difficulties
involved become extraordinary when both participants
in a communicative exchange have profoundly impaired
hearing (Von der Lieth 1978; Cicourel and Boese 1972).
It is not clear how far advocates of a natural or
synthetic approach in the teaching of oral language
are prepared to accept gestures or signs as legitimate modes of communication for young hearing
impaired children. Neither is it clear what steps
they would take in terms of monitoring, supervision
or surveillance of child/child communicative interactions.

A second explanation for the apparent failure
of oral methods is implicit in criticism of research
findings which suggest that some forms of manual
communication are beneficial. Ling, Ling and
Pflaster (1977), Nix (1975) and Owrid (1972), for
example, have noted that pupils for this research were
drawn mainly from residential schools where signing or

combined systems of communication prevailed in almost
every setting except the classroom. This sociolinguistic environment was held to be responsible for
the inadequate oral communication skills of pupils.
The argument, however, is nowhere pursued to any kind
of satisfactory conclusion. The purpose of the final
part of this paper is to examine this issue in some
detail.

Social Context and Language Usage in the Special School

Individuals with impaired hearing are often said
to be linguistically 'impoverished' or 'deprived'; their
language is diagnosed as being 'ungrammatical',
'primitive' or as 'having no structure'. In these
instances, as often as not, language is assumed to be
synonymous with standard usage in spoken or written
form (Fischer 1978; Lancioni 1981). Another related
assumption made about language and communication in
special schools for children with impaired hearing is
that the only linguistic interactions that occur are
those between adults and children, or at least those
are the only kind that count (Ivimey 1977).

Research findings suggest the existence of complex varieties of linguistic behaviour in communities
of individuals with impaired hearing. These range
from closed systems acquired or developed within a
small group to a native sign language capable of
expressing all the nuances and levels of its spoken
counterpart (Moores 1974; Schlesinger and Namir 1978;
Tervoort 1978; Wilbur 1976, 1979). Special schools
are no exception.

Special schooling involves gathering into one
place large numbers of children who have not
acquired an auditory-vocal channel of communication.
In these circumstances children will have to resort
to other than vocal channels of communication in
order to understand and be understood. Well docu-
mented evidence indicates that this is exactly
what they do (Cicourel and Boese 1972; Moores 1974;
Tervoort 1961). The urge to communicate obliges
hearing impaired children, often in the face of
adult disapproval or hostility, to construct gestural
linguistic systems or to surreptitiously acquire a
sign language from peers.

The existence of signing systems has been observed
even in school programmes which pursue strictly oral
methods (Cicourel and Boese 1972; Moores 1974). Some
of these systems may be unintelligible not only to
children with impaired hearing in other special schools

but also to pupils of other age groups in the same
school (Tervoort 1961). It has also been argued
that these linguistic systems are highly organised
and rule governed to a point where they must be considered as functioning in a symbolic way for the users
(Kretschmer and Kretschmer 1978, p. 89).

Indeed, one recent study of four children with
severe hearing impairment, aged from 1 : 6 to 4 : 0
years, described how symbolic communicative
behaviour could develop in the absence of an obvious
linguistic model (Goldin-Meadow and Feldman 1975).

Several areas of actual or potential conflict
arise out of this situation where the majority of
pupils are placed in school programmes that consciously exclude non-vocal methods of communication.
Firstly, there is a serious divergence between the
official communication system of the school and
the private systems of the pupils. Advocates of
strictly oral schooling have a number of ways of
dealing with this problem.

Schools can employ large numbers of well-
motivated staff to act as monitors or inter-
preters in child/child communicative exchanges.
This solution presents both practical and theoretical difficulties. Such low pupil-staff ratios
can hardly be achieved in view of the financial
constraints operating on special schools. If they
could be achieved, then an individualised tutoring
system based in ordinary schools would probably be
a more logical proposition. Furthermore, the
advisability of such an intense degree of supervision,
and its possible consequences for the social, emotional
and linguistic lives of pupils, must be questioned.

Schools can ignore alternative signing systems
which inevitably emerge in the absence of relatively
ideal staff-pupil ratios. This option assumes that
child/child communication is not important. Schools
can actively attempt to suppress unofficial communication systems, thus creating a situation of actual
conflict. This brings me to the second area of conflict in special schools.

To dismiss or suppress particular forms of
communicative behaviour will involve rejection of the
social and cultural norms and values which underlie
them. Labov (1972) points out that covert norms and
values associated with language usage are often
extremely difficult to elicit but are very powerful
nevertheless. Verbeck and Tervoort (1967) have, for
example, reported that children of all ages in special
schools in the United States, Belgium and the Netherlands,
tended to use signs as the preferred channel of
communication in their private conversations. An Irish
study (McDonnell 1980) found that although pupils with

profoundly impaired hearing placed the achievement of good
oral language skills at the top of their list of priorities,
non-vocal communication predominated in settings outside
the classroom.

It is probable that pupils see the use of oral
communication as appropriate in certain situations -
in the classroom or when being addressed by a teacher,
for example. Non-vocal communication may be perceived as appropriate in other situations, such as in
private conversations with peers. Indeed the tendency
of pupils who have the ability to speak to drop
their speech when communicating with hearing impaired
peers has been adverted to (Owrid 1972) and is something familiar to many teachers in special schools.
To apply Labov's (1972, p. 249) remarks about so-
called 'slovenly' speech in our context here, the fact
that children with impaired hearing do not use speech,
although they may be able to, may not be the result
of laziness or carelessness; speech may not be
appropriate in the situation as perceived and cate-
gorised by pupils. Therefore the active promotion of
oral communication as the official and only method of
communication in special schools may lead to conflict
not only in relation to the overt stylistic features
of communication but also in the more covert area of
norms and values which underlie, and in many senses
govern, linguistic behaviour.

Closely related to the issue of norms and values
is the notion of identity. Even very young children are
aware of the function of language in establishing group
identity, and use the appropriate variety to identify
with friends (Saville-Troike 1982, p. 189). Labov
(1972, pp. 304-5) has stressed the importance of the
influence of other children and of peers on linguistic
behaviour. Similarly, the hearing impaired child's
identity may be invested in a signing system which he
utilizes in his interactions with those who share his
deepest experiences. The pupil may also find that
maintenance of identity among peers requires the use
of such means of communication. Negative reactions
directed at linguistic behaviour can be perceived by
children as a negative view of themselves. As Baratz
(1968, p. 145) puts it, '... to devalue his language
... is to devalue the child'.

Finally, the development of attitudes towards
a language and its uses is of particular relevance
to the child with impaired hearing. The objective of
the school is to promote the use of oral communication
but this may involve a negative transfer across the

functions of language. The impact on communicative
performance must be considerable if one method of
communication is imposed and another devalued. Thus,
disagreeable or oppressive ways of dealing with the
issue of communication may frustrate the very
objective of special schooling.

Conclusion

Taken together the areas discussed above point
to a fundamental problem at the heart of special
schooling for children with impaired hearing in
Ireland and elsewhere. The declared objective of
special schooling is the development of oral language
in the pupils, but special schooling also involves
gathering together large numbers of children who,
in order to communicate with one another, must resort
to non-vocal channels of communication.

It must be emphasised that the point here is not
that oral communication is impossible for children
with impaired hearing. It is that if the objective
of special schooling is the development of oral language,
then there are prominent aspects of the special school
setting that are likely to make the exercise frust-
rating or even self-defeating, for both pupils and
school authorities. On the other hand, if special
schooling is to be maintained it seems logical to argue
that the legitimacy of some forms of manual communication must be recognised.

Critical difficulties, however, exist for
advocates of combined or total communication. Firstly,
as Kretschmer and Kretschmer (1978, p. 87) point out,
the mode of communication alone cannot account for all
the observed differences in the performances of
different groups of children exposed to different modes.
Secondly, there may be little correspondence between a
signing linguistic system used by pupils among themselves and one devised for use in the classroom.
Thirdly, parents are naturally anxious to have their
hearing impaired children acquire speech skills; oral
teaching methods are forcefully promoted and the contribution of signing systems to school achievement has
not yet been widely recognised or disseminated. It is
therefore difficult to estimate the extent to which
parents would accept a combined system of communication
for their children.

Among the hearing impaired themselves, however, there can be little doubt that sign language is the preferred mode of communication of the great majority, regardless of how they were educated. It has been argued (Cicourel and Boese 1972) that for them, English for example, is in reality a second language. Tervoort (1978) observes that pupils in special schools must be, to some extent, bilingual. Although research into sign languages and into the effects of a variety of communication methods is still in its infancy, it has brought about a greater understanding of the nature and role of motor-visual linguistic systems. During the past decade there has been widespread and critical questioning of the efficacy of strictly oral methods, not least by the deaf community itself. In a paper submitted at a seminar in 1981 (National Association for the Deaf, Seminar on the Education of Children with Impaired Hearing, Longford, May, 1981), members of St. Vincent's Deaf Community Centre, Dublin, urged the introduction of a combined method of communication into the ordinary curriculum of special schools. There is, therefore, a strong case for the use of a bilingual, or at least a bimodal system in schools for pupils with impaired hearing.

Cross-cultural and cross-linguistic activity is part of the daily experience of people with impaired hearing. It is time it became part of their schooling.

NOTES

1. A hearing impairment of 90 db or over in the crucial speech frequencies, 500 Hz - 2000 Hz, is commonly regarded as an audiometric definition of profound deafness (Ballantyne 1977; Quigley and Kretschmer 1982). My paper is primarily concerned with children having this degree of hearing loss.

2. It is necessary to point out that the meaning of the terms 'analytic' and 'synthetic' as used in the field of education of the hearing impaired is the reverse of their current meaning in the literature on, for example, teaching English as a foreign language.

REFERENCES

Ballantyne, J. (1977), Deafness, 3rd ed., Edinburgh: Churchill Livingstone.

Baratz, J. (1968), 'Language in the economically disadvantaged child: a perspective', American Speech and Hearing Association 10, pp. 143-5.

Brasel, K. and S. Quigley (1977), 'The influence of certain language and communication environments in early childhood on the development of language in deaf individuals', Journal of Speech and Hearing Research 20, pp. 95-107.

Brennan, M. (1975), 'Can deaf children acquire a language?', American Annals of the Deaf 120 (October), pp. 463-79.

Brown, R. (1973), A first language, Harmondsworth: Penguin Books.

Cicourel, A.V. and R.J. Boese (1972), 'Sign language acquisition and the teaching of deaf children', American Annals of the Deaf 117 (Feb.; June), pp. 27-33; 403-11.

Clark, M. (1978), 'Preparation of deaf children for hearing society', The Teacher of the Deaf 2 (Sept.), pp. 146-54.

Conrad, R. (1977a), 'The reading ability of deaf school leavers', British Journal of Educational Psychology 47, pp.138-48.

Conrad, R. (1977b), 'Lipreading by deaf and hearing children', British Journal of Educational Psychology 47, pp. 60-5.

Crystal, D. (1976), Child language, learning and linguistics, London: Edward Arnold.

Erber, N.P. (1972), 'Speech envelope cues as an acoustic aid to lipreading for profoundly deaf children', Journal of the Acoustical Society of America 51, pp. 1224-7.

Fisher, S.D. (1978), 'Sign language and creoles' in P. Siple (ed.), Understanding language through sign language research, London: Academic Press, pp. 309-31.

Goldin-Meadow, S. and H. Feldman (1975), 'The creation of a communication system: a study of deaf children of hearing parents', Sign Language Studies 8, pp. 225-34.

Henderson, P. (1976), Introduction, in Methods of communication currently used in the education of deaf children.

Ivimey, G.P. (1977), 'The perception of speech: an information processing approach', The Teacher of the Deaf 1 (May), pp. 102-9.

John, J.E.J. and J.N. Howarth (1973), 'An argument for oral communication', The Teacher of the Deaf 71 (March), pp. 102-9.

Kretschmer, R.R. and L.W. Kretschmer (1978), Language development and intervention in the hearing impaired, Baltimore: University Park Press.

Labov, W. (1972), Sociolinguistic patterns, Philadelphia: University of Pennsylvania Press.

Lancioni, G.E. (1981), 'Increasing the use of higher-level forms of communication in deaf children within a residential setting', The Teacher of the Deaf 5, pp. 77-82.

Lane, H. and F. Grosjean (1980), Recent perspectives on American Sign Language, Hillsdale, New Jersey: Lawrence Erlbaum Associates.

Lenneberg, E.H. (1968), 'A biological perspective of language', in R.C. Oldfield and J.C. Marshall (eds.), Language, Harmondsworth: Penguin Books, pp. 32-47.

Ling, D., A. Ling, and G. Pflaster (1977), 'Individualised educational programming for hearing impaired children', Volta Review 79, pp. 204-30.

McDonnell, P. (1980), 'Experiences of special schooling among pupils with impaired hearing', unpublished M.Ed. Thesis, University College, Dublin.

McNeill, D. (1970), The acquisition of language, London: Harper and Row.

Meadow, K.P. (1968), 'Early manual communication in relation to the deaf child's intellectual, social and communicative function', American Annals of the Deaf 113 (Jan.), pp. 29-41.

Methods of communication currently used in the education of deaf children (1976), Royal National Institute for the Deaf, 105 Gower Street, London.

Montgomery, G.W. (1966), 'Relationship of oral skills to manual communication in profoundly deaf adolescents', American Annals of the Deaf 111, pp. 557-65.

Moores, D.F. (1974), 'Non-vocal systems of verbal behaviour', in R.L. Schiefelbusch and L.L. Lloyd (eds.), Language perspectives: Acquisition, retardation and intervention, London: Macmillan, pp. 377-417.

Moores, D.F. (1978), Educating the deaf, Boston: Houghton Mifflin.

Morris, T. (1978), 'Some observations on the part played by oral teaching methods in perpetuating low standards of language achievement in severely and profoundly deaf pupils', The Teacher of the Deaf 2 (July), pp. 130-5.

Nix, G.W. (1975), 'Total communication: a review of studies offered in its support', Volta Review 77 (Nov.), pp. 470-94.

Owrid, H.L. (1972), 'Education and communication', Volta Review 74 (April), pp. 225-34.

Paper submitted at National Association for the Deaf Seminar on the Education of the Deaf, Longford, May, 1981, by St. Vincent's Deaf Community Centre, Dublin.

Pollack, D. (1964), 'Acoupedics: a uni-sensory approach to auditory training', Volta Review 66, pp. 400-409.

Plomp, R. (1978), 'Auditory handicap of hearing impairment and the limited benefit of hearing aids', Journal of the Acoustical Society of America 63.2, pp. 533-49.

Quigley, S.P. (1969), The influence of fingerspelling
on the development of language, communication and
educational achievement in deaf children,
Institute for Research on Exceptional Children,
University of Illinois, Urbana.
Quigley, S.P. and R.E. Kretschmer (1982), The education
of deaf children, London: Edward Arnold.
Reeves, J.K. (1976), 'The whole personality approach to
oralism in the education of the deaf' in Methods
of communication currently used in the education
of the deaf, pp. 9-17.
Saville-Troike, M. (1982), The ethnography of communication,
Oxford: Basil Blackwell.
Schlesinger, I.M. and L. Namir (eds.) (1978), Sign
language of the deaf, London: Academic Press.
Shah, C.P., D. Chandler and R. Dale (1978), 'Delay in
referral of children with impaired hearing',
Volta Review 80(May), pp. 206-15.
Siple, P. (ed.) (1978), Understanding language through
sign language research, London: Academic Press.
Stuckless, E.R. and J.W. Birch (1966), 'The influence
of early manual communication on linguistic
development in deaf children', American Annals
of the Deaf 111, pp. 452-60.
Tervoort, B. (1961), 'Esoteric symbolism in the
communicative behaviour of young children',
American Annals of the Deaf 106, pp. 436-80.
Tervoort, B. (1978), 'Bilingual interference' in
I.M. Schlesinger and L. Namir (eds.), Sign
language of the deaf, London: Academic Press,
pp. 169-240.
The education of children who are handicapped by impaired
hearing (1972), Report of a committee appointed by
the Minister for Education, Dublin: Stationery Office.
Vernon, McKay (1968), 'Fifty years of research on the
intelligence of the deaf and hard of hearing: a
survey of the literature and discussion of
implications', Journal of the Rehabilitation of
the Deaf 1, pp. 1-11.
Von der Lieth, L. (1978), 'Social-psychological aspects
of the use of sign language', in I.M. Schlesinger
and L. Namir (eds.), Sign language of the deaf,
pp. 315-32.
Wilbur, R. (1976), 'The linguistics of manual languages
and manual systems' in L.L. Llyod (ed.),
Communication assessment and intervention strategies,
Baltimore: University Park Press, pp. 424-91.
Wilbur, R. (1979), American Sign Language and sign systems,
Baltimore, University Park Press.

EXPRESSION OF CAUSATIVITY
IN ENGLISH AND HEBREW

Ezra Mentcher
The Technion
Haifa

Contrastive linguistics is concerned with establishing similarities and dissimilarities between languages irrespective of their genetical relationship.
A functionally important and almost universal linguistic
category, in which word-formation is closely linked to
syntax and semantics, is that of causativity. Causativity
implies compelling, persuading or causing somebody to do
something or causing something to happen. In many
languages this concept is morphologically materialized
in the verbal system by a special causative marker. In
others there are special deverbative verbs derived from
primary verbs and denoting the fact that the subject of
the sentence makes the object perform the action
expressed by the underlying verb.

The correlative verbs may be related to each other
in different ways. The causative verb may be (a) derived
from, (b) morphologically equal to but syntagmatically
different from, or (c) semantically related to but
lexically different from the underlying verb, which amounts
to derivation, conversion or suppletion respectively. In
analytical constructions the motivating verb is a component of a periphrastic structure (e.g. make somebody do
something).

Whereas a causative is by definition a transitive
verb, intransitivity is by no means a prerequisite of
the primary verb. Thus the Hebrew האכיל [1] 'feed'
presupposes a transitive verb אכל 'eat', which, at least
with this particular verb, leads to a bitransitive
construction הוא האכיל את יוסף את התפוח 'He fed the apple
to Joseph'. In this case causativization of the sentence
Joseph ate the apple increases the valence of the underlying verb eat by adding another agent and thus leads to
the twofold occurrence of a direct object (Rosen 1977,
p. 203).

In this paper a distinction will be drawn between
causatives proper and factitives. Whereas a causative
verb is opposed to a primary verb denoting an action or
state, factitives in Indo-European languages are transitive verbs derived from adjectives and, to a lesser
extent, from nouns and convey the meaning of 'cause to

be X', where X stands for the corresponding adjective
or noun. Thus sharpen means 'make sharp', heat
'make hot', etc. In a limited number of cases the
base of the derivative is a noun, e.g. cripple, 'make a
cripple of' (zero - derivation).

From the point of view of Hebrew, where in the
Biblical language the adjectives did not constitute an
autonomous part of speech but were participles of a
class of qualitative verbs (Rosen 1977, p. 416),
distinguishing between genuine causatives and factitives
makes little sense and is moreover both formally and
semantically difficult.

In both languages there is a regular relation in
terms of clause function between an adjective (noun) and
matching transitive verb expressing factitivity
(Quirk et al. 1972, p. 352).

Although this paper deals with a synchronic analysis
of causatives and factitives in the languages contrasted,
a historical view of these categories will help us to
see them in their right perspective. In Proto-Indo-
European there must have been a time where the
possibility of deriving causative verbs from primary ones
was almost limitless. The ancestral suffix added was
*eyo, giving corresponding reflexes in the different
languages of the family. In pre-Germanic it was -jan,
which could be affixed to the preterite stem of a strong
verb. This means of derivation characterized by phonetic
and morphological alternation is preserved in some
remnants (Engl. lay: lie, set: sit, etc.) but is no
longer productive. The reason for the abandonment of
this word-building means can be seen in the prolonged
process of phonetic and semantic evolution leading
to the dissociation of the causative from the base verb
in the mind of the speaker. Thus drench, which continues
the pre-English drenkjan, OE drencean, is the ablaut
grade of drinkan 'drink', of which it is the causative
derivative. Originally it meant 'administer drink (a
draught) of medicine to (an animal)', but will hardly
be perceived as a causative of drink by a speaker of
contemporary English because of the phonetic dis-
crepancy and shifting of meaning.

From the study of Biblical Hebrew as well as from
that of cognate languages we can infer that in pre-
Hebrew times there probably existed a transformational
relation between the Qal (the basic stem pattern) and
the Hif'il, a verbal stem characterized by the pattern

hiRRiR (R = any radical consonant), such that Hif'il
showed a causative or factitive meaning when opposed
to the Qal. However, even in Biblical times
approximately half of the Hif'il meanings could not
be derived from the basic meaning of the Qal (Jenni
1968, p. 251).

Another means of expressing causativity and factitivity in Biblical Hebrew was the Pi'el, traditionally regarded as an intensive stem. In a number
of cases both the Pi'el and Hif'il radical formations
could be used for transitivization and causativization
of an intransitive Qal with little or no semantic
differentiation between them. Even in modern Hebrew
some Pi'el and Hif'il stems derived from the same root
can be regarded as synonymous to a certain degree.
Thus both גמש and הגמיש mean 'make elastic' and are
factitives derived from גמיש 'elastic'. These forms,
while coinciding denotatively, may differ, however,
connotatively or syntagmatically.

In numerous cases the Pi'el was reinterpreted in
modern Hebrew as opposed to the Hitpa'el so that the
same relationship prevails as in the Qal: Hif'il
opposition (Rosen 1977, p. 202), e.g. התאחד 'unite (vi)':
איחד 'unite (vt)', and התאמן 'train oneself': אימן
'train (vt)' correlate in the same way as דלק 'burn (vi)':
הדליק 'ignite', etc.

Whereas the Hif'il stems still form a morphologically
distinct class of verbs and have not been affected by
sound change since Biblical times, the intervening
semantic evolution of one or both terms of the correlative pairs has led to a situation where only a part
of the Hif'il verbs can be considered causatives
proper when opposed to the underlying Qal stems.

This paper, after listing the means of expressing
causativity and factitivity in English, will then
analyze the Hif'il stems in Hebrew as constituting the
principal means of expressing the above-mentioned
categories in Hebrew. The contrastive analysis will
be limited to the causative and factitive stems among
them.

A. Means of expressing causativity and factitivity in
    modern English

I. As pointed out above, English has preserved a few

relics of the Old Germanic causatives, such as set, lay,
raise, fell, drench and others, which originally formed
correlative pairs with the primary strong verbs sit,
lie, rise, fall, drink respectively. Some of these
inherited causatives have retained their original
meaning in opposition to the motivating verb, e.g.
raise: rise, cf. The chemist raised the temperature vs.
The temperature rose.

Some lexicalized causatives have acquired a specialized
meaning and can be considered causatives only in a
restricted sense. Thus fell 'cause to fall' is mainly
used when speaking of a tree or a person (= 'strike down')
but would be inappropriate in speaking of another object.
Still others are in modern English phonetically and semantically too remote from their motivating verbs to be
considered causatives, cf. drench: drink, and others.

A few factitives also belong to this subdivision of
ancient derivatives as shown by their vocalic alternation, e.g. heat: hot, fill: full, gild: gold, etc.

To supplant this ancient and non-productive word-
building means modern English has developed a number
of other possibilities:

II. Derivation by means of affixes. These allow the
change of the grammatical class of the base so that
factitives can be formed from adjectives and nouns.
Both suffixes and prefixes are used for this purpose
with suffixation playing the major role.

1. Suffixes

   a) -ify (in learned words), e.g. amplify, simplify,
      liquefy (with a change of stem), beautify, etc.
   b) -ize (chiefly in technical words), e.g. legalize
      'make legal', publicize, popularize, modernize,
      etc.
   c) -ate (in borrowed and neo-classical words), e.g.
      validate, differentiate, debilitate, etc.

The suffixes listed above are limited in their productivity to Greek or Latin stems.

   d) -en, e.g. blacken, deafen, fatten, redden, sadden,
      sweeten, etc.

Derivatives from quality nouns are lengthen, heighten,
strengthen. The corresponding base nouns length, height
and strength are in turn derived from adjectives. The
suffix -en can be added to the comparative of an adjective

as in <u>worsen</u>. In many cases this scarcely productive
suffix conveys besides the factitive meaning of
'making (more) adj.' also the intransitive meaning of
'becoming (more) adj'. Thus <u>blacken</u> means both 'make
or become black'. This phenomenon is paralleled by
some ambivalent Hebrew factitives opposed to an
adjective, such as שחר 'black': השחיר 'make or become
black', לבן 'white': הלבין 'make or become white',
etc. An extreme case is the Hebrew הסמיק 'blush,
redden' possessing only an intransitive meaning.

    e) A few verbs show an irregular type of deri-
       vation from adjectives, such as <u>anger</u>: <u>angry</u>,
       <u>publish</u>: <u>public</u>, etc.

    2. <u>Prefixes</u>

    Different conversion prefixes are used to change the
base into a verb meaning 'to make (an object) X', where
X stands for an adjective or a noun.

    a) <u>en-</u> (<u>em-</u> before labials), e.g. <u>enrich</u>, <u>enable</u>,
       <u>enlarge</u>, <u>embitter</u>, <u>enslave</u>, etc.;
    b) <u>re-</u>, e.g. <u>refresh</u>, <u>renew</u>;
    c) <u>be-</u>, e.g. <u>becalm</u>, <u>belittle</u>, etc.;
    d) <u>pro-</u>, e.g. <u>prolong</u>.

Both prefixation and suffixation are used in deriving
the factitives <u>embolden</u>, <u>enliven</u>, <u>elongate</u>, <u>enlighten</u>,
<u>aggravate</u>, and others.

III.   Another means of transitivization and causativization widely used in modern English is <u>conversion</u>
implying a change in word class with a zero-suffix.
The following cases can be distinguished:

1) <u>adjective - verb</u>: <u>to dirty</u>, <u>lower</u>, <u>better</u>, <u>blind</u>,
<u>warm</u>, <u>cool</u>, etc. As shown by the examples, the
comparative degree of the adjective is sometimes used
for this purpose. Occasionally the adjective is con-
verted into a phrasal verb by the addition of a
particle, e.g. <u>smooth out</u>, <u>calm down</u>, etc.;

2) <u>intransitive verb - transitive verb</u>. By an extension
of the notion of conversion to changes of secondary
word-class we can consider the transitive use of
originally intransitive verbs a case of conversion
(Quirk et al. 1972, pp. 1015-1016). This kind of
transfer seems to be quite productive in contemporary
English, e.g. <u>to march</u>, <u>walk</u>, <u>budge</u>, <u>fly</u>, <u>stop</u>, <u>turn</u>,
<u>increase</u> and many more, cf. <u>The new recruits marched
home</u> vs. <u>The sergeant marched the new recruits home</u>.

    In deciding which of the two derivationally related
words is the base and which the derivative, one often
has to rely on intuition in the absence of any formal

indication or historical evidence (Adams 1973, pp. 38-39).
Thus the transitive walk is clearly secondary to the
intransitive verb. On the other hand, the intransitive
use of sell as in These clothes sell well is obviously
secondary to sell (vt) and therefore does not concern
us here.

It should also be noted here that although transitivization and causativization are overlapping processes
in that they both change verbal valence - the syntactic
status of a verb - (Rosen 1977, p. 200) - they are by
no means identical. We have already seen above that
the primary verb underlying a causative may itself be
transitive (eat, drink something) so that causativization
does not imply transitivization. Conversely, transitivization does not necessarily imply causativization
either. Thus climb is used intransitively in Monkeys
climb well and by conversion we can say The monkey
climbed a tree. However, this does not make climb a
causative verb since tree cannot be construed as the
subject of an intransitive climb (contrary to march
in the example quoted above), which would yield the
ungrammatical sentence *The tree climbed. As the
notions of transitivity and causativity do not coincide,
we cannot use passivization as a criterion of causativity, every causative verb being by definition
transitive and therefore capable of passivization. The
only valid transformational test of causativity is the
possibility of the object of the causative verb
becoming the subject of the underlying primary verb in
an Active-voice sentence, e.g. He walked his horse up
the hill →He caused his horse to walk up the hill,
whence His horse walked up the hill.

3) noun - verb. There are a number of transitive
desubstantival verbs derived by means of a zero-suffix
and meaning 'make (convert) the object into N'. In
other words the noun is the object complement of a
paraphrase sentence (Adams 1973, p. 44), e.g. to beggar,
cash, cripple, fool, group, orphan, phrase, structure,
etc. Thus fool (somebody) means 'make a fool of smb.'
Such verbs could be considered factitives on a par
with deadjectival factitives since they are based on the
same syntactic-semantic pattern, i.e. 'cause (the object)
to be (become) X' with X standing for either an adjective
or a noun.

IV.   Causativity and factitivity can also be expressed
by suppletion, i.e. by transitive verbs not derivationally
related to the primary verb or adjective that appears in
the deep structure in the course of transformational
derivation, such as kill 'cause to die', bring: come, e.g.

They brought the supplies yesterday→The supplies came
yesterday. It is interesting to note that in the
correlative pair lend: borrow it is the indirect object
of the causative verb which becomes the subject of the
underlying verb after application of the transformational
rules: I lent him a big sum of money→He borrowed a big
sum of money from me.

The implied subject of the underlying verb may even
be a prepositional object of the causative, e.g. feed:
eat, cf. She fed the porridge to the baby →The baby ate
the porridge.

Suppletive factitives abound in the neo-classical
vocabulary, e.g. rectify 'put right', rejuvenate 'make
young again', embellish 'make beautiful', refrigerate
'make cool', etc.

V. Moving from a predominantly synthetic to an analytic
structure English has evolved a series of causative
constructions using the verb cause in its central meaning
and make, have and get in idiomatic expressions.

1. cause + to + Inf.: The rain caused the weeds to grow.
2. get + to + Inf.: She got them to believe the story.
3. make + Inf.: Can you make this engine start?
   make + Past Part.: He made his power felt.
4. have + Inf.: I'll have them write a letter.
   have + Past Part.: You must have your hair cut.

The constructions containing a Past Participle express the
idea that the subject of the sentence causes something to be
done by an unspecified agent. In these passive forms -
more frequently used than the active ones - the Past
Participle is used as a predicate of result after the
object (Palmer and Blandford 1969, pp. 229-230).

There is no doubt that the analytical constructions
facilitate expression by providing a more abstract and
consequently more flexible way of expressing causativity.
These periphrastic structures have their parallels in
other Indo-European languages, cf. Germ. lassen + Infinitiv,
Fr. faire + infinitif. In these languages linguistic
change has led to a situation where relations formerly
expressed by affixes are now rendered by separate words
(Bloomfield 1970, p. 509).

B. Means of expressing causativity and factivity in
   Hebrew.

Here we shall have to consider in order of their
decreasing importance: 1. The Hif'il stems; 2. the

Pi'el stems; 3. suppletion; 4. the analytical means of expression; 5. the Šif'el stems. Derivation of causatives from underlying forms by means of affixes or by conversion is practically unknown in Hebrew.

I. <u>Principal means</u>.

The most important part in expressing causativity and factitivity is played by certain stem patterns (binyanim) of the verbal system inherited from Biblical Hebrew, viz. the Hif'il and Pi'el. Both these radical formations still constitute morphologically clear-cut stem patterns. Semantically, however, only a limited part of the verbs belonging to either pattern are easily definable as causatives or factitives when opposed to the underlying form, which, at least originally, must have been the Qal. Below are a few examples of cases where a distinct opposition is preserved:

1. <u>The Hi'fil</u>

   a) with causative meaning: הזכיר 'remind' : זכר 'remember', הדליק 'ignite, light' : דלק 'burn';
   b) with factitive meaning: הגדיל 'enlarge': גדול 'large', החליש 'weaken' : חלש 'be weak'.

2. <u>The Pi'el</u>

   a) with causative meaning: לימד 'teach' : למד 'learn', ביטל 'abolish, cancel' : בטל 'cease, stop (vi)';
   b) with factitive meaning: ליבן 'whiten, bleach' : לבן 'white'.

II. <u>Other means</u>.

3. Undoubtedly instances can be found in Hebrew where the categories discussed are expressed by verbs morphologically unrelated to the motivating word, i.e. by <u>suppletion</u>. A typical example is the Hebrew pair מת:הרג matched by the English <u>kill: die</u>. Another example is the isolated Hif'il השקה 'water, irrigate' semantically correlated with the Qal שתה 'drink', a verb which in turn lacks a Hif'il. On the whole, however, especially in the sphere of factitives, the proportion of suppletively used verbs is definitely smaller in Hebrew than in English since the former lacks the foreign-learned verbs originating from Latin such as the word <u>rectify</u> mentioned above.

4. It appears that <u>analytical means</u> to express causativity can also be used in Hebrew although to a lesser extent than in English. Thus it is perfectly acceptable to use constructions with גרם 'cause, bring about' followed by a direct or prepositional object. Another possibility is based on הביא אותו לידי or הביא אותו לכלל 'make someone, bring about'. The verbs כפה,אילץ,הכריח 'force, compel' can also be used in conjunction with an animate object and a main verb to express compulsion.

5. Finally, the <u>Old Semitic Šif'el pattern</u> is increasingly used to express causative meaning in a specialized way (Rosen 1977, p. 204). Thus we have שחזר 'recon-struct' : חזר 'came back' in addition to a regular Hif'il החזיר 'return (vt)'. We can also mention שכתב 're-write' : כתב 'write' : הכתיב 'dictate'; שעבד 'subjugate' : עבד 'work' : העביד 'employ', and others.

As already mentioned above, this paper will be restricted to a consideration of the causative and factitive Hif'il stems and disregard the other means listed.

C. Semantic classification of the Hif'il stems

I. Difficulties involved

Any attempt at classification in the realm of semantics is by nature difficult. Clear-cut distinctions cannot be made, borderlines are fluid, and in many cases a Hif'il belongs to two or more subdivisions simultaneously and can only arbitrarily be placed in one of them. A few examples will illustrate these points.

1. The first difficulty arises in considering <u>the second term of the correlative pair</u>. We assume that originally a Hif'il stem was opposed to a Qal. In the modern language, however, as a result of a semantic shift, a Hif'il can be semantically correlated with another verbal stem, say a Nif'al or Hitpa'el, whereas in opposition to the Qal it does not express causativity. Thus הדביק 'infect (with a disease)' can be regarded as a causative when opposed to נדבק 'become infected', but not to דבק 'stick, adhere'. Similarly, הגשים 'carry out, realize' is a causative when opposed to התגשם 'be realized, materialize', but not in relation to a non-existent Qal. There are cases where, from a synchronic point of view, the correlative term is a Nif'al, the Qal being obsolescent. Thus הפיץ 'scatter , disperse' must be seen in opposition to נפוץ 'be scattered' but not to the Biblical 'be scattered'.

Often we have to decide whether a Hif'il should be correlated with a Qal or with a noun, which would make it a factitive. Thus הטמיר 'nail down' can obviously not be considered a causative opposed to the Qal 'stiffen, bristle', but can morphologically and semantically be correlated with מסמר 'nail'.

2. **Polysemy** poses another problem. In the course of their historical development most Hif'il verbs have acquired a number of different meanings, only one of which can be considered causative. Synchronically we cannot tell which of the different meanings is dominant and consequently decide whether the verb should be considered a causative. For example הבריח is correlated with ברח 'flee, run away' only in its meaning 'cause to flee' but not in the sense of 'smuggle'.

In other cases the motivating Qal is polysemous and the Hif'il a causative solely with regard to one of the several meanings of the Qal. Thus אכל means 'eat, devour, consume, take away, destroy'. Only in opposition to the first meaning cited can האכיל 'feed, nourish' be considered a causative.

In numerous cases both the Qal and the Hif'il are polysemous, and we can form a correlative pair only by the appropriate choice of the individual terms of the opposition. For instance, הרביץ means 'beat, hit; cause to lie down; disseminate, teach' whereas רבץ is translated by 'lie down (animal); hang around'. Only when 'cause to lie down' is juxtaposed with 'lie down (animal)' can הרביץ be considered a causative.

3. It is sometimes difficult to differentiate between causatives proper and those with a narrowed meaning. Thus הכתיב 'dictate, cause to be written' is a Hif'il derived from כתב 'write'. In its literal sense 'cause to be written' it is a causative proper whereas meaning 'dictate (terms)' it has acquired a figurative meaning. The Hif'il הוליך can be interpreted literally as 'cause to walk' being a causative proper of הלך 'go, walk' or metaphorically with the specialized meaning of 'lead, direct'. It is difficult to decide which of these meanings is the central and which a peripheral one.

4. It is equally hard to make a clear-cut distinction between causatives and factitives in the Hebrew language. The Hif'il verbs can be classified unambiguously only when the correlative term is an adjective or a noun with no Qal recorded, as is the case in הלבין 'whiten' : לבן 'white' or in הלאים 'nationalize' : לאום 'nation'. Such a correlation would correspond to that prevailing in English between factitives and the adjectives (nouns) underlying them. Because of the presence of qualitative verbs in Hebrew it is much more difficult to assign a Hif'il to either of these subdivisions when it can be opposed both to a Qal and to an adjective. A case in point is הקשה 'make difficult' with two alternative terms of the opposition: the Qal קשה 'be difficult' and the adjective קשה 'hard, difficult'.

Classification is facilitated in cases where the
qualitative verb denoting a temporary or permanent
quality is characterized by a special paradigm in the
Qal formation, i.e. the Pa'el or Pa'ol pattern respectively (Bauer and Leander 1965, p. 54) with the
Future patterned upon the Yif'al model, e.g. כבד 'be
heavy', קטן 'be small'. The presence of the
adjectives כבד 'heavy' and קטן 'small' makes it even
easier to opt for the factive subdivision in
classifying the Hif'ils הכביד 'aggravate' and הקטין
'reduce'.

Notwithstanding these difficulties inherent in any
semantic classification we can broadly subdivide the
Hif'il verbs into the following categories, limiting
ourselves to a few typical illustrations of each.

II. Semantic categories

1. Causatives proper. Here an easily definable causative
relation is perceived when the Hif'il is contrasted with
the corresponding primary verb (not necessarily a Qal),
e.g. הדאיג 'cause anxiety': דאג 'be anxious'. In
opposition to a Nif'al we can quote הרדים 'put to sleep':
נרדם 'fall asleep', and matched by a Hitpa'el we have
הפליא 'amaze': התפלא 'be surprised'. As a rough
approximation about 34% of all Hif'ils can be considered
genuine causatives.

2. Specialized causatives. These verbs show a semantic
shift yielding a transferred or narrowed meaning. Thus
הוליך 'lead, direct' does not exactly mean 'walk
(somebody)' when opposed to הלך . The Hif'il החטיא in
its central meaning 'incite to sin' is opposed to חטא
'sin, transgress', but in the phrase החטיא את המטרה
'miss a target' it has acquired a marginal meaning
deflecting it from the underlying חטא . Proportionately
about 12% of the Hif'il stems could be assigned to this
category.

3. Factitives. We can group here a number of Hif'il
verbs opposed to a primary qualitative verb, as well
as denominative verbs opposed to an adjective or a
noun. As far as the qualitative verbs are concerned,
they can either be stative verbs expressing a continuous state and rendered in English by 'to be +
adjective' or else be dynamic verbs in the sense of
'to become + adjective'. Examples of the former type
are: בדד 'be alone': הבדיד 'isolate', גבה 'be high':
הגביה 'raise', whereas the latter type is exemplified
by התרחב 'become wider, widen (vi)' : הרחיב 'widen,
broaden (vt)', etc. A number of verbs combine both
aspects, such as זקן 'be (become) old': הזקין 'make old',
חשך 'be (become) dark': החשיך 'darken'.

According to the base we can distinguish:

a) deverbative factitives, e.g. החליש 'weaken': חלש
   'become weak', הגביר 'strengthen': גבר 'be strong',
   etc. A deverbative origin does not exclude the
   presence of related adjectives or nouns, e.g. חלש
   'weak' and גבר 'man' respectively;
b) deadjectival factitives, e.g. החמיר 'aggravate':
   חמור 'grave, serious', התפיל 'desalinate': תפל
   'unsalted, tepid', etc;
c) desubstantival factitives, e.g. הדגים 'exemplify':
   דגם 'model, sample', השליג 'cover with snow': שלג
   'snow'. Such denominatives suggest producing
   something - the object named by the noun - and
   are thus paralleled (Bauer and Leander 1965, p. 293)
   by the English factitives of the type <u>group</u>, <u>cripple</u>,
   etc.
   A little more than 10% of the Hif'il stems can be
   considered factitives.

4. <u>Non-causative Hif'ils</u>. This subdivision comprises
Hif'il verbs which, when opposed to the underlying Qal
or to any other secondary stem (Nif'al, Hit'pael), show
neither causative nor factitive meaning but differ in
meaning from the base verb. It is likely that such
a relationship obtains as a result of a historical
development in the course of which either of the two
stems or both have undergone a semantic change so that
the modern speaker does not perceive such Hif'ils to be
causative or factitive when compared with the Qal or any
other secondary stem. Thus הבחין 'distinguish' does not
mean 'cause to examine' as the Qal בחן suggests, the
verb האמיר 'raise (prices)' cannot be associated with אמר
'say, tell', etc. These examples can be easily
multiplied. A few types however deserve special
consideration. Thus in the pair החזיק 'hold, seize': חזק
'be strong' the Hif'il can be interpreted, in Jenni's
terminology, as an 'internal causative' (Jenni 1968,
p. 251) with deletion of the direct object of the
causative verb, i.e. 'make (the hand) hold (an object)'.

We can also mention here so-called declaratives of
the type הצדיק 'justify': צדק 'be right', הרשיע 'condemn,
convict': רשע 'sin, do evil'. These verbs express the
idea of declaring somebody to possess the quality named
by the primary verb.

Among the verbs of this category we can also quote
some denominatives conveying the idea of using something,
e.g. האזין 'listen': אזן 'ear', הלשין 'slander': לשון
'tongue', etc., as well as that of moving in a certain
direction, e.g. הדרים 'turn south': דרום 'south', etc.
About 16% of the total number of Hif'il stems analysed
can be assigned to this category.

5. <u>Hif'il verbs synonymous with the primary Qal</u>. While absolute synonyms are a rare phenomenon in language, it is worthwhile noting that in the course of semantic evolution some Hif'il verbs have come so close in meaning to the underlying Qal as to become near-synonymous. Evidently such verbs cannot be regarded as causatives. Thus both הטמין and טמן can be translated as 'hide, conceal', הלעיג and לעג both mean 'mock'. The Hif'il הוסיף 'add, increase' is synonymous with the Biblical Qal יסף; it is however a causative when opposed to the Nif'al נוסף 'be added'. Approximately 10% of the Hif'il verbs are to a varying degree synonymous with the underlying Qal.

6. <u>Extrasystemic Hif'il stems</u>. A Hif'il will be considered extrasystemic when it is either totally isolated in the verbal system or else when, in the absence of a Qal, the secondary stem present (esp. the Nif'al or Hitpa'el) cannot be regarded as forming a correlative pair with a causative Hif'il. Thus הלחים 'solder' is a totally isolated Hif'il and the only thing we can do is reconstruct a hypothetical Qal לחם (a homonym of the well-known לחם 'fight'). On the other hand הליין 'grumble' is not isolated since, in the absence of a Qal, we can find the Hitpa'el התלונן 'to complain'. However in this case the Hif'il does not express causativity when opposed to התלונן . As already noted, we can find a number of instances where the Hif'il formation coexists with a nearly synonymous Pi'el. In other cases with no Qal recorded the Pi'el and Hif'il meanings are widely divergent, e.g. המתין 'wait': מיתן 'moderate', etc. The percentage of extrasystemic Hif'il verbs can be put at about 18%.

In translating a Hif'il verb into English the translator can in numerous cases choose between synonymous means of expressing causativity belonging to different categories. Thus הגדיל in its transitive meaning can - depending on context - be translated as 'increase, enlarge, extend, expand, aggrandize', i.e. by means of verbs arrived at by conversion (increase), derivation (enlarge), aggrandize) and suppletion (extend, expand). Sometimes we may have to resort to a Passive Infinitive as in החניק 'strangle': נחנק 'be strangled' or to a more elaborate circumlocution as in הוריש 'leave as legacy': ירש 'inherit'.

In conclusion we can say that while in English, with the exception of a few residual forms, causativity is no longer expressed by deverbative causatives characterized by internal inflection, in modern Hebrew the inherited means of expressing causativity through the Hif'il radical formation has not fallen into oblivion. One of the reasons for the preservation of causative and factitive Hif'il verbs is the fact that shifts in semantic emphasis in one or both of the terms participating in the original Hif'il: Qal opposition have not been accompanied by a parallel phonetic change as was the case in English. The Hif'il stems are still associated in the mind of the speaker with the corresponding primary verbs, at least in the majority of cases.

167

The Hif'il verbs with a causative or factitive
meaning (semantic categories 1, 2 and 3 above) add up to
more than 50%, which is certainly an impressive figure
when compared with the negligible weight of the residual
causatives in English[2]. However, in view of the widely
divergent meanings expressed by the remainder of the
Hif'il verbs when opposed to the Qal, it would be a
mistake to indiscriminately label them causatives. There
is no one-to-one correspondence between the morphological
pattern and the semantics of the verbs, a lack of
correspondence which can be perceived with other
secondary verb stems as well.

NOTES

1. For the citation of Hebrew verbs the past tense 3rd
   person masculine singular form is used.

2. The numerical estimates arrived at in this paper
   are based on an analysis of the verb forms entered
   in the dictionaries:

   1. The Megiddo Modern Dictionary Hebrew-English,
      1977, Tel-Aviv: Megiddo Publishing Co.

   2. Handwörterbuch Hebräisch-Deutsch, 1978,
      Berlin/München: Langenscheidt-Achiasaf.

REFERENCES

Adams V. (1973), <u>An introduction to Modern English word-formation</u>, London: Longman.
Bauer H. and P. Leander (1965), <u>Historische Grammatik der hebräischen Sprachen</u>, Hildesheim: G. Olms.
Bloomfield L. (1970), <u>Language</u>, London: Allen and Unwin.
Jenni E. (1968), <u>Das hebräische Pi'el</u>, Zürich: EVZ-Verlag.
Palmer H. and F.C. Blandford (1969), <u>A grammar of spoken English</u>, Cambridge: Heffer.
Quirk R., S. Greenbaum et al. (1972), <u>A grammar of contemporary English</u>, London: Longman.
Rosen H.B. (1977), <u>Comtemporary Hebrew</u>, The Hague: Mouton.

YOUNG PUNJABI BILINGUALS IN NORTHERN IRELAND:
THEIR LANGUAGE COMPETENCE AND IDENTITY STRUCTURE

Mehroo Northover
Ulster Polytechnic

This paper does not contest the notion that language
as an expresser of ethnicity is a perfectly valid
construct for all groups of people and individuals.
Indeed, it is highly salient for some under certain
conditions. On the other hand, the use of a language
for personal interaction and schooling which is not
the same as the ethnic language or mother tongue, does
not necessarily hinder the development of the individual
in terms of achievement at school, or in terms of
gaining a rounded, stable personality. (This is expressed in terms of resolution of identification conflicts in respect of significant members of own and
Northern Irish groups). It is not to say that this
may not happen in some circumstances, particularly if
the second language is not sufficiently mastered.
However, the Northern Ireland sample of Punjabis demonstrates an example of second language skill and
educational attainment among Ss who show an awareness
of their distinctive ethnicity, at the same time
maintaining positive evaluations of their own Punjabi
as well as Northern Irish groups, and a positive
self-esteem.

INTRODUCTION

This pilot study was initiated in order to explore
how the second generation of a particular migrant
community which is relatively scattered within the
host country has adapted itself to its milieu in
terms of language, educational achievement and in
respect of salient values which differ from those
of its own group.

Before preliminary investigations took place,
certain assumptions were made regarding the second
generation Punjabis which were based in popular
images of migrant groups, their linguistic and
educational attainments, and their self-esteem.

Assumptions Preliminary to Qualitative Ethnographic
Study

1. It was assumed that there would be differences
other than physical features between second generation
Punjabis and their Northern Ireland peers. Such
differences would be expressed through:

a. food taboos (e.g. beef is generally unacceptable even to non-vegetarians);

b. belief in some form of the Hindu religion, rather than in some form of Christianity;

c. differences in the modes of parental control and authority, (more frequently positional than personal in orientation in Bernstein's terms);

d. certain values would derive almost exclusively from Punjabi norms, (more parental interference in the choice of spouse); other norms would differ quantitatively from those held in common with their Northern Irish peers, (less freedom in mixing with the opposite sex);

e. added to all these would be the difference in language.

2. Based on many attitudes expressed by teachers in England and popularly held stereotypes, it seemed valid to assume that the group would be bilingual and that their language competence in Punjabi would be far in excess of their competence in English. This would mean low achievement at CSE and O levels.

Introductions and contacts within the community led to participant-observation preliminary to firming up any of these hypotheses or lines of enquiry based on stereotypical assumptions. It soon became apparent that the Northern Ireland sample of immigrants from the Punjab and their offspring presented non-stereotypical sociolinguistic patterns and a high proportion went on to tertiary level education.

The language competence of the second generation lay primarily in English. Nearly all of them disclaimed active knowledge of Punjabi but claimed passive knowledge, i.e. an understanding of what was said to them in Punjabi by their parents, and some of the interaction carried out in Punjabi between the parents, or with same-generation relatives and friends from the Punjab. This was borne out by observation in the home. An aural comprehension test containing a number of cultural references to the Punjab and spoken in a formal register of Punjabi by a female speaker educated in the Punjab showed that nearly all of the respondents taking the test had a very limited understanding of Punjabi outside the domain of home.

3.a.   Before preliminary investigations took place, it
was also assumed that since the Punjabi language would be
the prime carrier of the socialisation process in the
home and that Punjabi values and cultural norms would
be stressed over Northern Irish values and norms,
certain patterns might emerge with regard to the extent
of language and cultural affiliation deriving from
their own group. It might be hypothesised that the
greater the strength of such affiliation and influence,
the more resistance might be offered to learning
English beyond the level necessary for everyday
communication and up to the level necessary for taking
CSE and O levels. This hypothesis would be all the
more acceptable if the Ss unquestionably accepted   or
had internalised that language has primordial and
inextricable ties with ethnicity and that a group loses
ethnic identity without its ethnic language.

        In fact, the pilot study revealed strong iden-
tifications with both groups but a greater proficiency
in the English language.

b.   Conversely, it might be hypothesised that if Ss
had predominant preference for the English language and
were   more proficient in it than in their Ll it
might indicate stronger affiliations for values of the
other group and a high degree of conflict in identification with own group.

        The pilot study did not reveal this tendency. It
does lend some counter-proof to the notion that ethnic-
language is inextricably bound with ethnic identity,
despite having high salience for group solidarity.

c.   With regard to the influence of a dual linguistic
system in an individual, it might be hypothesised that
the effect of having a language of the home which is not
the same as the language necessary for education or for
communication with the rest of society would have an
important impact on Ss in determining their self-concept
as being caught between two cultures. (The difficulty would
be to separate the influence of language from all the
surrounding variables of culture and physical features).
It could be argued that such a possibility exists, if it
is acknowledged that use of own-language is important for
the development of a confident stable personality since
it is an important means of cultural expression (Ervin-
Tripp's experiment with bilinguals showed intensification
of cultural beliefs and self-presentation when using own
language).

d.   Further, it could be said that where language competence in L2 was low, those Ss would continue to seek
their identifications with their own groups . Conversely,
proficiency in L2 would encourage the continuance of
communication with the other group. Providing the
reward from such communication was not outweighed by
alienation from the other group, conflict in identification with this out-group would continue to be low.

4.   An assumption also based in popular stereotyping,
and maintained by some studies done with Black Ss in
the US (Grier & Cobbs 1968; Wells & Marwell 1972),
would be that Punjabi second generation members,
belonging to a group with low social prestige ascribed
by members of the host society, might have a poor self-
image, low self-esteem, and would be foreclosed with
regard to high achievement at school or thereafter.
This would mean that a high proportion would leave
school at 16 years and before taking CSE and O levels.

    Investigations showed a high level of educational
attainments among Ss and in the group at large.
(See Table 1).

Methodology

    An intrinsic difficulty has been mentioned earlier
with regard to testing hypotheses 3.a. and 3.b., since
it is difficult to disentangle the influence of
language from other cultural variables in any particular S, and also to take into account the many
differences in biographical detail which might account
for differences in proficiency in languages.

    However, by using the concepts of Identity
Structure Analysis developed by P. Weinreich (1980),
and the methodology evolved by him, it is possible
to tease out Ss' identification conflicts with own and
other group. It is also possible to determine the
degree of consistency with which a person uses constructs relevant to ethnicity in evaluating significant members of both groups, e.g. if an S applies
the construct 'Is relaxed about mixing with the
opposite sex', believing it to be a positive value,
to his/her parents and finds that the parents are
uneasy with the opposite sex, this may lower the
'structural pressures' on the construct constraining
its current use if, on the whole, the parent is highly
evaluated. This might cause revision of the use of
this construct by S, and thus go some way toward
resolving conflict with parents on that dimension.

If Ss could be found with varying degrees of proficiency in English, their second language, this could be correlated by using concepts of ISA, with their strength in idealistic identification, contra identification and identification conflict with both groups and significant entities or members from each group.(These terms are explained in detail below).

With regard to hypothesis 4., the use of ISA would also indicate the self-image in terms of self-esteem and identity diffusion of Ss. The latter is a measure indicating the extent and strength of Ss' identifications across either or both groups.

As the numbers of young Punjabis available for the study were extremely small, and since none of them could be described as actively proficient in Punjabi, the pilot study was undertaken on the following lines:

THE PILOT STUDY

1. Linguistic Patterns by Generation

The first objective of the study was to continue participant-observation in the homes of members of the community and to establish who spoke which language to whom on a generational basis.

Among older members, two patterns revealed themselves, one for older females and one for older males. Among the parents, the father usually spoke very fluent English for communicative purposes, using many local idioms, and acquiring the local intonation of a rising note toward the end of the sentence. A number of them had studied up to matriculation and some beyond this level in India before migrating. This would mean a knowledge of English as spoken in India, which is close to written English in formality-use of full forms rather than elisions, e.g. 'it was not possible', rather than 'it wasn't possible'. Some of these language habits had become fossilised; the accent almost invariably remained heavily Punjabi. However, the intonation had become modified.

Among the older women, productive capacity in English varied from 'none or very little', to 'fluent for communicative purposes' in shops. When speaking to each other, parents did so in Punjabi despite the presence of a non Punjabi speaking observer-participant. Mothers spoke to their children in Punjabi, fathers spoke to all older generation males and females in Punjabi and tried to maintain Punjabi with younger generation members but with code-switching to English and code-mixing common items of vocabulary such as 'television', 'programme', etc.

As far as the younger generation to be observed is concerned, their production of Punjabi was usually none, or confined to a few words when speaking to their mothers. Siblings never spoke among themselves in Punjabi except in those families where some of the children had arrived at the age of ten or even older, and spoke Punjabi, or where they had been sent back to India for several crucial schooling years and retained their Punjabi.

They understood Punjabi of the type spoken in the domain of home between parents, but were not familiar with more formal registers of Punjabi.

2. A Brief Account of the Punjabis in Northern Ireland

The history of the community is purely oral and some of the general facts of migration were pieced together from individual accounts.

No written records exist regarding this migration which has been of an individual nature rather than a group migration as in the case of the Vietnamese. The numbers of families have been estimated at between 120 and 200. The migration stretches over a period of the last 30 to 35 years. Most families originate from a particular area of the Punjab in and around the district of Jullunder. Jullunder itself, although it has a large population qualifying it as a city, is nevertheless described as the 'mofussil'. This is a term meaning 'rural'. In UK terms, Jullunder would be comparable to Armagh, for instance, rather than Belfast, or Hereford rather than Bristol, in terms of parochialism, sophistication of civic amenities, entertainment, and so on, though of course this is only a comparison between types of cities and is not intended to be a comparison between Armagh or Hereford and Jullunder.

The families have arrived here individually, but on the basis of a family or village network, i.e. one member of the family or village may arrive here, and, on setting up a small business, may recommend that other members of the family or village follow and set up similar businesses, mainly in the drapery trade. Such a group is therefore, highly homogeneous in language, religion and socio-economic terms. Its members subcribe to similar norms in terms of material prosperity and education for their children, and aspirations for them with regard to marriage, career, continuation of tradition, a feeling of Indianness or Punjabiness, and the intention to preserve their religion. With regard to language, they felt they could not lose it since all spoke Punjabi in their homes but they found English necessary for communicative purposes and expected their children to learn English at school, and to become skilled in its use. Only a few families persisted in trying to make their children speak Punjabi in the home.

Since such a group represents what Mrs. Thatcher has described as an alien culture in our midst, and from the settlement of which Enoch Powell has predicted that rivers of blood will flow, the findings of this study are of interest in showing the growth of a community which describes itself as Punjabi, Irish, British and Indian at various times in the course of conversations and sees no conflict in such varying perceptions of itself.

3. The Young Subjects

The Punjabis tend to have large families. However, the number of second generation born in Northern Ireland or settled here before the age of five years, and now between the ages of 15 and 25 years, is very small. The difficulty of obtaining a sample from this number can be gauged when it is realised that only one male or female per family is eligible for the purpose of a study. The total number of those second generation persons between the ages of 15 and 25 years and still living in Northern Ireland would be below 150. It was decided to confine the sample to this age group as it covers that period just before and after school-leaving generally thought to be a crucial time for young immigrants putting themselves to the test in the employment market and mixing with the opposite sex with a view to selection of marriage partner - a choice which in the case of their Northern Irish peers is relatively free, but in their own case is restricted to a choice either from amongst their own group in Northern Ireland or England, or just as often from a relatively strange country called India. The restriction with regard to being born here or having arrived before the age of five years was in order to ensure uniformity of early schooling and introduction of Ss to the English language through school.

All Ss remembered periods when they had visited
India below the age of 10 years and had used Punjabi
only, or they had been told by their parents that
they had spoken only Punjabi in the home before the
age of five years and going to school in Northern Ireland.

Educational Achievements of Ss and Relationship with Second Language

Biographical and educational information on
10 Ss, 6 female and 4 male, was gathered by interview
of a semi-structured nature. Of these, only 1 S, a
female, was still at school; the others had gone on
to tertiary education and employment.

Table 1 shows the breakdown between Science and
Non-Science studies at CSE (I) and O levels among all
Ss. Science here = Maths, Physics, Chemistry, Biology,
Geography, Geology and Technical Drawing. Non-Science
here = Languages, Literature, History, Economics,
Sociology and Commerical Studies.

TABLE 1   Mean CSE (I) and O Levels per respondent

	Science A	Non-Science B	Science + Non-Science A	B
Females (6)	2.50	2.67	5.17	
Males (4)	4.25	3.25	7.50	

Ss of school-leaving age who were or had been in tertiary
education,

Females: 2 of 5   Males: 4 of 4

Interviews revealed that of the 10 Ss, 7 had failed
to secure offers of free grammar school places after the
11+ exam. Of these, 6 Ss went on to secondary schools,
1 to grammar school (by paying fees in the first year).

A study of a larger sample would have to be carried
out to determine if those children who have to master a
second language for the purposes of schooling from the
age of five years, or who before the age of 10 years
make a break with the second language for a period of
several months, are more likely to be late developers.
It would appear that learners in a second language can
learn the language of classroom and text-books to
achieve good results. It also appears that there is

some bias toward science subjects among the Ss. Low achievement at the 11+ stage is made up for in later years. Family and cultural values favour education which may be an added incentive to educational achievement. In a number of cases among families interviewed, parents had taken advantage of the local system of paying fees for the first year after entrance to grammar school to send children there who had not been offered places after the 11+. After a year's review, most had gone on as non-fee-paying pupils. Among Ss, teachers were one of the most highly evaluated groups within Ss' own value systems.

Second Generation Punjabis' Identifications with Own and Northern Irish Group Members

Ss were asked to fill out 'rating sheets' for the purpose of collecting data for Identity Structure Analysis. After computer processing, the output from this data was analysed for the purpose of determining the overall self-esteem of individuals within the group, their evaluations of own and other group members, their degree of identification conflicts with these. Certain constructs that were considered to be key issues of difference between young Punjabis and their Northern Irish counterparts, such as, 'Indian/Not at all Indian', 'Doesn't believe in mixing with the opposite sex/Quite relaxed about mixing with the opposite sex', were also analysed with a view to determining whether Ss considered these to be core evaluative dimensions in their perception of others.

Patterns of language competence of the Ss were established by means of participant-observation and by means of an aural test. By analysis of their Identity Structures, it was possible to quantify the strength of their cultural values deriving both from their Punjabi heritage and from their socialisation in the Northern Irish school system and their Northern Irish peer groups. Indeed their identification with Northern Irish groups is specific in terms of older generation such as teachers, peer groups, and a further division between Protestant and Catholic peers. Generally speaking, where Ss had loyalties with a particular peer group, their opinions were generalised to the entire group.

DISCUSSION OF FINDINGS WITHIN A CONCEPTUAL FRAMEWORK WITH PARTICULAR REFERENCE TO IDENTITY STRUCTURE ANALYSIS

Language and Ethnic Identification

In considering data from research among second generation Punjabis born in Northern Ireland and in the age group of 15 years to 25 years, some of the concepts of Identity, Idealistic and Contra Identification, Conflict in Identification, Social Identity, and Cultural Product of Identity, can be used to disentangle the mystique of language in the processes of socialisation, enculturation, education and self-definitions of identity.

By studying the case of young second generation Punjabis in Northern Ireland, it can be seen that language is not always a salient feature of cultural affiliation and identity. The lack of Punjabi language among respondents does not seem a deprivation of their cultural identity to them. Moreover, language is not a salient or significant feature of their construal system or identity structure.

An explanation for this may be afforded in the following manner. A view of language as an extension of identity has often been put forward, and hence its primordial importance for people seeking peoplehood or nationhood. However, an anthropological analysis of identity by Meyer Fortes (1982 unpublished and forthcoming 1983) puts forward the notion that to specify one's identity and to exhibit it or to make it evident for others to see, is an important feature of 'I-ness', e.g. one could say that only a hereditary chief or monarch has a ready-made identity, whereas most others need a 'product' of themselves to declare to others their identity. Such a product can be 'natural', such as, e.g., one's biological gender and its physical features. On the other hand, it can be a 'cultural' product; e.g. Van Gogh mutilated himself and cut off his ear rather than mutilate his own paintings - the cultural product of his identity (Fortes 1983).

Such a concept is useful in dispelling some of the mystique surrounding language and identity of the individual. For if language is regarded as a cultural product of self, or a social artefact locating the self in social dimensions recognisable to others (such

as, e.g., class, ethnicity or national loyalty), it must be considered an object of an individual's identity; it is seen to
have aspects of conscious use, a cultural product which
may be presented or withheld at will.

Any and every communicative act has the possibility
of disclosing identity (Hudson 1980), yet there must be
some aspects of communication where the need to exchange
information is far in excess of the need to present
oneself. It has been demonstrated in diglossic use or
in multi-lingual situations, that this need, which may
be described as a cognitive aspect of language, has to
be paramount in choice of code. People in Signapore,
e.g., will use English for purposes of learning technology, business transactions or travel, but may use
Chinese or Malay or Tamil or English in the domain
of home. Unless an exchange of information is in a
situation which also clearly demands the marking of
identity, language code or accent is not salient for
that particular purpose.

Language seen as a product fits the notion of
production at will when identity is desired to be
marked. (On the other hand, it does not exclude the
notion of code-switch and code-sliding taking place
below the level of consciousness (Blom and Gumperz
1972). We are not always in command of our internalised social responses, and language may also
respond to relaxation of inhibition. Similarly,
Goffman's dramaturgy of self-presentation does not
exclude presentation of facets of self below the
level of consciousness). From this it would also
follow that language is not inextricably bound with
identity and self-definition.

In the case of young Northern Irish Punjabis,
their knowledge of and fluency in the English language,
and their lack of fluency in Punjabi, is one of the
features they have in common with their Northern
Irish peers. At the same time, their knowledge of
English does not act as a barrier with their Punjabi
reference group. It does, though, create limited
modes of communication with their parents' generation.
However, despite evidence from Hess and Shipman (1972)
and Blank and Solomon (1972) on the influence that
language has on cognitive development, development of
cognitive constructs in Ss is not entirely by means of
language at home; the life-style acts as an alternative

mediating factor. This includes observance of religious customs and prayers, the degree and quality of parents' interest in school work, the organisation of leisure, their parents' cultural norms and expectations with regard to mixing and dating with the opposite sex, food taboos, the notion of restricted choice of marriage partners and some restriction on clothing on ceremonial occasions when females are expected to wear saris. It is to be remembered in this connection that many of the parents' own values are modified and attenuated by living in Northern Ireland, causing them to be well aware of the need for flexibility in the socialisation of their offspring.

For the offspring, countervailing norms are posed by neighbours, teachers, and white peers to certain values stressed by parents. How individuals in the course of their lives cope with differing modes of behaviour posed by individual and group models is related to the formation of and changes in their individual identifications with those entities with which they perceive many characteristics in common. Having become fluent in English for the purposes of schooling, they are competent to receive ideas and affect, and able to express themselves cognitively and affectively in the world outside home. At home they absorb values through observation of customs, direct discussion with at least one parent in English, and arrive at an understanding of the parental view-point through a passive understanding of Punjabi and socialisation into a particular life-style. Lack of the Punjabi language is not salient in the formation of their identity structures.

Language can be taken as being, occasionally and when intended, an 'expresser of paternity' (Fishman 1972), by individuals, politicians and groups who wish to make it salient. Language may also be conceived as one expression of an individual's ethnicity, and it may also help to focus on how language can be used as an emblem of ethnicity. If language is regarded as a product of identity, then it has the value of both being attached to identity and of having varying significance to individuals and groups. However, it can and has been used to create the belief that it is inseparable from ethnic and national identity and people can come to believe this to be the case.

Identity Structure

Identity is a loosely employed term in popular usage. It is also used with a variety of meanings within social psychology and a dichotomy has been made between Identity and Social Identity (Zavalloni 1980). It has also been subsumed as an important aspect of Self-Concept (Tajfel 1981). It is useful to see identity differentiated and refined into as many facets and aspects as may serve the analysis of a variety of behaviours - including language behaviour - and states of mind in individuals and groups. In the main, this paper has used concepts of Identity Structure developed by P. Weinreich (1980) and methodology deriving from these concepts for the measurement of certain indices of identity. It also refers later to concepts, specifically Social Identity, derived from inter-group theory (Tajfel 1981). It applies these concepts for clarification of issues raised here and extends them in the section on roles and role-relationship.

A primary distinction between Identity or I-ness and Social Identity may serve to focus on identity as an egocentric perception of self, based in a system of constructs which the ego uses to differentiate the characteristics of self and others (Weinreich 1982), and having a continuity in time. This concept serves to explain how states of empathy between individuals give rise to conflicts in identification. For it is only when one perceives shared attributes with another, and is ego-involved with them, that one may have idealistic identifications with those attributes which they possess and which the ego admires. Again, if people with whom one perceives oneself to be sharing empathetic identification have attributes which are unpleasant and from which one wishes to dissociate oneself, this is termed contra-identification. This is the basis of identification conflict with others. In the case of the Northern Irish Punjabis, that they evince some conflict in identification both with their own group and the Northern Irish is healthy, since it indicates empathetic identification with both groups.

Evaluative constructs which the Ss use may not always be compatibly applied to each of the entities which figure in their lives - e.g. when looking at the comparative ease with which their Northern Irish peers mix with the opposite sex, if they perceived that their own parents did not do this themselves, this would challenge the consistent use of the construct, 'Doesn't believe in mixing with the opposite sex/Quite relaxed about mixing with the opposite sex'. This would lower the stability of such a construct and in ISA terms, the 'Structural Pressure' (see Appendix, Table 4), on it would be low and the

construct might even be ready for reappraisal in its use.
It might also be used as a double standard, i.e. differently
applied for separate entities. If many key constructs are
in the process of such change, this aspect of a subject's
development is termed 'Identity Diffusion' (Weinreich 1980).
Two Ss in the course of the study were in such a state at
the time of interviewing. One was in the process of changing
key constructs related to identifications with own group. The
S had begun to construe his/her world in terms of identifications with the Northern Irish group and was moving
away from own group norms in order to resolve conflicts in
identification with own group.

Over a period of years, Punjabi young people come
to terms with the values of both groups. They perceive early on that 'There are differences between
Northern Irish and us/Northern Irish are same as us'.
Most signal conformity to their parents' and own-group
norms when they follow the traditional pattern of
selection of marriage partner being influenced by
parents' choice. They signal their adaptation to
Northern Irish groups by evaluating their peer group
highly with high idealistic identification with them,
low contra-identification and identification conflict,
as compared with their evaluation of their own group
on the same dimensions (see Appendix, Table 2).

A few other concepts developed in Identity
Structure Analysis (Weinreich 1980) and used in the
course of this paper and in tables   need some
explanation. 'Ego-involvement' with another constitutes
the responsiveness in quantity and strength of attributes a S construes another to possess. 'Evaluation of
another' is the overall assessment of another in terms
of positive and negative attributes that the Subject
construes in others. So that if a young Punjabi is
highly ego-involved with both groups and their representatives and has a high evaluation of both groups
within their value system, both groups are positively
significant for the subject (see Appendix, Table 2).

'Self-esteem' of an individual is the overall
assessment of the continuing relationship between a
person's past and current self-image, in accordance
with their value system. (See Appendix, Table 5).

'Identity Diffusion' is the overall dispersion
of and magnitude of an individual's identification
conflicts with significant others of both groups.
(See Table 5).

These are highly ellipted definitions of the
terms used and those wishing to use a methodology
deriving from these concepts should consult Weinreich
(1980).

184

Social Identity

This term has been defined variously. In one of its meanings it denotes an important facet of self-concept (Giles 1981). However, even in this definition it is consistently referred to as a separate concept and is apparently seen as loosely connected to personal identity or self-concept. A splitting-off of identity into the category of social identity, however, serves to show the extent to which identity is bound within a group, in this case an ethnic group. Giles et al. (1981) refer to the significance to an individual of belonging to a group. It is one of the most basic means of identifying oneself to describe oneself as belonging to a particular group which is distinct from some other group. However, some reflection on group membership reveals its varying nature for most people - e.g. a young Irishman who is aware of his Irishness may take this for granted and place little importance on this group membership. He may place much greater value on his membership of the group of lawyers in his country and this membership could be more salient to him than his Irishness. Thus, individuals belong to several groups and see themselves as members of different groups at different times. The priority of group membership is not necessarily fixed. At some other time, e.g. during a World Cup series, the same Irishman may suddenly proudly identify himself as an Irishman.

The usefulness of the concept of social identity may be extended by differentiating further between alter and ego-ascribed identity (Weinreich 1980). Others may look upon the young Punjabi group as 'Asians' or foreigners, or migrants, but they themselves, although they may be aware that they are described as such, need not subscribe to such an ascription. They may prefer to regard themselves as Irish, British, Indian or Punjabi-Irish. Thus, individuals are able to have metaperspectives on themselves, such as 'Me as my white friends see me', 'Me as Punjabis see me'. A young Punjabi may regard his/her view of him/herself as being Middle-class', or 'Employed', or being Northern Irish and sharing the values of Protestant peers at school, rather than Catholic peers in the same town, as being of greater significance than an alter-ascribed identity. Thus, alter-ascribed identity need not be congruent with ego-ascribed identity. Bearing this distinction in mind it is easier to conceive of Punjabis describing themselves as British, or Indian, or Irish, or Punjabi at various times. This also serves to explain how groups who may be ascribed a low status in their host society

nevertheless retain a strong and positive evaluation of
themselves and their own group, since they are able
to distinguish between alter-ascribed identity of the
stereotyped kind and their own perception of themselves.

The differentiation of social identity as a facet
of self-concept facilitates a view of the individual in
interaction with others, with own and other groups, whose
self-concept is constantly modified, attenuated and
redefined through the many and delicate inter-relation-
ships, whether at work, in the family, or when facing
a new situation. New values are formed by association
with new groups and in new relationships. Old values
are challenged. The self is a developing entity
growing out of the past with its genetic and cultural
heritage, maintaining itself in the present - sometimes
experiencing conflict in so doing - and aspiring
towards an ideal self in the future.

Role Relationship and Identity

A further incorporation into a many-faceted view
of Identity may lie in the exploration of role and
role-relationship. Giles (1981) states that high
occupational status of individuals, especially in
ethnic groups having hard, encapsulating boundaries,
may seek intra-group rather than inter-group
comparability. This would seem to acknowledge the
importance of role-relationship in the maintenance
of identity and the extent to which role confers
status; the value of role as a facet of identity
when the individual holds high status has been covered.
However, an individual's role dissociated from status
may also become a means of contributing to identity
formation in the following manner. By creating and
maintaining personal relationships, an individual could
increase or decrease self-evalutaion - e.g. a young
Punjabi in Northern Ireland who has a good relationship with a group can gain a favourable metapers-
pective of him/herself such as in 'Me as my white
friends see me', or 'Me as Punjabis see me. These are
important aspects of the Punjabi Ss' identity. The
two metaperspectives are compared for the group in
Table 3 (see Appendix).

Ego-involvement in a group with a high evaluation
of that group, strong idealistic identification with
it and low conflict in identification indicates
involvement with a group which is valued and contact
with it is rewarding. A person who is a member of a
group with little ego-involvement in that group, and
who is little known in that group, derives some enjoy-
ment from being a group member, e.g. a paid-up member

of the Labour Party. If, on the other hand, the member
is also heavily involved in party work, idealistic
identifications with the Labour Party and contra-
identifications with it due to a greater ego-involvement
will increase. It might be said, therefore, that through
role-relationships a person maintains, or increases,
idealistic and contra-identifications. If a person
increases the distance between him/herself and the group
or other individuals, the relationship becomes negligible
or withers away. (In cases where distance is increased
but the contra-identifications are not resolved, this
may only serve to put the conflict with the group out of
one's conscious mind. Nevertheless, it enables a person
to get on with other aspects of his/her life). Where
role-relationships are maintained, the resulting tension
and stresses of the relationship must feed back into
definitions of the other, as well as perceptions of
self.

If young Punjabis had little in the way of ego-
involvement, low indices of idealistic and contra-
identification with Northern Irish groups as compared
with their family group or own group, this would not
augur well for future relations between members of
the host society and generations of migrants born
in Northern Ireland. Withdrawal of role-relationship
with other groups would lead to total self-encapsulation
within their own group and to those dangerous positions
in society where ethnic groups are perceived as being
hostile to the general good because they seem preoccupied
with own-group values and disregarding of mainstream
concerns and opinions.

The importance of role-relationships in identity
maintenance is a psychological function. The process
of idealistic and contra-identification with individuals
and groups serves the maintenance and growth of an
individual's value system. If, however, the relationship between individuals loses significance, or suffers
loss of esteem in the eyes of the individual, then the
stability and importance ('structural pressures',
Weinreich 1980) of values associated and shared previously must also diminish, especially if generated in
the context of the relationship. It is for this
process of continuing to share values and value systems
that the web of role-relationships has high significance.
Maintaining the tension by increasing and decreasing
relations with family and Northern Irish peers increases
or decreases the stability of shared values.

CONCLUSION

This pilot study is limited to a sample of 10 Ss
in the very special circumstances of migration
afforded by the conditions of Northern Ireland. It is
not, therefore, intended to make generalisations from
this small study or to extrapolate broad principles
regarding all Punjabi migrants to the UK. However,
it has been intended to demonstrate certain
propositions below:

1. Recent sociolinguistic research has undertaken
   quantitative linguistic analysis among samples
   representing particular social classes and social
   networks (Milroy 1980; Labov Lang. Soc. 2;
   Bloom & Gumperz 1972). It has made a significant
   contribution toward the correlation of variations
   of language and the maintenance of social networks
   and group solidarity.

   Social psychologists by means of explanations arising
   in inter-group theory have contributed toward an
   understanding of the condition of psycholinguistic
   distinctiveness (Giles and Johnson 1981) and reasons
   why people revive ethnic language skills. They have
   also proposed explanations of why minority groups
   may seek to assimilate with the superordinate group,
   in which cases 'it may lead to alienation and a loss
   of cultural distinctiveness for those individuals who
   still value their ethnic group membership and see
   language as an important dimension of it'.

   The present study differs in its aim and methodo-
   logies from sociolinguistic studies of language
   maintenance. It presents a situation where the
   second generation of migrants do not maintain their
   mother tongue. It uses a theory of self-concept and
   identity (Weinreich 1980) to present and to analyse
   a process of ethnic identity maintenance despite the
   loss of active use of the ethnic language. By presenting empirical evidence of psychological process,
   it also differs from theoretical perspectives from
   Giles and Johnson (1981) and Giles and Byrne (1982).

2. An ethnographic study of a qualitative nature has
   been carried out prior to applying the methodology
   of Identity Structure Analysis (Weinreich 1980) and
   measuring in Ss their self-esteem and conflicts in
   identification with particular cultural values and
   affiliations. The ethnographic study by means of

participant-observation refuted certain stereotype beliefs, such as that migrant youngsters of Indian descent have poor proficiency levels in English as a second language. This may be true in certain cases, but the study demonstrates that this is not universally true. It also demonstrates that it is important that research should be directed toward establishing which educational, social, economic, psychological and cultural processes militate against L2 acquisition, and which conditions of this nature foster second language acquisition. It is important that such distinctions be established before detrimental stereotypical assumptions are made. That poor linguistic performance is prevalent among all second generation migrants may become a stereotype which influences the perception of teachers and employers alike. Such stereotypes can only be eliminated or modified by systematic studies of an empirical nature. Studies by Lambert in Canada (1972) have demonstrated effective methods of monitoring L2 acquisition under certain educational and social psychological conditions and refute general assumptions about bilingualism among English and French Canadian youngsters.

3. This study also strongly refutes the general stereotype held among host communities that individuals in migrant groups must have a low self-esteem, suffer from alienation in the host society, suffer culture conflict (a general and unspecified term), and may therefore be a poor risk as stable, law-abiding citizens. The riots of Brixton and Toxteth in 1982 - chiefly among Britons of West Indian descent - seemed to afford grounds for such speculation in private. It is claimed in this study that individuals and small groups may well be classifiable in the above manner. However, research should be undertaken to support or refute such claims now directed generally at minorities in Britain. In addition, specific research in Britain may be more useful than to generalise from findings of studies in the USA and other parts of Europe to minority groups in Britain. Wherever possible, a methodology should be adopted whereby claims regarding self-esteem, identity, culture conflict, etc., are quantifiable. The present study has used one methodology which by means of algebraic formulae, has translated concepts of identity structure into quantifiable terms.

APPENDIX

Table 2: Shows mean indices of Ss' construal of
significant members of both groups, own
and other.

Construal by Females & Males

(N) Entities	Mean of indices on entities				
	*Ego-Involvement	+Evaluation	Idlstc. Idfcn.	Contra Idtfn.	Idfcn. Con.
8 Father	4.38	0.527	0.731	0.233	0.366
10 Mother	4.46	0.360	0.638	0.327	0.409
9 Fav. Bro.	3.65	0.540	0.759	0.249	0.549
9 Fav. Sister	3.73	0.540	0.654	0.133	0.384
10 Teachers	2.18	0.464	0.498	0.110	0.226
7 Prot. Boys	2.95	0.247	0.456	0.313	0.326
5 R C Boys	3.10	0.381	0.585	0.205	0.291
9 Prot. girls	2.90	0.347	0.583	0.239	0.330
7 R C girls	3.81	0.310	0.543	0.222	0.326

* Max = 5.00
  Min = 0.00
+ Max = +1.00
  Min = -1.00

All the rest: Max = 1.00
              Min = 0.00

190

Table 3: Shows Metaperspectives 'Me as Punjabis see me'
(A) and 'Me as my white friends see me' (B)
crucial to Ss' relationships with own and other
group

(A)

(N)	Mean of all indices on Metaperspective 'Me as Punjabis see me'				
	*Ego-Involvement	+Evaluation	Idlstc. Idfcn.	Contra Idfcn.	Idtfcn. Conflict
Females (5)	2.91	0.328	0.449	0.116	0.135
Males (4)	3.78	0.468	0.651	0.282	0.309
F & M (9)	2.94	0.398	0.550	0.119	0.222

(B)

(N)	Mean of all indices on Metaperspective 'Me as my white friends see me'				
	*Ego-Involvement	+Evaluation	Idlstc. Idtfc.	Contra Idfcn.	Idtfcn. Conflict
Females (5)	3.62	0.542	0.668	0.102	0.344
Males (4)	3.67	0.761	0.802	0.136	0.216
F & M (9)	3.64	0.651	0.735	0.119	0.280

* Max = 5.00
  Min = 0.00

+Max =+1.00
 Min =-1.00

All other indices Max = 1.00
                  Min = 0.00

191

Table 4: Shows Mean Structural Pressures of Ss on key constructs concerning ethnicity. Range: Max = +100.00 to Min = -100.00. Values close to zero indicate inconsistent use of a construct. High + ve values indicate a desire to retain the current evaluative connotation. - ve values indicate pressures on S to reassess the evaluative significance the construct may have for them). Values are expressed under preferred polarity of Ss.

Key Constructs bearing on Ethnicity	Mean Strl. Pressures			
	(N)	Polarity 1	(N)	Polarity 2
Indian/Not at all Indian	(5)	22.91	(4)	61.47
Feels there are differences between NI & us/thinks NI same as us	(4)	57.41	(4)	30.34
Wants to please the Family/ Independent, goes his/her own way	(6)	20.99	(4)	64.74
Interested in religion/Has no wish to be involved	(8)	24.85	(2)	48.45
Respects tradition and interested in past/Not much interested in past	(6)	46.33	(4)	46.83
British/Not at all British	(5)	53.77	(4)	20.73
Strikes me as being Punjabi/ Doesn't seem at all Punjabi	(4)	19.78	(6)	51.68
Satisfied with what he/she is/ Would like to change and develop	(4)	43.55	(6)	20.86
Doesn't believe in mixing with the opposite sex/Quite relaxed about mixing with opposite sex		-	(9)	65.67

Table 5: Shows Mean values of Self-Esteem and Identity Diffusion for all Ss by gender F (6) & M (4)

Self-esteem Max = +1.00   Id. Diffusion Max = 1.00

          Min = -1.00   Min = 0.00

(N)	Self-esteem	Current Idty Diffusion	
Fs (6)	0.488	0.307	(Moderate)
Ms (4)	0.712	0.317	(Moderate)

BIBLIOGRAPHY

Bernstein, B. (1972), 'Social class, language and
    socialization' in A. Cashdan (ed.), Language in
    education, London: Routledge and Kegan Paul.
Blank, M. and F. Soloman, (1972), 'How shall the
    disadvantaged child be taught' in A. Cashdan (ed.),
    Language in education, London: Routledge and Kegan Paul.
Blom, J. and J. Gumperz, (1972), 'Social meaning in
    linguistic structures: code-switching in Norway',
    in J. Gumperz and D. Hymes (eds.), Directions in
    sociolinguistics, USA: Holt, Rinehart and Winston, Inc.
Ervin-Tripp, S. (1964), 'Language and TAT content in
    bilinguals', Jrnl. of Abnormal Psychology' 68,
    pp. 5oo-507.
Fishman, J. (1972), Readings in the sociology of language,
    The Hague: Mouton.
Fishman, J. et al. (eds.), (1968), Language problems
    of developing nations, New York: J. Wiley and Sons.
Fishman, J. (1972), Language in sociocultural change,
    Stanford: Stanford University Press.
Giles, H. and J. Byrnes (1982), 'An Inter-group approach
    to second language acquisition', Journal of Multilingual and
    Multicultural Development 3.1, pp. 17-40.
Giles, H. and P. Johnson, (1981), 'The role of language
    in ethnic group relations', in J. Turner and H. Giles,
    (eds.), Intergroup behaviour, Oxford: Basil Blackwell.
Grier, W. and P.M. Cobbs (1968), Black rage, New York:
    Basil Books.
Hudson, R. (1980), Sociolinguistics, Cambridge:
    Cambridge University Press.
Labov, W. (1973), 'The linguistic consequences of being a
    lame', Language in Society 2, pp. 81-115.
Milroy, L. (1980), Language and social networks,
    Oxford: Basil Blackwell.
Tajfel, H. (1981), Human groups and social categories,
    Cambridge: Cambridge University Press.
Wells, L.E. and J. Maxwell (1976), Self-esteem,
    Beverly Hills: Sage.
Weinreich, P. (1980), Manual for identity exploration
    using personal constructs, Birmingham: SSRC
    Research Unit on Ethnic Relations, University of
    Aston, Birmingham.
Zavalloni, M. (1980), 'Values' in H. Triandis and R.
    Brislin (eds.), Handbook of cross-cultural
    psychology, Social Psychology 5, Boston: Allyn
    and Bacon Inc.

THE INFLUENCE OF ENGLISH ON
MODERN SPOKEN HEBREW

Deborah Nothmann
University of Haifa

1   Introduction

At the same time that Theodor Herzl was writing his
prophetic book about the as yet non-existent Jewish state,
Altneuland (Old-New Land), Hebrew, the old-new language,
was undergoing a process of revival and rejuvenation.
Herzl had already claimed that he had founded this
Jewish state, at the first Zionist Congress in Basle in
1897. The new state needed a new language, able to cope
with the realities of the fast-approaching twentieth
century. A brave and commendable attempt was made to
revive old roots within the language so that modern
concepts could be expressed through them. At some
point the founding fathers lost control and the people
and events of the new times took over, at least partially. All languages borrow and change; out of necessity
Hebrew borrowed and changed more than most. This paper
deals with only one aspect of this process - the
addition of English words to Hebrew. Since Hebrew
lexicographers are by definition committed to the preservation and propagation of Hebrew roots, some of the
words included in this paper cannot be found in Hebrew
or Hebrew-English dictionaries. However, they can be
and are found in the language as spoken by Israelis and
as used in the Israeli communications media.

2   Reasons for Hebrew Borrowing from Other Languages

2.1 New Concepts, Foreign Concepts.

2.1.1 Lexical Voids

At various stages, the Jewish population of Israel
has found it necessary to adapt itself to conditions
that classical Hebrew or even early twentieth-century
Hebrew was not equipped to cope with. Developing the
rudiments of an army during British Mandatory times
necessitated to some extent the adoption of military
customs and their terms from the British Army (who in
turn may have got them from the United States Army)
that was so well known to the Jewish settlers. The
uniforms included what Americans called an Eisenhower
jacket and the Palestinian Jews referred to as a
/bateldres/. (In fact, it is still part of the uniform of Israeli soldiers.) The cheapest military

vehicle was the American-invented-and-named /djip/.
Kerosene (or paraffin) is still stored in a /djerikan/
and soldiers communicate with the help of a /vokitoki/.
In those days the most common method of getting around
in the country was by /tremp/ (mistakenly thought to
involve travelling in a vehicle), but you could always
be stopped at a /tshekpost/ where your wallet and your
/kitbeg/ could be inspected by the /si ai di/. Palestinian
Jews learned to prepare /stek/ on a /gril/ and eat it with
/tships/. For breakfast one ate /tost/ prepared in a
/toster/ and drank /inglish ti/. Babies thrived on
/kornflor/ and /kvaker/ and still do. Farmers had modern
equipment. Every kibbutz had a /kombain/ and some even
had a /shafeldozer/, now called a /shoofel/. And everyone knows that a /traktor/ is equipped with /pauertekof/.
If you had a radio, the /tyooner/ or the /amplifaier/
might be out of order. Roads were built with the help of
a /buldozer/. You rode on these roads in a /texi speishel/
if you didn't have a /praivet/, a /tender/ or a /semitreler/.
The /gir/ or /breks/ of any of these vehicles might be out
of order or you might get a /pantsher/ and all these would
have to be fixed at a /garazh/, as would the /stiring/ or
the /klatsh/. In time people got used to paying by /tshek/
or /shek/ with a /kros/ on it and to using /after shev/
before going out to engage in a /flirt/.

After the establishment of the State of Israel and
the departure of the British, economic conditions in the
country hit a new low. Anyone in the land of milk and
honey who possibly could located a long lost relative
in the land of opportunity, the United States of America.
With luck you could even get a /fridjider/ from one of
Uncle Sam's citizens. American CARE packages contained
a new fish, /toona/.

In time economic conditions improved, but Hebrew
speaking Israelis never gave up their admiration for all
things American. They became acquainted with the
/bauling/, /milkshek/, /popkorn/, /kreikerim/, /pankeks/
and /pai/, and their children learned how to solve
/pazelim/ and chew /babelgam/.

Israeli industry developed, but in many cases the
language was left behind. Dairies learned how to make
/kotedj/ cheese, textile factories produced /djins/ and
/taits/ made of /nailon stretsh/ and the people of
Tel Aviv started to go to the movies at the /draivin/.

But if you don't happen to live in Tel Aviv you can always
go to a /hepening/ or watch your son fall off his /sketbord/.
And all over Israel you can have your hair coiffured by
/fen/.

Some of these words are no longer voids. Hebrew, with
the help of the Hebrew Language Academy, has modernized
itself by finding equivalents for /buldozer/, /tshek/,
/fridjider/, /bauling/, /texi speishel/, /praivet/, /gir/,
/klatsh/, /breks/, /stiring/ and /garazh/, although their
solutions are not always acceptable to the man in the
street. No one plays the Hebrew equivalent of bowling,
very few people pay byanything but /tshek/, but they do
recognize the Hebrew words for bulldozer, taxi, automobile,
gear, puncture, refrigerator, clutch, steering, garage or
amplifier when they see them. In some cases Hebrew has
succeeded to such a degree that the English word may be
on the way out, or may already have died a natural death.
One seldom hears /fridjider/ today, and no one of the
younger generation knows what a /skvidji/ is; it was
once in common use for washing floors. Now it is a
/gumi/ if used at all.

2.1.2 Cultural Voids

There is a type of void that is not quite so readily
accepted by the Hebrew language; cultural voids have no
roots in Hebrew that can be modernized. Ham and bacon
have found their places in butcher shops that do not
observe the dietary laws; here you can buy /hem/ and
/bekon/ or /shinken/and /shpek/, depending on where one's
allegiances lie. Many restaurants, again the non-kosher
variety, feature /lobster/ and /shrimps/ on the menu.
Shrimps are often referred to by the Hebrew equivalent,
although I have yet to find this word in a Hebrew
dictionary.

Together with forbidden foods are cowboys, Indians
and spirituals. The word /boker/ usually refers to
Israeli and other non-American cowboys, while the
American term is reserved for the 'real' thing. The
Indians may possibly be one of the ten lost tribes,
but we do not have a word for them. Since only the
American Negro is associated with spirituals, the
Hebrew language has evidently deferred to English and
adopted /spirityooel/ as its own.

2.2 Snobbism

Another important motive for the adoption of a
foreign term is the desire to emulate the foreign
culture it is a part of. It is hard to find a native
Hebrew speaker of the middle class who does not say

/hai/, /bai/ and /aim veri sori/.[3] Everyone knows who is in /hai sosaieti/ and the places to shop are /dizengof senter/, /shop senter/ and that most modern tautology, /midel senter/. The most coveted dwelling is a /penthauz/ or a /kotedj/ (the more cosmopolitan/vila/ is passé). One relaxes at a /kauntri klab/ or /kantri klab/ where haute couture dictates that it is old-fashioned to wear the veteran Hebrew equivalent of shorts, which are 'in'. The anniversary of the birth of Jesus is known as /krismes/ even though Hebrew has a word for it.

There is a kind of snobbism for the most attractive features but also for the most outlandish, obnoxious or vulgar. (This is, of course, a subjective value judgement). Cursewords are an example of this. One finds well-bred, well-behaved Israeli youths using Anglo-Saxon four-letter words in situations where their American contemporaries wouldn't dare to.

3   Types of Acclimatization

When a foreign word enters a language there are invariably some changes made. These changes may be phonetic, morphologic, syntactic, orthographic and/or semantic. Since Hebrew is written with a different alphabet and different script from that of English, no English word can escape orthographic alteration. The same is true of the phonology of Hebrew. (The only English word I know of whose pronunciation has remained unchanged in Hebrew is the greeting /hai/. I find it very difficult to judge an Israeli's origins by the way he pronounces this word.) There are almost always morphological changes. The syntactic and semantic structure of these words changes less consistently, but these alterations are still quite common.

3.1 Phonetic Changes

Since most phonetic changes are actually allophonic I shall not discuss them. More significant are the phonemic changes that occur in the process of transfer. Vowels and consonants may change and consonants may get lost in the shuffle.

3.1.1   Vowel Shifts

It is possible to say /boling/ in Hebrew, but no one does. The word is /bauling/. Often tape becomes /taip/, probably because of the ambiguous transliteration (TIIP), which could be pronounced either /teip/ or /taip/. For the same reason we have /speishel/, meaning a taxi. Country often becomes /kauntri/ and one eats a /kreiker/ because of lack of knowledge of correct English pronunciation.

198

/Kauntri/ is the mistake of a nation, as is /bauling/, but /kreiker/ has probably been inflicted on the populace by an advertiser or a manufacturer who should have devoted more time to studying English.

3.1.2 Consonant Shifts

Hebrew does not have the unvoiced affricate /tsh/ represented in the alphabet, but one of the Israeli Jewish child's most popular heroes is a monkey called /tshipopo/. As a result most Hebrew speakers acquire the ability to pronounce /tsh/ rather early in life. Nevertheless, many people pay by /shek/ rather than /tshek/.

During Mandatory times many people in Israel knew English either because they served in the government or the army or because they had learned it at school. The German Jews knew English, but had different ways of pronouncing the same letters. This is the only explanation I have for pronouncing shoveldozer /shafeldozer/ or /shofeldozer/.

3.1.3 Consonants Dropped

Every language has its characteristic consonant clusters and words may have to change upon entering a new language. /Ost/ is common at the end of English words or syllables, but not at the end of Hebrew ones. As a result exhaust (n.) becomes /egzoz/ and roast beef becomes /rosbif/ or /rozbif/.

/S/ or /z/ at the end of a word, after other consonants, seems to be too much of a load for the average Israeli, who wears [an] /overol/, studies at the university for a /master/, and has trouble with the collective /gir/ in his car.

Since the prevalent pronunciation in Israel is that of Jews who spoke (or speak) languages lacking an unvoiced glottal fricative, this sound is often dropped both from veteran Hebrew words and the new additions from English. In one case at least the result is a set of homophones where none existed in English. There is no differentiation between overalls and overhaul. Both are pronounced /overol/, with only the context left to decide the issue.

3.1.4 Consonant Changed -

Sometimes there seems to be no rhyme or reason for changes that occur. For instance, I have no explanation for walkie-talkie becoming /hokitoki/.

3.2 Morphologic Changes

3.2.1 Dropped Morphemes

Sometimes more than a consonant is deleted when an English word joins Hebrew. After-duty pass becomes /after/, good-bye becomes /bai/ (in English too, but not consistently and exclusively), roller becomes /rol/ and fuck-up is shortened to /fak/.

3.2.2 Plural Suffixes

Most English words which have found a place in Hebrew have assumed the Hebrew plural. Everyone is at home with /boilerim/, /bebisiterim/, /blenderim/ and /bosim/ and the overwhelming majority of English words incorporated into Hebrew have Hebrew plural endings. More unusual are those words that have not yet been fully adopted: /tisyooz/, /tisherts/, /pankeiks/, /kornfleks/, /spirityooels/ and others.

Some words have two plurals. One, the English, is considered part of the word, not the plural suffix, and so the word acquires the Hebrew plural suffix: /breksim/, /djinzim/[4] and /tshipsim/[4] are the ones that come to mind.

Sometimes the singular ending of an English word sounds like a Hebrew plural. When this word is used in Hebrew it acquires a new singular form in keeping with Hebrew phonology. The seal beam of a car is, in Hebrew, /silv/ in the singular and /silbim/ in the plural.

In other cases the English plural suffix is dropped for phonologic reasons. But once that happens the word is treated as a singular form. Gears is /gir/ in the singular and /girim/ in the plural.

3.2.3 New Word Families

A few words have become so acclimatized that they have developed new extended forms that are in keeping with modern Hebrew morphology. A /tremp/ is indulged in by a /trempist/ who waits for a ride at the /trempiada/, and grilled /stek/ is sold and eaten in a /stekia/.

3.2.4 Adjectives that do not Acquire Agreement

Another difficulty presents itself when an English adjective joins Hebrew. English adjectives do not show agreement, whereas Hebrew adjectives do. The result is that Israelis wear 'socks stretch' and buy 'deodorant in [a] spray'. In other words, English premodifiers become Hebrew postmodifiers without assuming agreement.

3.3 Syntactic Changes

3.3.1 Syntactic Shifts and Non-Shifts

3.3.1.1 Syntactic Voids

For syntactic reasons /es o es/ is a void. It is a noun, and the Hebrew equivalent is a verbal imperative.

3.3.1.2 Apparent Syntactic Shifts

Sometimes a word seems to have shifted to a different syntactic category but what has really happened is that the word or phrase was shortened. /After/, meaning after-duty-pass, is a noun, not an adverb. /Speishel/ has undergone a similar process. It is a noun replacing /teksi speishel/, where it appears as an adjective.

3.3.1.3 Syntactic Non-Shifts

When a phrase rather than a word finds its place in Hebrew, the result can be a violation of Hebrew syntactic structure. This is what happens with many phrases having snob appeal. The aforementioned /aim veri sori/, /dizengof senter/, /shop senter/, /midel senter/ and /kantri klab/ are examples of this. In each of these, there is a premodifier that normally does not exist in Hebrew. In addition, /aim veri sori/ contains a copulative verb where none would appear in a present tense Hebrew utterance.

3.3.2 Syntactic Specification

A word is borrowed in order to fulfil a specific function. /Bos/ functions as a noun, so as to provide a colloquial term where only a literary or officialese one was in evidence - /ma'avid/. The use of /bos/ as a verb was not needed and so was never incorporated into Hebrew. To brake a car is, in the borrowed form, 'to make brakes' or, in the original Hebrew, /livlom/, (to brake). /Gir/ also left its verb behind, as did /tost/, /fyooz/, /flirt/ and /kombain/. The same is true of /klatsh/, /kros/, /shit/, /shans/ and others.

3.4 Semantic Changes

3.4.1 Semantic Shifts

Where word borrowing is concerned, there seem to be two kinds of semantic shifts: (a) the meaning of the word

changes upon entering the new language and (b) the meaning
of the word changes after the word has been in the new
language for some time.

To the best of my knowledge, examples for (a) would be
/tremp/, /trafik/, /kotedj/. As stated earlier, /tremp/
means hitchhiking and always has. In British English
tramp means 'to hike' with no riding involved. /Trafik/
in Hebrew refers not to 'traffic' but to the policeman
or the headquarters dealing with traffic supervision. In
Israel a /kotedj/ is a status symbol with at least two levels.
A /dirat kotedj/ is a duplex apartment. This has very little
to do with the simple country house the native English
speaker knows as a cottage. Perhaps the dream of every
housing development dweller is a house of one's own. By the
time he has the money for it, he needs more of a status symbol
and lo and behold, the cottage becomes a miniature palace.

Examples of (b), delayed semantic modification,
are /djob/, /teip/, /pantsher/ and /fen/. Originally,
/djob/ meant a special task, as in

I have a job for you to do.

However, this /djob/ was a very specific one; it was an
underground activity, some action to be carried out
against the British who had, willy nilly, supplied the
word. Eventually /djob/ assumed most of the meanings
job has in English. /Teip/ was originally the tape
used in a tape recorder, but has since assumed the
meaning of 'tape recorder' as well. /Pantsher/ was
originally a puncture or flat tyre but has so acclimatized itself as to take on the metaphoric meaning of
'mishap' and is now a polyseme. /Fen/ was originally a
portable hair dryer that blows (like a fan, and is
therefore also an example of (a)) hot or cold air to dry
it, with the help of a brush or comb to style the hair.
Now it can mean simply the act of styling the hair with
a brush while drying it with a blow dryer. /Djob/, /teip/
and /pantsher/ are also examples of semantic specification,
which will be discussed next.

3.4.2 Semantic Specification

In any language, words acquire new meanings as the
speakers of that language develop new concepts or find
related situations needing some form of expression.
Dictionaries often list five, ten or more meanings for
a single word. But when a word with multiple meanings
is borrowed by another language, the chances are that
most of the meanings will be left behind. Switch is a
case in point. The Random House American college
dictionary lists eight meanings of the noun switch, only
one of which is the definition of the Hebrew /svitsh/:

5. _Elect._ a device for turning on or off or directing an electric current, or making or breaking a circuit.

The same is true of /tranzit/, which is only a specific type of vehicle, or /tisyoo/, which is only a paper handkerchief. /Tships/ are made solely of potatoes and /rosbif/ is a specific cut of beef for roasting, not just any beef that has already been roasted (which makes /rosbif/ an example of semantic shift).

Another type of semantic specification is the designation of specific landmarks and institutions. There is only one /refaineri/ in Israel - the one in Haifa Bay for refining petroleum. All other refineries in or out of Israel are denoted in the original, unsullied Hebrew. There is a historical reason for this. The Haifa Bay refinery was the only one in Palestine at the time of the British mandate and was British owned. For some reason, the only road junction in Israel still known as a /tshekpost/ is the one in Haifa Bay where the road leading to the /refaineri/ joins the road to the Jezreel Valley.

3.4.3 Semantic Voids and Gridding

It sometimes happens that a new English addition to Hebrew has one or more designational synonyms in the lexicon of veteran Hebrew words or among other additions from English or other languages,but that these words denote different things. For instance, /sprei/, /erosol/, /risoos/ and /shprits/ all have something to do with spraying, but they are used in different situations. /Sprei/ is used for cosmetic purposes (even if the substance to be sprayed comes in an aerosol can), /erosol/ is the term for industrial and household products and /risoos/, from a Hebrew root, is for agricultural use. There is some overlapping between /sprei/ and /erosol/, but this is usually a matter of stylistic register; women are more inclined to use /sprei/ and men usually use /erosol/. /Shprits/ is used mainly for non-work situation, as when children turn a water hose on each other, or for a drink of wine and soda water. It is also the term used for a type of house painting or for stuccoing. All of these meanings are originally German, as is the word itself.

3.5 Stylistic Levels and Registers

As has been pointed out, some English words in Hebrew are stylistic voids. I would consider any English word a stylistic void if its Hebrew synonym is to be found only in a dictionary, an official document or in a translation of an English literary work. Such is the

case with /bauling/, /master/, /em ei/, /pai/ and /tshek/.
/Pai/ is more complicated than the others. The Hebrew
/pashtida/ can also mean 'pudding' or 'custard'. When
it means 'pie' it is the work of a translator trying to
make a text intelligible to the Hebrew reader or protecting the 'purity' of the Hebrew language.

There are also differences in stylistic levels where
the veteran English word and the later Hebrew addition
are both in common use. Examples of these are: /svitsh/-
/mafsek/, /overol/-/shipoots/, /teip rekorder/-/maklit kol/,
/tisyoo/-/mimxatat nyar/, /texi/-/monit/, /trafik/-/shoter
tnu'a/, /fer/-/hogen/, and /pantsher/-/takala/. In all
these cases the Hebrew word is on a higher stylistic level.
This is almost a general rule.

Then there is the question of register. As one of our
writers has pointed out, Israel is a country where parents
learn the mother tongue from their children; where the
mother's tongue is not the mother tongue (Kishon n.d.).
A great many English words were adopted before the
Hebrew Language Academy came up with equivalents based
on Hebrew roots. /Fifti fifti/, /breks/, /refaineri/,
/svitsh/, /boiler/, /djob/, /sendvitsh/ and /fridjider/
are used more by the older generation than are their
modern Hebrew counterparts. The younger generation is
composed mainly of people who were educated in Israeli
schools and who know Hebrew better than many of their
parents.

This situation exists not only where different
generations are concerned, but in professional jargons as
well. The Academy often sees the need for a word <u>after</u>
the speakers of Hebrew have discovered the deficiency and
have corrected it with a loan word. If the word the
Academy proposes actually 'takes', then the chances are
that the loan word will become less and less popular,
often to the point where it returns from whence it came.
This is what happened to /stiring/ and what is happening
to /klatsh/, /breks/ and other mechanical terms. For
a while, fewer and fewer doctors were heard saying
/roomatik fiver/; at least temporarily, the Hebrew term
took its place. (The medical profession seems to be
wavering in its allegiances. Only time will tell which
term will win.) /Lipstik/ used to be very popular; now
/sifton/ or the newer /sfaton/ are more in use. (However,
some cosmetic saleswomen are going back to the English,
probably to create snob appeal.) Psychologists no longer
talk about /kompleksim/, but about /tasbixim/.

4. Conclusion

The process of borrowing and returning is one that
will probably continue for some time, if not forever.
I am sure that someone writing a paper on this subject
ten years from now will cite words that are at present
not used by Hebrew speakers, and that many of the words
cited in this paper will no longer be in use in
another decade. There was a time when Hebrew borrowed
/sandal/ and /xatul/ from the Greeks. Like so many
others, this loan was never repaid. At the time these
words were borrowed, there were probably a great many
other Greek words in use by Hebrew speakers that have
not stood the test of time. Today, fewer and fewer
people are using /egzoz/, /overol/ and /amplifaier/.
But /after/, /bauling/ and /bateldres/ are holding their
own.

English words in Hebrew often fill a stylistic gap.
One reason for this is the fact that so many people
have been working so earnestly to modernize Hebrew and
give it equal status with other modern languages,
that .they have ignored the necessary spontaneity of a
spoken language, something that is developed by the
speakers of any tongue. So few generations of
Palestinian and Israeli Jews have used their language
on a day-to-day basis, and so few Palestinian and Israeli
Jews used Hebrew as their sole language that Hebrew has
not really had a chance to develop all its levels to the
extent that other languages have. Since Israel is such
a small country, and since so many people in the country
find it necessary to use more than one language, it is
only natural to turn to our almost universal second
language, one that represents an extremely influential
part of the world, for the words that Hebrew has not
yet developed and perhaps never will. This is not to be
condemned, but accepted, as it is in other languages.
Germans say <u>brand-neu</u> without understanding what <u>brand</u> is.
It does not matter; they still know what they mean by
<u>brand-neu</u>. The French (and now the Israelis) eat lunch
at a drugstore that sells no drugs, but they know where
to get a meal. Why should Israelis be any different?
Even more to the point, how can they be?

NOTES

1. Since other European languages also have /tshek/ or
/shek/, I cannot be sure that Hebrew got this word from
English. However, since /kros/ definitely came from
English I think it reasonable to assume that /tshek/
did as well.

2. <u>Nylon</u> is another international word. According to
the German <u>Fremdwörterlexikon</u> by Richard von Kienle
(München: Heinz Peter, 1965), the word originally meant
'Now <u>You</u> <u>Look</u> <u>Out</u> Nipon', and came from English. But only
in <u>England</u> <u>were</u> <u>polythene</u> bags referred to as nylon. Since the
same confusion has occurred in Israel, it is hard to say
where /nailon/ came from.

3. /Aim veri sori/ is not only a sabra phrase. This is
something one hears from almost every foreign-born Ashkenazi
and from many foreign-born Sephardi Jews as well.

4. Some people use only the English plural; others find
it necessary to add the Hebrew /im/.

5. Again, this is also true of the German, which makes
it difficult to know if the word was borrowed directly
from English or was introduced into Hebrew by German-
Jewish immigrants.

REFERENCES

Kishon E. (n.d.), 'This is the land', in Y. Padan (ed.),
      25 + Kishon, Israel: Ministry of Defence.
The American college dictionary (1970), New York: Random
      House.

ENGLISH WORDS AND EXPRESSIONS IN THE IRISH OF INIS MEÁIN[1] AND THE USE OF ENGLISH BY THE LOCAL COMMUNITY

Ciarán Ó Coigligh
Coláiste Phádraig
Dublin

The first section of this paper will comprise an account and an examination of the English words and expressions in the Irish of five members of one family and five members of another family. The second section will concern itself with the speaking of English on the island.

With regard to the first five mentioned above, two (the parents) are monoglot Irish speakers in their late sixties who have never left the island except for short visits of a business, medical or holiday nature to Connemara, Galway city or Co. Clare. Their three children learned to speak English while attending an English-speaking boarding school in Galway city. The youngest works in a knitting factory on the island which is run by a local Comharchumann (Co-operative). The second works as a nurse in Galway city, and the eldest teaches at primary level in the Midlands. The other five - three boys and two girls - are children between the ages of four and fourteen. One has yet to begin his schooling; three attend the local primary school; and the eldest is boarding in an English-speaking secondary school in Tuam, Co. Galway.

From the point of view of contact with the two languages - Irish and English - the two families on which this study is based are fairly typical of the families on the island.

The English words and phrases will be discussed in the context of the following: (i) functions; (ii) notions; (iii) topics; (iv) situations; (v) grammar; (vi) displacement or otherwise of native words/expressions; (vii) frequency. Reference will be made also to the use of modern Irish terminology of the Revival period.

As far as the speaking of English on the island is concerned, one will attempt to examine the degree of contact on the part of the local community with English, the occasions on which English is spoken and also the attitude of the community to Irish and English.

Functions

Of the four categories - functions, notions, topics, situations[2] - that of functions[3] is the one which is least influenced by or dependent on borrowings from English. The following examples - thirteen in all - are taken in alphabetical order rather than in order of frequency:

1. All right (adverb): used (i) to express that fact that one is not opposed to something; and (ii) to grant forgiveness. Frequently all right, a mhac ('all right, son') etc., that is, followed by an appropriate vocative, in both instances. Where granting forgiveness is involved the expression is very often preceded by the substantive verb, e.g. tá sé all right, a mhac ('it's all right, son'), etc. Current Irish equivalents are (i) tá go maith ('good'), ceart go leor ('good enough'); (ii) tá tú ceart/tá sé ceart ('you're all right'/ it's all right'), etc.

2. By dad (preposition+noun; asservation): used in both initial utterances and responses (i) as an asservation and (ii) as an emphasizer. Current Irish equivalents for asservation - dar Dia ('by God'), dar diagaí ('by godie'), dar fia ('by deer'), dar fiagaí ('by deer hunter') - clearly illustrate the shared tendency of speakers of both Irish and English to employ euphemism in the particular instance, by dad being a distortion of by God. The Irish equivalents for emphasis are invariably preceded or followed by the substantive verb, e.g. tá, a mh'anam / a mh'anam go bhfuil ('there is, by my soul'), etc. tá go deimhin / go deimhin tá ('there is indeed'/'indeed there is').

3. Bye bye (contraction?; valediction): used when taking leave of a child or when a child takes leave of the speaker. Irish equivalents: slán agat ('farewell') when speaker takes leave, slán leat ('farewell') or more commonly go ngnóthaí Dia dhuit ('may God increase you') when child leaves.

4. (Good)bye (contraction of the phrase God be with you; valediction): used (i) when taking leave or (ii) when another takes leave. Understood by informant[4] to have been introduced by Yanks, i.e. returned emigrants to America. Irish equivalents are as for 3, plus lá / tráthnóna / oíche m(h)aith ('good day / afternoon / night') spoken by the one who takes leave and the response to which is Go ngnóthaí Dia dhuit.

5. <u>Good morning</u> (adjective+noun; salutation): heard
only once. The Irish equivalent <u>Dia dhuit</u>, etc.,
<u>ar maidin</u> (lit. 'God be with you, this morning') is
not widely used and questions such as <u>an bhfuil an tae
thíos agat?</u> ('have you made the tea?'), or expressions
of opinion such as <u>tá sé in am agat</u> ('it's time for
you [to be out of bed]') in the private domain and
reference to the weather in the public domain are
preferred as methods of initiating discourse.

6. (a) <u>Happy birthday</u> / (b) <u>Happy Christmas</u> / (c) <u>Happy
Easter</u> / (d) <u>Happy New Year</u> (adjective+noun; salutation).
Response (a): <u>go raibh maith agat</u> ('thank you'); (b), (c),
(d), <u>an rud céanna duit féin</u> ('the same to you') which is
a direct translation from the English. Irish equivalents
(a) <u>go maire tú an lá</u> (lit. 'may you live the day').
Responses: <u>go maire tú féin</u> ('may you yourself live');
<u>go raibh maith agat</u> ('thank you'); (b) <u>mo chuid den
Nollaig ort</u> (lit. 'may you have my portion of the
Christmas fare'). Responses: <u>agus agat féin</u> ('the same
to you'); <u>go mba hé dhuit</u>. (d) Irish equivalent: <u>mo
chuid den bhliain nua ort</u>. Responses: as for (b).
These greetings have been introduced by Yanks or
returned emigrants to America or by those working
outside the island or studying in English-medium schools
according to informant 3.

7. <u>Hello</u> (noun; salutation): universally used on the
phone; primarily used by younger people in face-to-face
encounters. Humorous response: <u>cac bó</u> (lit. 'cow dung'),
used by children. The Irish equivalent <u>Dia dhuit /
dhaoibh</u> is not widely used except with strangers and
among younger age-group. People are acknowledged by
reference to the weather for the most part: <u>tá sé go
breá</u>, <u>garbh</u>, etc. ('it is fine, rough' etc.).

8. <u>No</u> adverb: used by very young children to express
a strongly negative response whether expressing
disagreement, disapproval, denying, declining
invitations, refusing to do things, withholding
permission. Parental exposure to English usage in
America and other parts is responsible.

9. <u>Okay</u> (slang): used to express the fact that one
is not opposed to something; to grant forgiveness.
Irish equivalents: <u>tá go maith</u>, <u>ceart go leor</u>;
<u>tá tú ceart</u>, <u>tá sé ceart</u>, etc.

10. <u>Sorry</u> (adjective): used (i) to express apology, e.g.
<u>sorry, a mhac</u>, etc.; (ii) (as noun) to express regret,
e.g. <u>bhí an-sorry orm</u>. Irish equivalents: (i) <u>gabh mo
leithscéal</u>, (ii) <u>tá caitheamh ina dhiadh agam</u>, etc.,
<u>tá aiféala orm</u>, etc.

11. Thanks (plural noun): used to express gratitude / appreciation, e.g. thanks, a mhac, etc. Used by younger people influenced by English-medium schooling and life in non-Gaeltacht environment. Irish equivalents: go raibh maith agat, etc., go méadaí Dia thú; nár laga Dia thú.

12. Well (interjection): used to introduce utterance and/or response and also to cover a pause. Irish equivalents: muise, ara.

13. Wish (noun): to invite another to make a wish or to refer to wishing on the part of oneself or another, e.g., dean(aigi) wish anois. Irish equivalent: guí (substantive), guígh (verb, 3rd sing.). There is a modern quasi-folkloristic dimension to the concept of wishing which appears not to have existed in the Irish tradition.
The above thirteen examples (or twelve if one ignores example 5 which occurred only once) comprise the entire range of functions for which English is used whether seldom, occasionally or invariably.

Notions[5]

The following thirteen examples indicate some of the more obvious and significant features of the modern English borrowings on the semantic level.

1. appointment: used only in the sense of a pre-arranged meeting with a professional person, i.e. a doctor, a dentist, etc. Used only by younger people. The older people use more circumlocutory phrases, e.g. Tá orm etc. a bheith ann ('I must be there'), etc., Caithfidh mé a bheith ann ('It is necessary that I be there'), etc., as there is no single-word equivalent in the local dialect. It is worth noting that the borrowed verbal noun meetáil is preferred to the Irish verbal noun casadh + the preposition le in referring to prearranged and/or more or less inevitable meetings on the mainland.

2. bite: used by old and young, the word has a broader local semantic range than the Irish equivalent plaic which though having less currency is used interchangeably in referring to food, i.e. bain bite as/bain plaic as ('take a bite of it'); but bhain an mada bite as mo cheathrú ('the dog took a bite out of my calf').

3. blast: as well as carrying a meaning closely related to 'explosion' as is the case in English, this word has been subjected to semantic development to produce the following interesting usages: tá blast air, i.e. tá drochaimsir ag teacht ('there is bad weather on the way'); tá blast air le hól ('he is swollen from drink').

4. engaged: this word has currency only in the speech of the younger people. Older speakers and some younger ones use such expressions as ag socrú síos ('settling down') and ag bualadh faoin saol (lit. 'embarking on (married) life'). The modernity of the concept is evidenced by

the fact that 'made marriages' (cleamhnaisí) were a
feature of island life at least until the very late
sixties and possibly even later.

5. fireáilte: meaning 'quick tempered', this is an
example of the adoption of a euphemism to serve the
concept most often indicated by the use of the equally
euphemistic obann, e.g. tá sé chomh fireáilte / hobann.

6. gleas (gléas): interestingly this Irish word used
in the phrase tá gleas in d'éadan is thought by
younger speakers to be the English word glass.

7. handy: the word seems to refer to the fact that
something is of immediate convenience or usefulness
as opposed to the word fóintiúil which seems to imply
potential usefulness. This distinction is speculative
and limited by the fact that often the words are used
interchangeably.

8. plabar starch: this expression gives an interesting
example of the use of an English word to emphasise a
concept word to which it is totally semantically
unrelated. The expression may be translated as 'utter
rubbish'.

9. quarantine: the adoption of this word has been
accompanied by a slight alteration of the basic concept.
As currently used in Inis Meáin the word implies (i)
a (lengthy) period of time; (ii) a (lengthy) period
of time in a non-native environment.

10. raid: this word seems to have almost completely
displaced the Irish noun ionsaí when an assault on
a human being is not in question while ionsaí is
invariably used as the verbal noun of the verb
ionsaigh, the forms of which have suffered no anglicization.

11. rough: the use of this as in tá sé chomh rough implies
misbehaviour and physical abuse as the following
explanation testifies: a bheith ag ladhráil ar dhuine agus
á ghortú ('to (man)handle someone and hurt him in the
process').[6] The Irish form garbh is invariably used where
this element of rough handling is absent, e.g. lá garbh
('a rough day') lámha garbha ('rough hands'). Rough
is current in the speech of the younger people while
gránna ('horrible') or mímhúinte for instance would serve
the purpose in the speech of older people.

12. sight: the use of sight in preference to the Irish
amharc seems to be a matter of emphasis. The sentence
ní bhfuair mé amharc ar bith air ('I didn't see him/

it at all', lit. '... get any sight of ...') emphasises the fact of not having seen whereas the sentence Ní raibh sight air ('he/it wasn't to be seen', lit.
'there wasn't a sight of him') emphasises the absence of the
object (from sight).

13. turn: implying an occasion or a journey, this word
is interchangeable with turas, trip, geábh, babhta.
However the following three sentences indicate unique
usages in the case of the first and second and an
interesting example of turn meaning 'return (visit)' in
the third: Cé air a bhfuil turn an tsagairt? ('On whom
does the responsibility for bringing the priest to say
mass on this occasion lie?'). Cé hé fear an turn?
('On which man rests the obligation to bring the priest
(to say mass on this occasion)?'). Beidh turn eile fós
ort sula n-imeoidh tú ('you will return once again before
you finally leave').

Topics [7]

Personal identification: date of birth

1. nineteen fourteen: the English form is almost always
used by older people in referring to date of birth
whereas younger people invariably use the Irish form
(naoi déag (a) ceathair déag in this instance). This
reflects the use of English as a medium of instruction
in the local national school prior to the setting up of
the Irish Free State and the transition to the use of
Irish after the establishment of same.

House and home: household equipment, furniture, bedclothes
etc.

2. bag plastic: this form is no more common than the form
máilín plastic. The use of bag implies a small bag (as
the diminutive máilín indicates) acquired in a shop as
opposed to a sack (mála garbh) or very big bag. Bagín is
also current.

Education: students' and teachers' materials

3. copy(book): there is no Irish equivalent in the
local dialect. Copies is the plural form invariably
used. The use of copy(book) suggests the influence
of written English on the cover of the copybook.

Leisure time activities and entertainment: sports and
keep-fit

4. football: what is interesting about the use of this
word is that it seems to be most commonly used after
the verbal noun ag bualadh ('playing') or to qualify the
noun game. In all other cases the Irish plural form
báireachaí seems to have greater currency, e.g. beidh
báireachaí ann amáireach ('there will be a game tomorrow',
lit '... games ...').

Intellectual and social topics: fashion

5. breastpin: there is no Irish equivalent in the local
dialect. The word broach which is current has a
restricted particular meaning indicating value or
desirability, e.g. is gearr le broach thú ('you're great')
and is not interchangeable with breastpin as in fuair mé
breastpin cloichiní as Meiriceá ('I got a breastpin with
small stones from America').

Travel and transport: private transport

6. motor: this word is used only to indicate hurry and
is not interchangeable with the word carr which is
current, e.g. Chuaigh sé siar agus motor air ('he went
back in a hurry', lit. 'with a motor on him').

Farming and rural life

7. trammel: this is one of the very few English words
employed in discussion of traditional currach fishing.
It refers to a specific type of fishing net while líon
is the general Irish term. By contrast discussion of
modern fishing methods occasions the use of a far
greater number of English borrowings such as oilers,
engine, radar, etc.

Urban life: varieties of urban development (shopping
precincts, etc.)

8. shopping centre: this is used by young and old
alike but mostly by females. No Irish equivalent
in the local dialect.

Shopping and service industries: varieties of shops

9. supermarket: used by young and old alike but mostly
by females. No Irish equivalent in the local dialect.

Food and drink: meat

10. mild cured: this term is used to refer to shop
bacon as opposed to home-cured bacon (muiceoil shaillte)
as the following sentence indicates: cheannaigh mé píosa
deas maiciúr ('mild cured') sa siopa.

Public and professional services: hospital

11. appendix: this is mostly used by younger people and
may indicate a perception on their part that peindic,
the term employed by older people is 'bad English' and
therefore to be avoided.

Languages

12. Italian: reference is rarely made to languages other than Irish or English. The Irish equivalents of 'German' (Gearmáinis) and 'French' (Fraincis) seem to be used by both young and old while Italian, though infrequently referred to, seems to be preferred to Eadáinis (dialectal form) or Iodáilis (standard form).

Climate and weather: weather

13. breeze there seems to be no Irish equivalent in the local dialect and sentences such as tá breeze maith ann ('there is a strong breeze') are used by people of all ages.

Grammar and Syntax

Gender: A majority of borrowings are given a masculine gender as is evidenced by the fact that of the eight months January, February, May, June, July, August, September, October only August is feminine as indicated by the aspiration of the adjective in the expression August bhrocach ('filthy August').

There is a noticeable tendency to maintain the nominative form in the genitive case. This tendency is even more marked in relation to English borrowings, e.g. moustache bhreá ('a fine moustache') but dath an mhoustache ('the colour of the moustache') and not dath na moustache; an oven but doras an oven. However, the historically correct usage is found in phrases such as barr na slipe ('the top of the slip').

The placing of t before a masculine noun qualified by the article in the nominative case is eclectic, e.g. an egg beater but an t-article as is its use in the genitive, e.g. lucht an supermarket. The aspiration of words beginning with the consonant f is equally eclectic, e.g. níl aon fhlash againn, lucht an fhactory, dhá fhilling, doras an freezer, doras an fridge, dúirt sé liom an toilet a flusháil. Adjectives qualifying borrowed plural forms are invariably aspirated, e.g. batteries mhóra, boots dheasa, tablets ghránna. Alternative plural forms are a feature of Irish in general and of English borrowings in particular, e.g. covers/coverachaí, pegs/pegannaí.

The use of the adjective plastic as a substantive is noteworthy, e.g. an bhfuil aon phlastic agaibh, ('have you a plastic bag?'), the word plastic meaning 'plastic bag'.

Syntax: The adoption of the English convention of placing the adjective before the noun rather than after as is customary in Irish seems to arise from an awareness of the adjective not as an adjective but as the initial element in the noun as suggested by the example black pudding bán ('white pudding', lit. 'white black pudding'). Other examples are icing set, pressure cooker, septic tank, tin can, t-shirt, washing-up liquid, community centre, eye-shadow, school steward. The imposition of Irish syntax on similar borrowings occurs also, as in bag plastic, jumper v-neck. In many instances the two syntactical forms have equal currency as in (e)lectric blanket/pluid (e)lectricity; i dTeach an Chustaim/sa gCustom House.

The English borrowings in the main fall into the following grammatical categories:

nouns:	e.g. (i)(singular) appointment
	(ii)(plural) peas;
verbal nouns:	blastáil;
adjectival nouns:	defrostáilte;
adjectives:	pink

Many of the borrowings have come from America rather than from the Galltacht (English-speaking areas in Ireland) or from England, e.g. crackers, freezer, pocket-(book), sidewalk.

I have ignored the area of phonetics. However, it must be pointed out that the pronunciation of words such as slash, slice, toast seems to be greatly influenced by the speaker's knowledge or lack of knowledge of English and in particular by his or her awareness of what the more acceptable English form is throughout the Galltacht or English-speaking part of the country.

Situations[8]

The people of Inis Meáin are a community under attack. Their culture in general and their language in particular are under severe and continuous attack. Inis Meáin is universally accepted as being one of the strongest Gaeltacht or Irish-speaking areas in the country if not the strongest. It has a population of 257 people: fifteen are under school-attendance age, thirty are children attending the local National School and eighteen work in the local Comharchumann (Co-operative). Apart from the Comharchumann (Co-operative), there are two shops, a primary school, a church, a public house, a hall, a post-office, a museum and an air strip on the island.

It is estimated that one-third of the population of the island are monoglot Irish speakers. A majority of the homes on the island have a television set and a radio. Growing affluence has created a situation whereby the public house has become the major centre of social activity. Here conversation is impeded by the persistent playing of records, mostly in English, and by the dominance of the television or the radio. Further anglicisation takes place in summer and during major holidays with the influx of holiday-makers who tend to dominate the scene with the singing of (lively) ballads or pop songs in English.

The return of islanders on a large scale for annual and/or seasonal vacations, often accompanied by English-speaking spouses and/or offspring, is a phenomenon which weakens the hegemony of Irish as the sole interpersonal means of communication in the home.

Irish is the language of the <u>Comharchumann</u> (Co-operative), the school, the post-office, the <u>two shops</u>, the public house and the church, although in the case of the latter the language used in informal encounters depends on the ability of the priest stationed on the island at any given time as well as his disposition.

There is an Irish-medium comprehensive school on Inis Mór. Some students from Inis Meáin attend this school, while others attend Irish-medium or English-medium schools on the mainland. There may be a growing tendency on the part of parents to opt for English-medium second-level schools because of a perception that the children do not attain a sufficiently high standard in English in the National School.

Older islanders recall that English was the medium of instruction in the National School prior to the setting-up of the Irish Free State in 1922. Hence the fact that some older people correspond solely in English while the younger age groups have (some) written competence in both languages.

The buying from and selling of stock to visiting <u>jabairí</u> ('dealers') is invariably conducted through <u>the medium</u> of English. Inis Meáin has been exposed to the influence of holiday-makers at least since the end of the last century. This influence seems to have been benign for the most part as many of the visitors were enthusiastic students of the language and often competent speakers.

There are only four couples on the island rearing
children through the medium of English: in one case the
mother is English and only recently come to live on the
island; another mother is from the Galltacht and the two
other mothers are sisters from the Connemara Gaeltacht
where the rearing of children through English has
become increasingly widespread.

With the exception of monoglot Irish speakers,
islanders almost never attempt to use Irish in tran-
sacting business in Galway city unless they are certain
that those with thom they are dealing have a high level
of competence in Irish and are positively disposed.

Informant 3 felt that céilíochaí ('evenings of
Irish dancing'), cookery and other classes, and the
organization of sports activities, where attention
would be given to the cultivation of a terminology in
Irish to meet the people's needs would be of great
benefit. The informant also felt that occasional
public meetings at which matters of a linguistic and or
cultural nature might be discussed would also be a very
positive influence. The majority of islanders married
to non-native Irish speakers and living in the Galltacht
rear their children as monoglot English speakers. This
is equally the case where a married island couple are
living in America or England. English words such as
bicycle and sweets are more acceptable than the Irish
equivalents rothar and milseáin, given popular currency
in the Revival period.

The founding of a Coláiste Gaeilge (Irish (Summer)
College) has added a new significant dimension to the
life of the island intimately linked with Irish. It
has also increased the incidence of spoken English on
the island.

What is to be done in order that Irish may continue to be the vernacular of Inis Meáin? It is
necessary that an English Primary School syllabus be
produced that will accommodate the needs of children
whose home and communal language is Irish; that Raidió
na Gaeltachta provide a comprehensive service; that
an Irish-medium television station be established to
provide a range of programmes to accommodate all age
groups; that an Irish-medium newspaper giving comprehensive coverage of material of local concern and
appropriate coverage of national and international
affairs be established; that the local teachers be
motivated to ensure a high standard of oral and written

Irish and to assist the children in integrating modern
Irish terminology into the local dialect where the
local dialect proves inadequate. Colleges of Education
must ensure that student teachers are competent to
deal with the realities of teaching in Inis Meáin and
similar environments.

Bainisteoir ('manager'), monarcha ('factory'),
ball ('member of committee'), scarannaí ('shares'),
gineadóirí ('generators'), coiste ('committee') cumann
('association'), cruinniú ('meeting'), cluiche ('game')
comharchumann ('co-operative'), scéim ('scheme'),
ceirnín ('record'), píolóta ('pilot') oifig ('office'),
cóisir ('party'), siopadóireacht ('shopping'), are
modern Irish terms in common use in the Irish of Inis
Meáin. Almost without exception they relate to the
public domain. For the most part they have been introduced,
promoted and encouraged by the Bainisteoir or 'Manager'
of the local Comharchumann ('Co-operative') and the baill
('members') of Coiste an Chomharchumainn ('the Co-operative
Committee'). This is clear evidence of the positive results
that can be obtained when a policy of language maintenance
and promotion is pursued with sincerity, dedication and
tact. The private domain is less easily influenced without
the aid of Irish-medium radio and television stations.

Of the thirty children currently on the school roll
five are being reared through the medium of English, i.e.
1/6th. Of the fifteen children under the school-going
age five also are being reared through English, i.e. 1/3rd.
The implications of these figures are obvious.

Ultimately the viability of Inis Meáin as an Irish-
speaking area depends on the achievement of a situation
where an all-Irish-speaking upbringing is seen as a
distinct advantage. This is dependent on the vigorous and
sincere implementation by the State and other significant
institutions of policies supportive of Irish as a
vernacular.

I wish to acknowledge the generous assistance, the
informed criticism and the sustained interest of Máirín
Mhaidhcil Ní Chualáin, Baile An Mhothair, Inis Meáin.

1. Inis Meáin is one of the three islands situated in Galway Bay.

2. For the purposes of this article and in order to provide myself with appropriate categories for the words and expressions under discussion I have used Institiúid Teangeolaíochta Éireann, Skeleton Syllabus (Principles and Guidelines), Revised Version, September 1980. Functions and situations refer to the purposes and contexts of communication while notions and topics refer to the concepts to be communicated, (ibid., p. 3).

3. Functions (are) the communicative acts the (speaker) should be able to perform and respond to; what he should be able to do with the language (e.g. identify things, suggest a course of action, express doubt, greet people). Exponents of functions (are) syntactic patterns in association with particular lexical items and idioms appropriate to the speech acts in question (ibid., pp. 3, 4, 5).

4. The eldest daughter of the first family. See paragraph two.

5. Notions: the basic general meanings the (speaker) should be able to express and understand ... (e.g. location, number, past reference, contrast). Exponents of ... notions: ... the basic grammatical categories, structures and processes, as well as some of the general vocabulary. (ibid., pp. 3, 4).

6. See note 3.

7. Topics: the more specific areas of meaning to which the (speaker) should have access ... (e.g. house and home, education, travel and transport, urban life, food and drink). Exponents of ... topics: ... vocabulary and expression specific to particular centres of interest. For example ... trades, professions, occupations ... (ibid., pp. 3, 4, 5).

8. Situations: the circumstances under which the (speaker) should be able to operate through the ... language – in terms of the physical context of communication, the social and psychological roles of the participants, and the medium of communication. ... the exponents of situations are somewhat different in character, consisting in discursive descriptions of culture-specific aspects of physical context, social and physical context, social and psychological role, and medium of communication ... (e.g. formal/informal, spoken/ written) (ibid., pp. 3, 4, 5).

BIBLIOGRAPHY

An Coiste Gnó, Conradh na Gaeilge (1983), Géarchéim na Gaeilge, Baile Átha Cliath: Clódhanna Teo.

An Coiste um Thaighde ar Dhearcadh an Phobail i dTaobh na Gaeilge / Committee on Language Attitudes Research (1975), Tuarascáil / Report, Baile Átha Cliath: Oifig an tSoláthair.

Bord na Gaeilge (1983), Action Plan for Irish / Plean Gníomhaíochta don Ghaeilge 1983-1986, Dublin.

Comhar na Múinteoirí Gaeilge (1981), Tuarascáil: Bunoideachas trí Ghaeilge sa Ghaeltacht, Baile Átha Cliath.

Conradh na Gaeilge (1976), Polasaí Gaeltachta, Baile Átha Cliath and Corcaigh: Clódhanna Teo.

Institiúid Teangeolaíochta Éireann (1980), Skeleton Syllabus (Principles and Guidelines), Revised Version, September 1980, Modern Languages Syllabus Project for Post-Primary Schools, Dublin.

Institiúid Teangeolaíochta Éireann (1982), Taighde Sochtheangeolaíochta agus Teangeolaíochta sa Ghaeltacht: Riachtanais an Lae Inniu, Baile Átha Cliath.

Mac an Iomaire, P. (1983), 'Tionchar na Tionsclaíochta ar Ghaeilge Chonamara Theas', Teangeolas 16. Spring 1983, pp. 9-18.

Mackey, W.F. (1972), Irish Language Promotion: Potentials and Constraints, Dublin: Institiúid Teangeolaíochta Éireann.

Tovey, H. (1978), Language Policy and Socioeconomic Development in Ireland, Dublin: Institiúid Teangeolaíochta Éireann.

THE VALUE OF LITERARY TRANSLATION IN LANGUAGE TEACHING

Cormac Ó Cuilleanáin
Glasthule
Co. Dublin

This paper is directed to professional linguists and language teachers. Its author cannot lay claim to either of those qualifications, having only a limited experience of language teaching and an elementary acquaintance with the concerns of applied linguistics. My interest in the subject of the paper stems mainly from the fact that I have made a study of literature in a foreign language, namely Italian, and that I have done professional translation work from that same language. Also, during my undergraduate days, the translation of literary texts was widely used as a convenient means of examining linguistic competence, whatever about teaching that competence. All of this tends to give me a bias in favour of literary translation and a vested interest in its standing as a didactic method. But although the paper claims amateur status, it will be supported by reference to statements made by real experts in the hope that some of its suggestions may be of use to professional linguists, who might wish to consider its arguments in the light of current theory.

When discussing the educational merits of literary translation, one needs to establish first of all that literary language is not necessarily a negation of common language; on the contrary, it can conform to the requirements of everyday usage, and may indeed be seen as a central part of the language. Having staked this claim for creative language, the next step will be to look at some different types and applications of translation, and consider their possible uses in language teaching. Bringing the first two terms of our title together, it remains to consider literary translation, and how this particular practice may contribute to an understanding of the target language. The main conclusion here, paradoxically, will be that the merit of teaching translation is to teach <u>untranslatableness,</u> bringing to the student a real sense of what is typical of one language and not of another. For translation is essentially an unsatisfactory art, yet one which is implicit in all attempts to communicate by means of language. The failures of translation, that is to say, are the failures of language itself, and these are failures which language teachers must set out to teach.

What, then, is literary language? Is it a separate
system of communication, or merely a marginal application
of the rules of 'ordinary' language? Are there 'literature universals' which cross language boundaries, or
will the language student have to master separately the
literary norms of a target language, in order to read its
literature? For example, one recent article suggested
that the transition from ordinary to literary language
can present a greater barrier than the transition from
mother-tongue to foreign language, so its authors
approach the study of two Spanish poems through a
series of exercises designed to introduce the student
to poetic devices and emotive uses of language. (1)
Thus, they combine a study of figurative language with
a study of Spanish, but it is questionable whether this
adds up to a single subject called 'Figurative Spanish'.
The methods proposed are based on a distinction drawn by
I.A. Richards in <u>Principles of literary criticism:</u>

> There are two totally distinct uses of language... A
> statement may be used for the sake of the <u>reference</u>,
> true or false, which it causes. This is the
> <u>scientific</u> use of language. But it may also be
> used for the sake of the effects in emotion and
> attitude produced by the reference it occasions.
> This is the <u>emotive</u> use of language (2).

These definitions offer a useful key to the intentionally
artistic use of language, but leave aside the unintentional bias which every language imposes on the
reality to which it refers. Edward Sapir put that
factor in a creative context: 'every language is itself
a collective art of expression', while Benjamin Lee
Whorf noted the distortions contained in the most
'inexpressive' descriptive language:

> It is the 'plainest' English which contains the
> greatest number of unconscious assumptions about
> nature. This is the trouble with schemes like
> Basic English, in which an eviscerated British
> English, with its concealed premises working
> harder than ever, is to be fobbed off on an
> unsuspecting world as the essence of pure
> Reason itself (3).

Questions of expression, therefore, have a bearing on
the simple everyday uses of language, and simplified
or basic constructions do not enjoy any 'neutral' or
'objective' status, however useful they may be in the
early stages of language learning. From this linguistic perspective, the distinction between 'scientific'
and 'emotive' uses of language looks a good deal less

absolute. Of course there is a need to appreciate the
special nature of creative language, and to codify it
systematically for teaching purposes. It may not be
possible to maintain a logical or linguistic distinction between creative and neutral language, but a
social or cultural distinction has obvious attractions.
In his educational book, <u>Pour une nouvelle pédagogie
du texte littéraire</u>, Michel Benamou distinguishes
literature from ordinary discourse or simple reportage
under the three headings of <u>écart</u>, <u>structure</u> and
<u>connotation</u> (deviation, patterning, allusion).
According to Benamou's working definition, these three
features set literary language apart from a merely
adequate use of language, 'le discours que tiendrait
un locuteur plausible dans telle ou telle situation'(4).
This criterion avoids terms like the 'linguistic norm',
and considers such factors as the speaker's circumstances, social situation and medium of expression; but
the requirement of plausibility in non-literary speech
itself sounds a somewhat literary criterion. Still,
the yardstick of opposition to ordinary language is also
broadly acceptable to a literary theorist like Jonathan
Culler, who writes:

> Poetry lies at the centre of the literary experience
> because it is the form that most clearly asserts the
> specificity of literature, its difference from
> ordinary discourse by an empirical individual about
> the world (5).

The introduction of terms like 'empirical' and 'plausible'
will prompt some caution in judging the linguistic
status of this 'ordinary' language. Indeed, 'ordinariness'
would seem to be a social rather than a linguistic norm.
And even the empiricism is not based on real observation, but rather on expectation, which is a cultural
rather than a social phenomenon. People do not, in
fact, say utterly predictable things in given situations,
and their feelings are just as likely to be poetic as
prosaic.

   In spite of these reservations, Benamou's working
definition does provide a useful key to the teaching
of literary style, preparing the reader, as he claims,
linguistically and psychologically for the proper
expectation (<u>juste attente</u>) of what ought to be said
in each situation, so that they may then feel the

proper surprise when the text deviates from the proper
course. One should, however, be quite clear that this
juste attente is prescribed by culture, not by linguistics or psychology. Both the 'expected' and the
'literary' forms of language are determined by
cultural convention. Both share the same linguistic
basis of acceptability, but operate on different levels
of appropriateness.

In claiming a central position for literary
expression within the world of language, as against the
claims of plain prose, one cannot avoid considering
the relation of literature to ordinary speech. If
speech is regarded by modern linguistics as the primary
mode of language (6), its new prestige might seem to
imply a downgrading of literary production, particularly
poetry, as material for the linguistic discourse; while
prose, as an approximate transcription of speech, would
enjoy a rather more privileged position. In fact, a
closer examination of the relationship between poetry,
prose and the spoken language reveals a very different
state of affairs.

Northrop Frye, in _The well-tempered critic_, attacks
the confusion of prose with the language of ordinary
speech. The confusion, he argues, arises from an
educational problem compounded by a critical one:

> Very early in our education we are made familiar
> with the distinction between verse and prose.
> The conviction gradually forces itself on us
> that when we mean what we say we write prose,
> and that verse is an ingenious but fundamentally
> perverse way of distorting ordinary prose
> statements... Embedded in it is the purely
> critical assumption that prose is the language
> of ordinary speech ... The language of ordinary
> speech is called prose only because it is not
> distinguished from prose. Actual prose is the
> expression or imitation of directed thinking or
> controlled description in words, and its unit is
> the sentence. It does not follow that all prose
> is descriptive or thoughtful, much less logical,
> but only that prose imitates, in its rhythm and
> structure the verbal expression of a conscious and
> rational mind (7).

There are certain articulate people, Frye modestly admits,
who have mastered the difficult idiom of prose, and
speak a conversational version of it. But most of us
speak in a babbling stream of consciousness, using units

of rhythm largely innocent of syntax, putting into words
our 'daydreaming, remembering, worrying, associating,
brooding and mooning'.

The irregular rhythm of ordinary speech may be
conventionalized in two ways. One way is to impose
a pattern of recurrence on it; the other is to impose
the logical and semantic pattern of the sentence. We
have verse when the arrangement of words is dominated
by recurrent rhythm and sound, prose when it is
dominated by the syntactical relation of subject and
predicate. Of the two, verse is much the simpler
and more primitive type ...

In Frye's interpretation, then, the rhythmic repe-
titiousness of ordinary speech, following 'the paths
of private association', is far from the ordered logic
of plain prose and close to the private, illogical,
associative paths of poetry. And George Steiner
claims in <u>After Babel</u> that all developed language has
a private core, preserving the secret codes of intimate groups. 'At its intimate centre, in the zone
of familial or totemic immediacy, our language is
most economic of explanation, most dense with inten-
tionality and compacted implication.' Likewise,
poetry 'deploys with least regard to routine or
conventional transparency, those energies of
covertness and of invention which are the crux of human
speech'. The baffling shorthand of poetry therefore
appears as a condition of its intimate form of address;
the reader is drawn into a close core of communication
where much can be left unsaid. As Steiner suggests,
'we speak first to ourselves, then to those nearest us
in kinship and locale' (8). This is one reason why the
reader may feel like an eavesdropper, and the poet may
be 'not heard but overheard', as John Stuart Mill
observed (9).

All very well in theory, but can the private
idiolect of a poet's personal language really offer
special insights into a target language? Surely
private thoughts lie beyond the scope of language
study?

That objection is quite mistaken, according to
the theory of language and personal consciousness
put forward by Raymond Williams in <u>Marxism and literature</u>.
The signifying element of language has the capacity to
become an <u>inner sign</u>, part of an active practical
consciousness.

Thus, in addition to its social and material existence between actual individuals, the sign is also part of a verbally constituted consciousness which allows individuals to use signs of their own initiative, whether in acts of social communication or in practices which, not being manifestly social, can be interpreted as personal or private (10).

And this view of personal thought shaped by language receives linguistic support from Whorf, who rejected the view that language serves only for the communi-cation of thought. Language, he implies, not only communicates thought but functions ∴ its inception. On the phonological plane of language, 'significant behaviour is ruled by pattern from outside the focus of personal consciousness'. Similarly, on the higher plane of expressing thoughts, 'thinking also follows a network of tracks laid down in the given language ... The individual is utterly unaware of this organization and is constrained completely within its unbreakable bonds' (11).

Now it might be thought that poetry transcends the bonds of predetermined thought, mastering language and bending it to creative ends. But a more useful idea of the poet's work might be based on Eliot's alternative image of the poet as the servant, not the master, of the language; the poet might be seen as scouting out the hidden network of tracks laid down in the language. In claiming this particular linguistic function for literature, it is relevant in the present context to recall Robert Frost's famous definition of poetry as 'that which gets lost from verse and prose in translation'. Thus, if creative language holds a special position in the life of a language, one which the language learner would do well to explore, it is equally true that the linguistic function of creative language is particularly well revealed through the process of trying to translate it. We will return to Frost's definition later on.

Lastly, it might be objected that in spite of the claims that are made for literature, creative language does frequently violate the codes of normal usage, and is thus unsuitable as language learning material. It is true that poetry, like everyday speech, may often be delinquent in this regard, and one might speculate how far the violation can go before a poem ceases to be an acceptable linguistic utterance. Far more interesting in the present context is the fact that literature may adhere meticulously to the rules of grammar, while still remaining specifically poetic. One only has to think of the impeccable grammatical order underlying John Betjeman's poetic order. Ultimately, the distinctive 'distance' of creative

literature would seem to reside in its own coherent
autonomous system of significance, which coexists with
the rules of language and can itself be codified in ways
that look something like linguistic rules, as with the
hierarchical grammar of narration postulated by Roland
Barthes (12). It is an open question how far one can
analyse the 'grammar of poetry'. Jonathan Culler, in
Structuralist poetics, argues the need for a theory
of 'literary competence', underlying 'literary
performance', and claims that criticism must try to
determine 'how far it is possible to account for meaning
in literature on the hypothesis that minimal semantic
features combine in rule-governed ways to produce large-
scale semantic effects' (13). But in his book on
Saussure, Culler admits that the toughest semiotic code
to crack will always be the aesthetic code, which constantly transcends and negates its own vocabulary:

> as soon as an aesthetic code comes to be generally
> perceived as a code ··· works of art tend to move
> beyond this code. They question, parody, and
> generally undermine the code while exploring
> its possible mutations and extensions. One might
> even say that much of the interest of works of
> art lies in the ways in which they explore and
> modify the codes which they seem to be using,
> and this makes semiological investigation of
> those systems both highly relevant and
> extremely difficult (14).

Whatever its additional rules and procedures,
literature is linguistically creative. And if a
language generates its epics as surely as its helicopter repair manuals, then a creative sense of
language is a useful target for the language learner.
Sapir speaks of the complete fusion of structure and
thought in a literary masterpiece: 'with Heine, for
instance, one is under the illusion that the universe
speaks German' (15). Such a native-speaker illusion is
surely a reputable educational goal.

Before returning to the question of how literature
and translation may interact, it may be useful at this
stage to mention some of the various types and uses
of translation.

Roman Jakobson identified three types of translation:
intralingual translation or 'rewording', interlingual
translation or 'translation proper', and intersemiotic

translation or 'transmutation' by which verbal signs are interpreted into a non-verbal sign system (16). We are concerned here with the teaching of translation proper, but this is not the only type of translation which arises in langauge learning. Even in the native language, translation is inescapable. As W.H. Auden says, 'to read is to translate, for no two persons' experience is the same' (17). In native language reading, the translation process is intralingual, but the same ability to reword texts should be attainable at a more advanced level of reading in a foreign language, representing a stage of greater refinement than simple interlingual translation.

One practical use of interlingual translation in language teaching is the naming of equivalent words in the mother-tongue as a way of conveying the meaning of units in the target language, while emphasising the differences in linguistic usage as against the mother-tongue. This contrastive practice of 'semantic demonstration' was defined by Harold Palmer as being more flexible and more accurate, in certain situations, than the Direct Method techniques of contextualising, paraphrasing or defining the new word with others from the target language, or indeed simply finding one of the things the word refers to and pointing at it. A modern supporter of Palmer's view, Mr. Jimmy Thomas, asks whether we really need to take the student to the zoo to teach him the word for 'elephant'. Practical considerations aside, this would not even theoretically be the best way of teaching 'elephant', as the word and the concept are far more powerful and more flexible, as elements of language and culture, than one beast of the species could ever be (18).

Another pedagogical use of interlingual translation is to teach rules in the target language. A Canadian article by H.S. Frank Collins gives several interesting examples of semi-literary translation, where students were asked to put English slogans into their French-Canadian equivalents. The exercise provided some interesting cultural contrasts, and a useful grammatical point emerged from the comparison of two versions of the Avis catchphrase.

If a student were to translate 'We try harder' by 'Nous essayons plus fort', this would provide the instructor with an excellent opportunity to remind his students that French does not normally favour the use of the comparative or superlative unless both or all objects being compared are made explicit. The absence of the comparative in 'On y met du coeur' would reinforce that lesson ...(19)

Apart from the practical business of teaching foreign languages, translation has an important role to play in the scientific study of the differences between languages. Whorf's work on linguistic relativity, for example, rests largely on the non-translatability of concepts from one language into the grammar of another. More generally, Jakobson urges that 'any comparison of two languages implies an examination of their mutual translatability; widespread practice of interlingual communication, particularly translating activities, must be kept under constant scrutiny by linguistic science' (20). Translation equivalence, of a complex kind, provides a common denominator for the contrastive analysis of two languages (21). Similarly, it has been suggested that a comparison of different translations of the standard classics into English is 'one of the simplest ways of showing what is expected at various times in answer to the question of "What is Poetry?"' (22).

Among the many uses of translation outside the fields of pedagogy, linguistic science and cultural studies, there are cases in which the precise formal correspondence of the linguistic forms used is of very minor concern. Richard Brislin, in his editor's introduction to the composite volume Translation: applications and research (23), cites the experiments in translation conducted by American military planners in the process of 'Vietnamisation' of the Vietnam war. Technical documents had to be translated wholesale in the drive to transfer American technological functions to the Vietnamese themselves. The aim of these translations was not linguistic equivalence, but the transfer of skills to the target population. The efficacy of these translations was gauged not by philological analysis but by such techniques as 'knowledge-testing' the information received by Vietnamese receptors of the translations, and even 'performance-testing' the helicopters serviced according to the various translations of the maintenance manual. A bad translation produced 11% error-free performance in the helicopter maintenance task, while a good translation raised this to 71%. Actually, 71% reliability is not a very reassuring standard when applied to helicopters; one foreign correspondent noted that 'the lack of helicopter maintenance expertise displayed by the South Vietnamese almost guaranteed a horrendous accident rate' (24).

Turning from this most depressingly unliterary of
translation problems, we may briefly consider the
concrete questions of how translation might be introduced to a foreign language course. Its place in the
course may be less controversial now than a few years
ago, as Wolfram Wilss, Professor of translation at the
University of Saarbrücken, points out:

> It is a well-known fact that under the influence
> of behavioristic learning theory as developed by
> Skinner, the role of translation into foreign-
> language teaching has been critically assessed.
> The issue is still controversial; whereas at first
> the grammar-translation method, under the impact
> of the direct method, was widely regarded as
> irrelevant for language teaching, there are now
> indications on an increasing scale that, owing to
> the progress of cognitive-code learning theory,
> translation is re-establishing itself as a useful
> and legitimate tool of foreign language teaching
> with a markedly higher degree of didactic and
> methodological sophistication than previously (25).

Exactly what type of translation should be used, and
when it should be introduced, remain matters for debate.
In the early stages of self-expression, translation may
have an inhibiting effect on the imagination of a student projecting himself into a new language community.
But in a more reflective phase of learning, the practice
of literary translation, which means treating the
original text as if the exact forms of the words carry
the meaning, can have great benefits in terms of an
intuitive sense of language. This goes beyond simple
knowledge of a foreign language. In the words of Whorf,
'we handle even our plain English with much greater
effect if we direct it from the vantage point of a
multilingual awareness' (26). The ability to use one's
native language, understanding something of its genius
by contrast with foreign languages, and sensing its
relative position within the whole human faculty of
language, is probably the most important of all the
educational benefits conferred by the study of foreign
languages.

On a more mundane note, a recent American article
on a college translation seminar claims that translation at advanced level can be an aid to better
composition in the target language, as well as expanding
vocabulary. The author goes on to describe the benefits of an experiment in the creative translation of
Proust. The students gained an enhanced sense of the

sounds and connotations of French words, while incidentally
improving their mastery of English (27). These two results
from one operation would be hard to achieve in any other
way. To take one fundamental point, how better to learn
the meaning and appropriate use of the imperfect tense in
French than by experiencing its usage in French literature,
and noting its non-availability in English? In an
analysis of Scott-Moncrieff's version of Combray, David
Lodge makes precisely that point: English has no
imperfect tense; therefore it is impossible to render
the effects of Proust's prose style accurately in
English. Lodge's other criticisms of the phonological
and syntactical inadequacies of Scott-Moncrieff's
translation might seem too detailed to be of interest
to the hard-bitten foreign language instructor, but
the Romance languages' command of the imperfect tense
is too important a contrast to be ignored, and the use
of translation in learning it too productive to be
neglected (28).

We are now at the crux of the question: how can
literary translation have a value in language teaching,
when it is a self-contradictory activity? Not only is
poetry lost in translation, but the problem is not
even confined to foreign language versions. Coleridge's
'infallible test of a blameless style' was 'its
untranslatableness in words of the same language without
injury to the meaning' (29). But the strictness of this
definition may be self-defeating; how can we know whether
meaning has been lost unless we interpret that meaning
and judge its equivalence to alternative formulations in
the same language? After all, as Eugene Nida points
out, 'loss of information is part of any communicative
process'; thus, 'if one is to insist that translation must
involve no loss of information whatsoever, then obviously
not only translating but all communication is impossible' (30).
And the principle of translation is central to any act of
understanding. We already have the authority of Auden
to set against Frost: 'To read is to translate'. And
as Alastair Reid wrote in the first issue of Delos, the
journal of translation, 'the problem ... is not a
question of what gets lost in translation ... but rather
... what gets lost ... between love or desperation - ...
and its coming into words ... what gets lost ... is not
what gets lost in translation, but rather what gets lost
in language itself' (31).

Perhaps the greatest merit, and the greatest problem,
in the translation of foreign texts is that it explores
untranslatableness: what can and cannot be taken over.
Untranslatable elements are, by definition, characteristic
of one language but not of another, and the highest

concentration of characteristic forms is likely to be found in poetry. Literary translation, then, is a valuable enterprise doomed to almost certain failure.

In a more extended paper, one might discuss some of the skills specific to literary translation, and how they might best be imparted. A tactful sense of the limits of translation is obviously a prime requisite: to know what cannot be attempted. One must not be too timid, of course. Jakobson says that because the pun reigns over poetic art, poetry by definition is untranslatable (32). But Auden, while conceding that semantic relationships based on phonemic similarity are beyond translation, argues that the case is different for elements not based on verbal experience, as for example 'images, similes and metaphors which are drawn from sensory experience' (33). Obviously, these should be attempted. Likewise, the translator cannot shirk trying to render the distinctive literary form of the original. Ideally, the translation of a poem should be another poem; but even when perfect formal imitation is achieved, the effort may be wasted if the receptor culture does not understand the medium: Eugene Nida points out that a complete seventeen-syllable haiku will not carry the same significance for a literate English speaker as for a literate Japanese (34). It has been suggested that concepts to be translated should be divided into culture-specific, or 'emic' elements, and universal or 'etic' elements; and that it is by definition impossible to translate an emic concept (35). But the limits of cross-cultural understanding lie outside the scope of the present paper.

The possible ramifications of the art of translation are endless, and one could pursue them at length, once the basic value of the enterprise has been established. One particular warning, however, sounded in the seventeenth century by Wentworth Dillon, fourth Earl of Roscommon, might be relevant here. His <u>Essay on translated verse</u>, an early theoretical work in rhyming couplets, contains the statement that 'Excursions are inexpiably bad, And 'tis much safer to leave out than add' (36). Bearing this in mind, I will not attempt here to anatomize the procedures of teaching translation, nor is there time to go into such esoteric questions as the translatableness of dialect expression, or even to consider Steiner's speculations as to the relative meanings accorded in different cultures to that most baffling linguistic sign: silence (37).

REFERENCES

(1)   Spinelli, E. and S.A. Williams (1981), 'From language to literature: teaching figurative language in the college foreign language class', Foreign Language Annals 14.1, pp. 37-43.

(2)   (1926), London, pp. 261, 267.

(3)   (Repr. 1974), Language, thought and reality, Cambridge, Mass., p. 244.

(4)   (1971), Paris, pp. 7-8.

(5)   (1975), Structuralist poetics: structuralism, linguistics and the study of literature, London, p. 162.

(6)   Chapman, R. (1973), Linguistics and literature, London, p. 32.

(7)   (1963), Bloomington and London, pp. 17-21.

(8)   (1975, repr. 1977), After Babel: aspects of language and translation, Oxford, p. 231.

(9)   Quoted in N. Frye (1957), Anatomy of criticism, Princetown, p. 5.

(10)   (1977), Oxford, p. 40.

(11)   Whorf (1974), p. 256.

(12)   · (1966), 'Introduction à l'analyse structurale des récits', Communications 8, pp. 1-27.

(13)   pp. 115, 76.

(14)   (1976), Saussure, London, pp. 100-101.

(15)   Sapir, E. (1921), Language: an introduction to the study of speech, New York (reissued, London 1978), pp. 221, 225.

(16)   Jakobson, R. (1959), 'On linguistic aspects of translation', in R. A. Brower (ed.), (1959), On translation, Cambridge, Mass., pp. 232-239 (pp. 232-233).

(17)   (1975), The Dyer's Hand, London, p. 3.

(18)   Palmer, H.E. (1968), The scientific study and teaching of languages, edited by David Harper, London, pp. 60-68; Jimmy Thomas (1976), 'Translation, language teaching and the bilingual assumption', TESOL Quarterly 10.4, pp. 404-410 (p. 405).

(19)   Frank Collins, H.S. (1977), 'Translation and the teacher of French', Canadian Modern Language Review, 33.4, pp. 532-534.

(20)   Jakobson (1959), p. 234.

(21)   James, C. (1980), Contrastive analysis, Harlow.

(22)   Brower, R.A. (1959), 'Seven Agamemnons', in Brower (ed.) (1959), pp. 173-195 (p. 173).

(23)   (1976), New York, pp. 12-19.

(24)   Behr, E. (1982), 'Anyone here been raped and speaks English?': A foreign correspondent's life behind the lines, paperback edition, London, p. 282.

(25)   'Perspectives and limitations of a didactic framework
        for the teaching of translation', in Brislin, (ed.) (1976),
        pp. 117-134, (p. 117).
(26)   Whorf, (1974), p. 244.
(27)   Myers O'Connor, N. (1979), 'Translation as re-
        creation: an experiment at Middlebury College',
        French Review 53.1, pp. 60-67.
(28)   (1966 repr. 1979), Language of fiction: essays in
        criticism and verbal anaylsis of the English novel,
        London, pp. 20-23.
(29)   Burnshaw, S. (ed.) (1964), The poem itself,
        Harmondsworth, pp. xi-xiii.
(30)   Nida, E. (1976), 'A framework for the analysis and
        evaluation of theories of translation', in Brislin, (ed.)
        (1976), pp. 47-91, (p. 63).
(31)   Reid, A. (1968), 'Lo que se pierde/What gets lost',
        Delos: A Journal on and of Translation 1,   p. 5.
(32)   Jakobson (1959), p. 238.
(33)   Auden (1975), p. 23.
(34)   Nida (1976), p. 52.
(35)   Triandis, H.C. (1976), 'Approaches towards minimizing
        translation' in Brislin (ed). (1976), pp. 229-243 (p. 229).
(36)   Dillon, W. (1797), The poetical works of Went. Dillon,
        Earl of Roscommon, with the life of the author,
        British Library, Strand, London, vv. 216-17.
(37)   Steiner (1977), p. 18.

CROSS-LINGUISTIC SPEECH ACT STUDIES: THEORETICAL AND EMPIRICAL ISSUES*

Elite Olshtain and
Shoshana Blum-Kulka
The Hebrew University of
Jerusalem

'A Polynesian child, on hearing his mother say "Don't do that Johnny", will normally (if amenable) reply "yes" meaning he will obey his mother and cease doing whatever it was. This can easily be misinterpreted by a teacher as impudence when in fact it is a courteous reply' (Understanding Polynesians, No. 12, New Zealand Government pamphlet, no date).

Cross-cultural comparative studies of discourse (Ochs-Keenan 1976; Lein and Brenneis 1978; Tannen 1979) have repeatedly shown that rules of speaking are culturally determined and vary from culture to culture. It has also been shown that cross-cultural differences in expectations of linguistic behaviour, interpretive strategies and signalling devices can lead to breakdowns in inter-group communication (Gumperz 1978). One such case is the Polynesian child (see quote) whose affirmative response to a negative command might be interpreted by an English speaker not as signalling compliance (which would be signalled by deeds, not words) but rather as showing understanding ('Yes, I heard you') which is impudent from a child to a mother in western cultures.

In recent years the relevance of cross-cultural differences in interactional styles has become increasingly clear to students of first and second language acquisition. It became almost a common-place to quote Hymes (1964) to the effect that communicative competence depends on more than the rules of lexicon, grammar and phonology of the language or languages spoken in one's community and that the competent speaker knows not only these but also the socio-cultural rules of appropriate speech usage which dictate the choice of linguistic variants in context and often carry social meaning.

It follows, that in order to become a competent speaker in any language, the learner needs to acquire the socio-cultural rules of appropriate speech usage. Though it is still far from clear what the entire system of rules of speech for any language consists of,

theoretical and empirical work, focusing on certain areas
such as speech act performance (Searle 1979; Gordon and
Lakoff 1975) have shown the grammatical, pragmatic and
social aspects of language use to be interdependent in
complex ways. Speech acts constitute an aspect
of language which is often highly complex in the mapping
of form and meaning and yet in which the choice of the
specific way for realizing the act involves high social
stakes for both speaker and hearer (Brown and Levinson
1978). One of the most basic issues in speech act
studies is the question of universality: assuming that
speech act realization rules demonstrate an inter-
relationship between various types of phenomena, is
it possible to determine the degree to which the nature
of this interdependence varies from culture to culture
and language to language?

This issue is especially relevant in the context of
second language studies, since cross-linguistic
differences in speech act realization rules might explain
communicative failures of the language learner. Studies
that adopted this perspective (Blum-Kulka 1982;
Olshtain and Cohen 1981; House and Kasper 1981) have
established empirically cross-linguistic differences in
speech act realization rules in respect to certain speech
acts, and have also shown that language learners indeed
tend to transfer rules of speaking from their native
language. Yet, the complexity of the theoretical and
methodological issues involved in this line of research
has prevented fast progress in the area. Our goal in
this paper is to discuss these issues in an attempt to
suggest a possible empirical framework for the cross-
linguistic study of speech act patterns.

Theoretical considerations

Our first concern is to suggest ways for setting up
parameters for cross-linguistic comparability with
respect to two speech acts which we have studied in
detail so far: requests and apologies. The theoretical
framework and the empirical solutions that we are
going to discuss, address themselves to the major
question of setting up degrees of equivalence on two
different levels: the sociocultural level and the level
of pragmalinguistic realizations.

The sociocultural level presents the speaker with
at least two types of constraints:

1. constraints on performance, i.e., the social and cultural norms that affect the speaker's decision to perform or not to perform a given act (make a request, apologize or not)

2. constraints on strategy selection within the speech act: i.e., the features of the social context which determine the way the act is actually performed, given both the pragmatic information and the potential strategies available in any language (for example, the level of directness in which a request is being performed).

The level of pragmalinguistic realizations relates to the fact that the pragmatic force of the speech act has to be mapped on to a linguistic token. This seems to involve two sub-levels:

1. the relationship between illocutionary intent (what you want to mean) and the linguistic repertoire: i.e., the range of potential realizations that any language makes available for the performance of a given speech act (subsequently referred to as the speech act set).

2. the actual choice of a strategy and its realization in a certain grammatical and lexical form (e.g. choosing the form 'will you' versus 'can you' to make a request in English).

It seems reasonable to assume that features of social context such as distance and power between interlocutors play a significant role in governing choice of speech act strategies in all cultures, although they may be assessed differently in different cultures and thus lead to varied realizations when compared cross-culturally.[1] Therefore, we are concerned on the one hand with the establishment of universal features of speech act performance and on the other hand with the description of cross-cultural differences. Such differences between universal and language-specific features will be of interest both at the sociocultural and the pragmalinguistic levels.

On the sociocultural level we might find some situations which call for the performance of a speech act, apologizing, for instance, regardless of the language being spoken; in other situations, one culture might reject entirely the need to apologize while another culture does not. Furthermore, once the choice has been made to

perform the act of apologizing, conventions in one language
may prefer the apology to be expressed through an explanation
of external circumstances which lead to the situation
calling for an apology, while in another language it would
be necessary to apologize overtly. Thus, constraints on
performance of the speech act and on strategy selection
within the speech act may vary considerably from language
to language.

On the pragmalinguistic level there might be
differences between languages in terms of the <u>procedures</u>[2]
available for the realization of an act. In English, for
instance, asking for a menu at a restaurant would most
probably be realized in a 'could + verb' question such
as: 'Could I have a menu, please?' This realization makes
reference to Searle's 'preparatory condition' of ability
on the part of the speaker, while in Hebrew the most
likely realization is 'Efŝar lekabel et hatafrit?'
(literally, 'Is it possible to get the menu?'). The
Hebrew realization makes reference to a pre-condition of
the possibility of realizing the act, a procedure which
does not have a conventional counterpart in English.

At the level of linguistic realization, we may
find that in a given situation a certain formulaic
expression is the most frequently selected form in a
variety of languages, but that the actual linguistic form
selected for use may be language specific and so could not
be arrived at by simply translating from one language to
the other. When bumping into a lady at the supermarket,
for instance, the English speaker is most likely to
express regret by saying 'I'm sorry', while the Hebrew
speaker does so by saying 'slixa', which literally means
'forgiveness'.

Finally, even if we find that two or more languages
use similar choices both at the sociocultural and the
pragmalinguistic levels, they may still differ in the
degree of intensity with which the speech act is carried
out. For example, the speaker of English will tend to
apologize more profusely when late for a meeting than
will the speaker of Hebrew.

In view of what has been said so far, our main quest
in speech act studies is to find parameters which allow

effective cross-linguistic comparability as well as
language-specific descriptions.

Requests and apologies

The present paper concerns two different types of
speech acts: requests and apologies. As we shall try to
show, these two acts differ in basic ways.

Requests express the speaker's expectation towards
some prospective action - verbal or non-verbal - by the
hearer. Thus, as suggested by Brown and Levinson (1978)
all types of requests impinge upon the private territory of the hearer. All languages seem to provide their
speakers with a wide variety of direct and indirect
strategies for making requests: this variation is
motivated, universally, according to Brown and Levinson,
by the need to minimize the impingement, or threat to
face, involved in requesting behaviour. Another phenomenon observed about requests (Searle 1975; Labov
and Fanshel 1977) is the seemingly systematic relationship between the pragmatic precondition necessary for the
performance of the act and its linguistic realization.
This relationship is observable in verbal patterns referred
to as 'conventional indirect speech acts', which provide
speakers across languages with linguistically fixed
utterances that 'count' habitually as requests (such as
'could you...').

The act of apologizing is rather different, since it is
called for after some behaviour or action has resulted in the
violation of social norms, or before such an infraction is
about to happen. When an action or an utterance (or the lack
of either) results in the fact that one or more persons perceive themselves as deserving an apology, the culpable
person(s) is (are) expected to apologize. The speaker therefore
intends to placate the hearer and to restore thereby his/her own
social status (Edmondson and House 1981). According to
Searle (1979) a person who apologizes for doing A, expresses
regret at having done so. It is therefore clear that here there
is no threat to the hearer's face - on the contrary, apologies
by their very nature are hearer-supportive acts, that threaten
the speaker's face.

For cross-linguistic analysis, Olshtain and Cohen
(in press) have proposed the notion of a 'speech act set'.
This notion was developed in an attempt to better define the relations holding between illocutionary
intent and linguistic repertoire. For any given act,

the set encompasses the maximal range of strategies available
for the performance of the act. Empirically, the acts of
requesting and apologizing necessitate different criteria
in establishing their respective speech act sets.

In the case of apologies we are concerned, on the
one hand, with formulaic routines ('I'm sorry') and,
on the other, with an open-ended variety of possible
utterances, which by their propositional content express
notions associated with the speech act of apology, used
in addition to or instead of the formulaic expressions.
In the case of requests, the speech act set consists of
at least three basic categories, two of which can be
defined using linguistic and pragmalinguistic formal
criteria. Together these three categories form a scale
of directness which seems to be shared by all languages.
The first category consists of the direct, linguistically
marked ways for making requests (such as imperatives and
performatives). The second category, which is the most
difficult one to compare across languages, consists of those
indirect strategies which are conventionally used for
requesting in a given language, such as 'could you' or
'would you' in English. The third category consists of
the open-ended set of indirect hints, such as 'It is cold in
here' used as a request to close the window. These basic
categories for analyzing apologies and requests can serve
as a basis for setting up cross-linguistically comparable
speech act sets for each respective act. Thus in comparing apologies across languages, it would be interesting
to note the nature of the formulaic routine expressions in
each, as well the relative role in usage of the basic notions
of apologizing. For requests such a comparison should
yield the language specific variations in the group of direct
and conventionally indirect strategies, as well as the major
types of the context-bound open-ended set of indirect ones.

Empirical considerations

From a methodological standpoint, which then are the
tools for data collection which would enable cross-
linguistic comparisons? Our main objective here is to
establish patterns of usage as related to social constraints, i.e., to discover the preferences of native
speakers of different languages across socially varied
situations. Ethnographic research can tap such differences
for a given language; for instance, via data collection of

a given act in natural situations (Blum-Kulka, Danet and
Gerson 1983). But for cross-linguistic research there is
a need to control social variables in ways that ensure
cross-cultural comparability. One way to achieve this
objective is via controlled data collection procedures,
such as a discourse completion test. This technique,
originally developed for comparing the speech act performance patterns of native and non-native speakers (Blum-
Kulka 1982), is based on presenting respondents with
incomplete discourse sequences that represent socially
defined situations. Respondents are asked to complete
the discourse by providing the missing utterance(s). For
example:

<u>At a teachers' meeting</u>
Teacher: When is the next meeting?
Principal: Next Wednesday at 8.00. We'll have to
            notify the people who aren't here tonight.
            Richard _____
Richard: O.K.

The discourse completion test allows researchers to control
basic social parameters of the situation such as the
setting, status of speaker and hearer and the relative
social distance between speaker and hearer. The delimited
context serves to elicit the realization of the speech act
in question (in the example - a request) and the mani-
pulation of social parameters across situations is meant to
establish the variation in strategies (for the same act)
relative to social parameters.[3]

The approach described above focuses on the speaker's
point of view; it taps native speakers' preferences across
socially varied situations. Given a cross-cultural
research framework, it can tell us to what extent the
observed variation in usage is culture and language
dependent. Native speakers' 'preferences' in completing
an item on a discourse completion test represent the
strategy or strategies used by the majority of native
speakers in a given situation. However, such an approach
does not provide us with the hearer's point of view, namely
with the extent to which different strategies from the
provided range would be acceptable in the given situation.
Thus, performance data alone cannot tell us directly[4] the
range of acceptable strategies, nor the extent to which
infrequently used strategies might be still considered
acceptable in a given speech community. This aspect of
cross-linguistic speech act study requires the development
of another instrument for data collection - a speech act
pattern <u>acceptability test</u>.

The data discussed in this section was obtained by the use of an acceptability study, carried out among speakers of English and Hebrew. Our goal in the following is to show how this type of instrument can serve to establish levels of agreement among native speakers on the relative acceptability of a variety of realizations for a given speech act in a socially specified situation.

Our test consists of four request and four apology situations. Each item supplies a description of the particular situation, followed by six realizations of the request or apology in question (the realizations are from actual responses collected via a discourse completion test). The set of utterances provided in each item represents: a) formal, polite variants of the request or apology; b) informal, intimate-language variants; c) direct, blunt variants.[5] For example, item 1 on the test (English version) reads as follows:

Item 1:

Ruth, a friend of yours at the university, comes up to you after class and tells you that she has finally found an apartment to rent. The only problem is that she has to pay $200 - immediately, and at present she only has $100. She turns to you and says:
a. How about lending me the money?
b. So do me a favor and lend me the money.
c. Do you want to lend me the money?
d. I'd appreciate it if you could lend me the money.
e. Could you possibly lend me the money?
f. Lend me the money, please.

As can be seen from this example, the social variables of power, namely (+) or (-) dominance, distance which is (+) or (-) familiarity between speaker and hearer, and sex of speaker (the sex of the respondent will be specified on the questionnaire) are supplied for the respondent as part of the situation. In the item given above ('Ruth, a friend of yours') presents respondents with the following: female speaker, (-) dominance and (-) distance. These factors are being manipulated in the situations; thus the request to a subordinate at work represents (+) dominance and (-) distance, and the request from a policeman to a driver is considered as representing (+) dominance and (+) distance.

Respondents[6] for the acceptability test were asked to rate each of the six realizations on a scale of appropriateness (relative to the situation) from 1 to 3. Thus, in the example given above, 'asking a friend for a loan', respondents had to evaluate each of the six choices (a-f) independently as: 1 = most appropriate, 2 = more or less appropriate, 3 = not appropriate. Table One illustrates the distribution of the ratings for the situation 'asking for a loan'.

Table One: Distribution of ratings - asking for a loan
(Item 1. English version, n = 172)

Realization	Most appropriate	More or less approp.	Not approp.	
	%	%	%	
a. How about lending me the money?	7	40	53	100
b. So do me a favor and lend me the money.	2	25	73	100
c. Do you want to lend me the money?	7	49	44	100
d. I'd appreciate it if you could lend me the money.	60	36	4	100
e. Could you possibly lend me the money?	85	12	3	100
f. Lend me the money, please.	5	42	53	100

The strategy judged most appropriate by 84.8% of the informants - 'Could you possibly lend me the money?' (1e) qualifies as a non-presumptuous, conventionally indirect way for making the request. More than half of the English speakers (60.1%) seem also to accept the very formal, indirect way for approaching the subject, i.e., 'I'd appreciate it if you could lend me the money' (1d). On the other hand, the same speakers seem to feel uncomfortable with a more intimate approach, as represented by 1a - 'How about lending me the money? (rejected by 53.1%) and definitely uncomfortable with the direct (and presumptuous) 'So do me a favor and lend me the money' (rejected by 73.5%).

The most striking feature of Table One is the degree of agreement exhibited by native speakers on some of the realizations. We had originally been concerned with the fact that on an acceptability test native speakers might tend to cluster around the middle, choosing the rating of 2, which would obscure the full range of acceptability. Yet, quite contrary to our fears, our native speakers tended to accept or reject certain choices. Thus three of the realizations (a, b and f) were judged by more than half of the respondents as not acceptable. It is also interesting to note the range of acceptable patterns (see (d) and (e) on Table One). The tolerance exhibited by the informants for more than one strategy in a given situation (see (d) and (e) on Table One) is taken to reflect natural variability in actual usage. The collection of productive data alone may not provide an opportunity to observe the true range of variability, hence the special value of the judgment test.

Furthermore, it is our belief that a judgment test can help establish degrees of equivalence between two or more languages both at the sociocultural and pragmalinguistic levels. The responses on the judgment test point to the frequency of usage of a range of variants as related to social constraints, enabling us to discover the preferences that native speakers of different languages have across socially varied situations. In order to illustrate this point, we shall consider results for the apology situations comparatively from the two test versions: Hebrew and English. Table Two presents only the choices that exhibit relatively high levels of agreement (more than 50%) in at least one of the two languages which are being compared. (Equivalent choices were given in both languages.)

Table Two: Distribution of 'Most appropriate' ratings for three apology situations
(English n = 172, Hebrew n = 260)

Situation 1: A young man/woman bumps into you at the supermarket and some of your groceries spill onto the floor. S/he turns to you and says:

English		Hebrew	
I'm really sorry.		I'm sorry.	94%
Here, let me help you.	89%	Sorry!	86%

Situation 2: You arranged to meet a (student) friend to get some notes for an exam. You waited for an hour and he/she didn't show up. You call him/her up and he/she says:

English		Hebrew	
I'm afraid I forgot about the meeting. When can I bring it to you?	62%	I'm really very sorry; it is very unpleasant for me. It's my fault. It won't happen again.	50%
		I was held up on my way and couldn't make it.	50%

Situation 3:   In a discussion at work, you were offended
               by something that one of your colleagues said.
               He/she comes up to you afterwards and says:

English	Hebrew
I'm really sorry if I offended you. I didn't mean to. 76%	I'm really sorry. I didn't mean it personally. 84%
	I said what I meant. 32%

The first interesting difference between English and
Hebrew which becomes evident from examining Table Two is
the fact that English responses tend to cluster significantly around one single choice while Hebrew
responses are often equally divided between two, either
similar or very different realizations. Furthermore,
some preferred strategies are shared by both languages
while others exhibit considerable difference. In situation
1, for instance, Hebrew speakers tend to prefer the short,
impersonal apology (Sorry/I'm sorry), while speakers of
English feel the need to intensify the apology (I'm really
sorry). This result is in line with previous findings
(Cohen and Olshtain 1981, Blum-Kulka 1982) in which
cross-linguistic comparisons between English and Hebrew
show significant differences between the two cultures:
while Hebrew speakers, as a group prefer the more
direct, straightforward and unmitigated choices. English
speakers tend to soften their choices and often prefer
more indirect realizations.

Situation 2 in Table Two is particularly interesting
because Hebrew speakers exhibit here opposing trends:
while half of the informants accept a profuse apology
which is very similar to the English preferred version
(a choice that is even more mitigated than the English
one), half of the informants also accept an explanation
which contains no overt apology at all. These two
choices are like complete opposites on a negative-positive
politeness scale as suggested by Brown and Levinson (1978).

Situation 3 was presented here especially in order to
illustrate the fact that agreement on the 'rejection' of
a strategy might be just as important as agreement on
its selection. The first choices selected by both languages
were very close in form and received high ratings both in
English (76%) and in Hebrew (84%). Another choice,
however, 'I said what I meant', was totally rejected by
English speakers, yet sounded acceptable to 32% of the
Hebrew respondents. This result indicates a much higher
level of tolerance among Hebrew speakers for the 'truthful'
and unmitigated realization, even in a case where the
hearer's face is greatly threatened by the act.[7]

Conclusion

In summing up our methodological stand, it seems to us that in order to gain insights into speech act performance across languages we should ideally follow a three-phase procedure:

a) phase one - is based on ethnographic data collection analyzed qualitatively and quantitatively.

b) phase two - translates the hypotheses from phase one to controlled data collection instruments that focus on the speaker's point of view. Open-ended instrumentation such as discourse-completion tests and role-playing is useful for this phase.

c) phase three - refines the hypotheses about speech act behaviour and shifts the focus to the hearer's point of view. At this stage, research is particularly interested in establishing the range of acceptability as exhibited by native speakers in a particular language.

Phase-two- and phase-three-type studies can and should be carried out cross-culturally. In both types of instrumentation it is possible to control for contextual information, as we have seen, and therefore the realization can be compared across languages and cultures.

NOTES

1. For example, in an ethnographic study of the language of requesting in Israeli society, based on 477 naturally occurring request tokens the analysis of the distribution of request types relative to the social parameters of distance and power revealed the following:

a) As separate variables, both distance and power were shown to have a statistically significant effect on the distribution of strategy types;

b) However, on a multiple regression analysis that took into account a set of predictor variables (such as age of speaker and hearer, sex, goal of the request and relative distance and power of speaker and hearer and setting) relative distance and power accounted for only 1% of the variance of strategy types while the variable of 'goal of request' accounted for 19%. This result was interpreted to mean that in Israeli society relative power and distance are rarely assessed as very crucial, a fact that partly explains the general 'directness' in Israeli interactionsl style (Blum-Kulka, Danet and Gerson 1983).

2. By 'procedure' we mean the contextual feature standardly referred to in verbalizing the act.
3. A research project aimed at the study of cross-cultural patterns of speech act realization (CCSARP) currently underway uses the discourse completion test as the basic data collection instrument. The project focuses at this stage on two speech acts (requests and apologies) in the following languages: American English (Wolfson and Rintell), British English (Thomas), Australian English (Ventola), Danish (Kasper and Faerch), German (House and Vollmer), Canadian French (Weitzman) and Hebrew (Blum-Kulka and Olshtain). The discourse completion test developed by the research team includes 16 items, 8 for requests and 8 for apologies, varied across setting and relative status and power. The test has been translated (with minor changes in the descriptions of the settings to accommodate cross-cultural differences) into the languages studied. The results will enable us to make a cross-cultural comparison of the realization patterns of requests and apologies in controlled situations across the languages studied.
4. Obviously if 85% of native speakers use a certain strategy in one situation, that strategy must be an acceptable one. But the level of acceptability of all the other strategies used remains unclear, unless directly looked at.
5. The division to the three groups was inspired by Brown and Levinson's (1978) categories of negative-politeness strategies (group a), positive politeness strategies (group b) and 'bald on record' strategies (group c).
6. The test was administered to 400 college students, 200 in Hebrew (Israelis) and 200 in English (American students at the Hebrew University). The data presented here is from native speakers of Hebrew (260) and American English (172).
7. For further elaboration on the last point see Blum-Kulka and Olshtain (1983).

* We are indebted to Andrew Cohen for reading the paper at the 'Language Across Cultures' conference and for his useful comments and editorial suggestions.

REFERENCES

Blum-Kulka, Sh. (1982), 'Learning to say what you mean in a second language; a study of the speech act perfor- mance of Hebrew second language learners', Applied Linguistics 3.1

Blum-Kulka Sh. and E. Olshtain (1983), 'The ethos of Israeli directness', paper presented at the First Annual Colloquium on Pragmatics and Second Language Learning, TESOL Convention, Toronto.

Blum-Kulka Sh., B. Danet and R. Gerson (1983), 'The language of requesting in Israeli society', paper presented at the Language and Social Psychology Conference, Bristol

Brown P. and S. Levinson (1978), 'Universals of language usage: politeness phenomena', in C. Goody (ed.), Questions and Politeness, Cambridge University Press, pp. 56-311

Cohen A.D. and E. Olshtain (1981), 'Developing a measure of sociocultural competence: the case of apology' Language Learning, 31.1

Edmondson W. and S. House (1981), Let's talk and talk about it, Urban and Schwarzenberg

Gordon D. and G. Lakoff (1975), 'Conversational postulates' in P. Cole and J. Morgan (eds.), Syntax and Semantics, 3, Speech Acts, New York and London: Academic Press

Gumperz J. (1978), 'The conversational analysis of interethnic communication' in Ross (ed.), Interethnic communication, Southern Anthropological Society Proceedings, Athens: University of Georgia Press

House J. and G. Kasper (1981), 'Politeness markers in English and German' in F. Coulmas (ed.), Conversational routine, The Hague: Mouton, pp. 157-185

Hymes D. (1964), 'Directions in (ethno) linguistic theory', American Anthropologist, G6, 3.2, pp. 6-56

Labov W. and D. Fanshel (1977), Therapeutic discourse, New York and London: Academic Press

Lein L. and D. Brenneis (1978), 'Children's disputes in three speech communities', Language in Society, 7, pp. 299-323

Olshtain E. and A.D. Cohen (in press), 'Apology: a speech act set' to appear in N. Wolfson and E. Judd, (eds.), TESOL and sociolinguistics research, Rowley, Mass.: Newbury House

Ochs Keenan E. (1976), 'The universality of conversational postulates', Language in Society, 5, pp. 67-80

Searle J. (1975), 'Indirect speech acts', in Cole and Morgan (eds.), Syntax and Semantics, 3, Speech Acts, New York and London: Academic Press, pp. 59-82

Searle J. (1979), Expression and meaning, Cambridge: Cambridge University Press

CONTRASTIVE ETHOLOGY OF LANGUAGE

Michael Pickering
University of Turku

In his foundational book, <u>Language across cultures</u>, Robert Lado devoted a final chapter to cultural contrasts, of which he gave some vivid examples. In a slightly earlier epoch, the work of the anthropological linguists Sapir and Whorf had focussed attention on the possible influence of specific language structures on culture-specific patterns of thought. Neither the study of culture contrasts nor the Sapir-Whorf hypothesis has been adopted in any applied linguistic research programme known to me, while the contrastive analysis of languages has given rise to a number of programmes, as well as considerable controversy. Culture contrastive analysis is I think no more problematic, perhaps less problematic than language contrastive analysis. The comparative study of language and culture, however, has made little progress at a theoretical level; yet it would be of considerable value to applied linguists if results in this area could be obtained. For many linguists - except those anthropologists who are bolder in forwarding their intuitions - the neglect of the language-culture relationship is founded on doubts about whether grammatical structure is really non-arbitrary in its relation to the external, non-linguistic world. The dispute between those who deny that language is significantly externally motivated and those who believe that it is in some important degree motivated by differences in the structure of external reality is a very old dispute. The problem of the substantive connection between language and culture still remains, however, and the bridge between the two is difficult to cross. In this paper, I want to suggest a new approach which may enable us to cross the bridge, and after outlining the approach, I shall give an example of the kind of analysis which is entailed.

It should be pointed out, perhaps, that where culture is concerned, a linguist is not necessarily trained in the skills required for obtaining suitable data. We may need, therefore, in a trans-disciplinary spirit, to consult anthropologists, sociologists, psychologists, ethnologists, historians, even journalistic commentators,

indeed any sources which may be of help. I shall refer
in this paper to just three reports - one from ethnology,
one from sociology   (a student production) and one from
psychology - which deal scientifically with constrasts
between Finnish and other cultures from a general or
Finnish viewpoint. (This material will however more
than suffice to show how we may proceed in an analysis).

Given, then, that we have some scientific cultural
data, which in the present instance is largely descriptive, as opposed to experimental, we need to consider what areas of language may be illuminated by
these data. Before turning to this question, however,
we must ask whether, since data on language and culture
are available, we can find a suitable mediating construct between them. It would not be wise, I think,
to follow Whorf, and quite useless to engage in naive
psychology. A recent Whorfian study of Finnish has
appeared (Leino 1981) which, interesting as it is,
uses only notional mediating constructs, in particular
time and causation. We should make a fresh start and
select a theoretical apparatus which is broad enough
to encompass all varieties of language structure and of
cultural forms. With this level of generality in view,
and also in the hope of progressing beyond nominal
data to an ordinal scale, I propose to use one set of
fundamental concepts from the epistemology of Jean
Piaget as the mediating construct. There is no intended
reference here to Piaget's developmental psychology,
which has already been applied to psycholinguistic
development (e.g. Sinclair-de-Svart 1969). It should
be understood that the concepts can be applied time-
lessly and without reference to development. The
reader will already have noticed that the title of this
paper contains the word 'ethology'. The use of this
word is intended to suggest the connection with
biology of human behaviour which is intrinsic to the
Piagetian theory, and in particular to the concepts
of 'assimilation' and 'accommodation' which also correspond respectively to the implicative and explicative
functions of intelligence (Piaget 1956). I shall use
'assimilation' or 'implicative' and 'accommodation' or
'explicative' according to context with the same general
meaning.

I shall assume that the organisation of a language
and the organisation of a culture are a system of
assimilations, which have been adapted over the course
of time both to the external reality and to one another
so as to form a coherent whole. I shall also follow
Michael Halliday in assuming that in the organisation
of a language there is a cline or continuum from

grammar to lexis, and I shall adopt a term used by
Dan Slobin, the term 'grammaticisation', to denote the
degree in which a particular form is actually assimilated to the grammar.

Part of the inspiration for the present study
derives from a study by the anthropological linguist
John L. Fischer of the Micronesian societies of Truk
and Ponape (Fischer 1964). Fischer makes a statement,
in a very concrete context, which may be paralleled
with the statement I have just made on the language-
culture relation. He says: 'I do not see how these
particular divergencies in linguistic development
(sc. between the related languages of Truk and Ponape)
can be explained in terms of psychomotor economy of
speech alone, although I think such an explanation
would be appropriate if the entire social and cultural
context were taken into account at the same time'.
(Fischer 1964, p. 180). I believe he is right, in
that an isolated account of the development of grammaticised forms in terms of mechanical, phonetic change
would be insufficient: grammaticisation would be
motivated also by higher level processes.

Slobin's statement on this topic (Slobin 1980,
p. 232) which agrees with Fischer's, though the
emphasis is different, is formulated in such a way
that it can be fairly easily translated into the
terms of the assimilation/accommodation construct
which I am proposing. Slobin says that the process
of grammaticisation occurs 'in part because the
integrity of separate surface elements tends to
be eroded by phonological change and by shortcuts
of rapid everyday speech and because metaphors are
extended beyond their original domain'. Translated
then into our construct, this says that phonological
assimilation is assimilation in the Piagetian sense,
where the assimilated sound becomes part of a
neighbouring sound, and metaphorisation is
generalising, or possibly distorting, assimilation
in the Piagetian sense, whereby concrete lexical
meanings of words become abstract grammatical
meanings. It is possibly true that we need not go
beyond a view of phonological change which considers
the way in which a social group externally represents
itself - cf. the successes of William Labov and his
followers in the study of social stratification;

but this approach I believe will be insufficient to explain the internal relations between language and culture.

To summarise what I have said so far, I would postulate the following: the grammaticised part of a language is that end of a cline from grammar to lexis which is the organised (and persisting) form for expressing what is also implicated in the organised forms of the culture. As a concrete example from the domain of syntax, consider the personal pronouns: the basic forms of these pronouns express the structure of social communication (in this instance, a universal structure) as speaker (I), addressee (you) and topic (he, she, it). Language is thus adapted in the same sense that the rest of culture is adapted, and the rules of a language constitute its structure in the same way as the norms of a culture constitute the cultural structure.

A point to be emphasised here is that the construction of a cline from implicative to explicative, corresponding to the cline from grammar to lexis, enables us to compare and contrast languages, not simply in terms of their grammatical structures, but in terms of a higher order property of these structures, namely, their degree of grammaticisation, which we have postulated to be their degree of implicativeness. We may now ask: can this cline be constructed in practice, and, what is its status in theory? I shall try to show first that it can be constructed in practice by comparing very limited areas in two genetically unrelated languages, English and Finnish. I will then discuss the theoretical status of the construct, before using it to compare the Finnish and English cultures, where we shall have to be content however with an opposition in place of a cline.

The choice of an area for comparison is difficult, given the small amount of cultural data available, but I shall maximise the chances of success by taking a very small area in which (a) there are sharp differences between the two languages and (b) there is a certain amount of good quality data available on the cultures. Before considering the area in question, that is, the modal verbs of the class often termed deontic modals, I should like to make at least two remarks on the historical aspect of the language-culture relation. Firstly, it is of course generally believed that cultural change is more rapid than language change, implying a lag in the relationship. I shall not contest this, but simply note that the abstract level of the culture which I shall be considering may well be just that level which changes as slowly as the language does. Secondly, it is well-known that external influences, of one language on another, can vary from totally transforming impact to very moderate effects. On the other hand, it is recognised that grammatical forms change more slowly than lexical forms, and it may be relevant to add that, as Kari Sajavaara has observed, the influence of English on Finnish - which is already claimed to be the most conservative of the Finno-Ugric languages - has been relatively slight. And thirdly - to broach a wider issue - the influence of Norman French on English may well help to explain why the English modals became grammaticised more than the Finnish modals did, while the influence or lack of influence on Finnish of the Swedish language may assist in accounting for the lesser grammaticisation of Finnish modals: in short, a culture is extended in time, and I am here disregarding without dismissing the temporal aspects of the totality.

We now examine, by means of the table below, the translational correspondences between the English and Finnish deontic modal verbs. I may mention in parenthesis that all the Finnish modals can appear in the conditional mood, and, in principle at least, in the potential mood. Most of them can be preceded by at least two modals, taitaa (I suppose it is ...) and mahtaa (is likely to ...); tarvita can be preceded by voida (can). (That Finnish can here make more distinctions than English is very typical of the relation between the languages).

FINNISH		ENGLISH	
subject: genitive (or locative) case	verb	subject: nominative case	verb
Minun or Mun	pitää tehdä se	I	could, might, must do it
	täytyy tehdä se		must, am obliged, am compelled to do it
	pitäisi tehdä se		should, ought to do it
	täytyisi tehdä se		must, have to do it
	tarvitsee tehdä se		need to do it
	on pakko tehdä se		have to, am bound to do it
	on määrä tehdä se		am expected, supposed to do it
	on tehtävä sen		am to do it
	tulee tehdä se		ought to, am to, am obliged to do it
(in Ostro- bothnian dialect)	saa tehdä se		can, am allowed to do it

The 'equivalents', of which the sources are
dictionaries and personal informants, are given from
the Finnish point of view only. Note also that the
modals are restricted, in Finnish, to those which
are followed by the first infinitive, but this
group in fact includes all the deontics.

Below is the analysis of the modal verbs in
both languages according to the cline of grammaticisation.

MORE   . LESS
GRAMMATICISED   GRAMMATICISED

assimilative/implicative pole accommodative/explicative pole

FINNISH	täytyy, täytyisi	pitää pitäisi
ENGLISH	must	have to
	should	ought to
FINNISH		tarvitsee
ENGLISH		need to
FINNISH		saa
ENGLISH	(may) can	am allowed to
		tulee
		am obliged to
		am bound to
FINNISH		on pakko
ENGLISH		am supposed to
FINNISH		on määrä
FINNISH		on tehtävä
ENGLISH		am to be ...

The points of difference between Finnish and English
concern

(1) saa/can and pitäisi or pitää/should; täytyy
    is also less grammaticised than must because
    it is closely related to the lexical verb
    täyttää (complete).
(2) the subject of all the Finnish deontic modals
    is an oblique case which is now identical with
    the genitive but was originally locative;
    similarly there are English periphrastic modals
    with passive verb forms, so that their subjects
    are grammatically different from those of
    active verbs; but these, being periphrastic,
    are less grammaticised than any of the Finnish
    modals save two.

We can conclude, therefore that at least for the basic
deontic modals of duty and permission, English is
decisively more implicative than Finnish. This is
the main finding to be borne in mind.

I hope now to have shown that the cline of grammaticisation can be constructed. What, then, will be its status in general theory? I refer here to the work of two Dutch psychologists, Van de Vijver and Poortinga, who have recently distinguished cultural universals in relation to the statistical data types (Van de Vijver and Poortinga 1982). Thus according to them there are 'conceptual universals' (nominal data), 'weak (or functionally equivalent) universals' (ordinal data), 'strong universals' (metric data) and 'strict (or scalar equivalent) universals' (metric data with the same scale origin in different cultures). The grammaticisation scale can certainly apply for status as a weak universal of language. It may also be that it is it stronger than a weak universal, inasmuch as a zero point on the ordinal scale, the point of maximal grammaticisation, can be established in principle. While, as I said earlier, it is hard to conceive of conventional experiments which could be performed, there is a sense in which a language as such can be regarded as an experiment in vivo, from which observed scale differences could be obtained and correlated. On the other hand, with the available data on cultures, it may not be possible to construct a scale, but merely an opposition of more and less assimilation/implicativeness for the chosen area, and this is what has been attained in the present study, as we shall now see.

The culture area assumed to correspond to the deontic modals is the specific orientation to duty, or social role performance. The fact that in this area data is available on Finnish culture and on English culture, at least from the Finnish viewpoint, is the reason for having chosen the deontic modals as a language area. A clear connecting link between the language and culture is suggested by the ethnologist Frank Neal (1978) who concretises 'preoccupation with role' in Finland as emphasis on the deontic modal 'I should' ('Minun pitäisi'). 'Preoccupation with role' is a judgment on the basis of high factor loadings found by Kuusinen (1969) in the 'semantic differential' study termed 'A Finnish implicit theory of personality', the results of which Neal estimates to be 'a direct analogy to almost every and only obsessional defence mechanisms' (p. 42). Taking this assertion as a starting point, I have looked at other reports. A Finnish student of sociology, Vieno Kennedy, states in her report on married Finnish women living in England (1982) that 'the ideal type of Finnish woman to live happily in England seems to be someone who was alienated by Finland's cultural authoritarianism. She also concludes that 'once the Finns get used to England's "inferiority", to the dirt and the general slovenly state of affairs, they often begin to enjoy themselves, because mental freedom more than compensates for lack

of order'. On the relation between the 'obsessional'
personality syndrome and the desire for order and
authority, one may consult Fisher and Greenberg
(1977, esp. p. 152 and p. 157), who have surveyed
the scientific credibility of Freudian constructs.
Without endorsing any implied value judgments, I
would take Kennedy's statements as confirming, in a
general way and from the Finnish point of view, the
statements of Neal. According to Neal, the preoccupation with role in Finnish culture stems from the
obsessional need 'to submit to a harsh, poorly
integrated conscience in terms of "external necessity"'.
Since parental strictness must surely underlie the
development of such a character as Neal proposes, it
would be interesting to know whether in fact Finns do
introject conflicting aspects of the parent, as Neal
implies by his 'poorly integrated conscience'. Limited
supporting information here comes from a Rorschach test
recently administered on a normal population by
Mattlar et al. (1978) which showed several striking
differences between Finnish and 'international' norms,
among them a high percentage of responses involving
fairytale and mythical personages. Internationally,
these responses are interpreted as rejection of the
parental and nurturing role, as are other childlike
responses. In pointing out, as they do, that the
responses are normal for Finland, the authors are
not necessarily denying that this type of response
implied lack of parental role integration. Thus
the Rorschach evidence does seem to be in accord with
Neal's characterisation on the basis of Kuusinen's
study.

   How can this characterisation be interpreted in
the theory that I propose? The integration of parental,
and generally of social role I assume to be due to the
assimilative/implicative function. If in Finland this
basic role is not fully and harmoniously internalised,
the performance of duty becomes an accommodation to
external social requirements, due to the accommo-
dative/explicative function. This interpretation
can then be placed in correspondence with the
accommodative/explicative rating of the deontic modal
pitäisi or pitää (should). Similar considerations apply
to saa (may, can). On the other hand, English can and

should are assimilative/implicative, and can be placed
in correspondence with the English context, in which
duty will be reconciled with pleasure. We can also
infer a correspondence between the genitive (locative)
subject of the Finnish modals and the unpleasurable
view of duty. The genitive or locative subject makes
the doer of an action its owner or location rather than
its responsible initiator; on the other hand, the English
subject of can and should is nominative and as much a
responsible initiator as the subject of any lexical
verb in the active voice; this would correspond to the
integration of social role.

In conclusion, let me emphasise that no thorough
test for the proposed theoretical construct has been
described in this paper. There does exist concordant
evidence for it in other areas of Finnish and English
language and culture, not reported here, but this
evidence would not count for or against the general
value of the mediating construct. Such evidence can
only be gathered from the study of a number of languages
and cultures which are sufficiently different from one
another in their histories and contemporary forms. If
the theoretical construct is satisfactory it will function
as at least a weak universal of language and culture.

REFERENCES

Baldwin, A. (1979), Theories of child development (Piaget
  pp. 171-300), New York.
Fischer, J.L. (1964), 'Syntax and social structure:
  Truk and Ponape' in W. Bright (ed.), Sociolinguistics,
  The Hague, pp. 168-182.
Fisher, S. and R.P. Greenberg (1977), The scientific
  credibility of Freud's theories and therapy, New York.
Kennedy, V. (1982), 'English life for the Finnish wife',
  Siirtolaisuus/Migration 4 (Institute of Migration
  Studies, Turku).
Kuusinen, J. (1972), 'Affective and denotative studies of
  personality ratings', Journal of Personality and
  Social Psychology 12.3, pp. 181-188; reviewed by
  E. Putanen in Psychiatria Fennica (1972), pp, 26-29.
Lado, R. (1957), Linguistics across cultures, Ann Arbor.
Leino. P. (1981), 'Ajaako suomenkieli ajatelemaan
  suomalaisesti?' ('Does a Finnish speaker tend to have
  Finnish intentions?'), Suomen Antropologi (Finnish
  Anthropologist) 4, pp. 163-176.
Mattlar, C.E., K. Lantela and T. Maunu (1979),
  Rorschachin testin populaarivastaukset ja normaali-
  pöytäkirjan sisältö suomalaisessa terveessä
  aikuisväestössä (Popular Rorschach content responses
  in a healthy Finnish population), Turku: Rehabilitation
  Research Centre.
Neal, F. (1978), 'Towards an ethos typology: Durkheim
  revisited', Psychiatria Fennica, pp. 26-29.
Piaget, J. (1952), The origins of intelligence in
  children, London.
Sinclair-de-Svart, H. (1969), 'Developmental psycholinguistics'
  in D. Elkind and J.H. Flavel (eds.), Studies in
  cognitive development: Essays in honour of Jean Piaget,
  New York, pp. 315-336.
Slobin, D. (1980), 'The repeated path between transparency
  and opacity in language', in U. Bellugi and M.
  Studdert-Kennedy (eds.), Biological constraints on
  linguistic form, Basel, pp. 229-243.
Van de Vijver Fons, J.R. and H. Poortinga Ype (1982),
  'Cross-cultural generalisation and universality',
  Journal of Cross-Cultural Psychology 13.4, pp. 387-408.

A FIRST ENCOUNTER WITH DUTCH:
PERCEIVED LANGUAGE DISTANCE AND LANGUAGE
TRANSFER AS FACTORS IN COMPREHENSION

David Singleton and David Little
Trinity College
Dublin

1. Introductory

This paper reports on an experiment designed to test
the general hypothesis that in situations where people
are faced with the task of trying to understand
utterances in a language they do not know, they will be
assisted by any experience they have of other languages
which are related to the unfamiliar language, and that,
in such situations, the closer the relation between the
languages they know and the unfamiliar language, the
more successful they will be in extracting meaning from
the utterances in question. Clearly, the above hypothesis
relates to the familiar concept of 'positive transfer'
or 'facilitation'. It is also linked to the perhaps
somewhat less familiar idea that the language learner's
perception of the 'distance' or degree of typological
relatedness between languages strongly influences the
extent to which he attempts to transfer from one
language to another.

The latter notion has been thoroughly explored in
recent years, notably by Kellerman (1977, 1979), who
points out that it has a fair amount of direct and
indirect support from a number of studies (e.g. Oller and
Ziahosseiny 1970; Whinnom 1971; Ringbom and Palmberg 1976;
Schachter, Tyson and Diffley 1976). Much of the evidence
pertains to the distance between a learner's native
language and his target language; however, some evidence
(e.g. Sjöholm 1976; Schachter, Tyson and Diffley 1976 -
cf. Jordens 1977) suggests that 'the learner is capable
of becoming sensitive to the fact that TLa is closer to
TLb than the NL' (Kellerman 1977, p. 95), and that he
may as a consequence transfer more readily between
target languages than between native language and target
language. Singleton's (1981, 1982) case study of an
Anglophone subject who uses Spanish as a preferred
source of transfers when speaking French confirms
Kellerman's insight.

The above-mentioned studies focus on language
distance and language transfer as factors in the
productive use of a language which constitutes a
genuine learning target for the individual(s)
investigated. The present paper, in contrast, is concerned with an experiment probing the operation of the
same factors in the reception of an unidentified
language which is unknown to the experimental subjects.

The experiment includes the classic procedure of dividing the subjects into two groups according to their language background and setting each group precisely the same comprehension task. However, in order to gain some insight into subjects' perceptions of the task and the strategies they employed in completing it - information of a kind which is notoriously difficult to get at by means of objective observation (cf. Glahn 1980, p. 127) - some introspective evidence was also gathered. Subjects were asked to engage in 'self-observation' (Cohen and Hosenfeld 1981, pp. 286-8), specifically, 'immediate retrospection' (ibid.). A more directly 'interventionist' method of eliciting such data (cf. Cohen 1983a) was not employed because it was feared that such an approach might prove disruptive. However, it should be noted that Cohen (personal communication and 1983b) suggests that 'interventionist' methods are in fact both applicable and fruitful in small-scale experimental contexts.

2.   The experiment

The experiment set out to test our general hypothesis by hypothesizing specifically that Anglophones with no knowledge of any Germanic language apart from English would derive some sense from an oral/written text in Dutch, but that Anglophones with a reasonable command of German but with no knowledge of any other Germanic language apart from English would derive considerably more sense from the same text.

The text used in the experiment (see Appendix) was created by asking a native-speaker of Dutch to present her curriculum vitae in a register which was as far as possible neutral between spoken and written styles. The native-speaker was recorded speaking the text (slowly, but not unnaturally so), and a typescript of its written version was also prepared.

The subjects for the experiment were recruited from amongst first-year students of French and German in Trinity College, Dublin. A strong attempt was made to recruit 20 students with a knowledge of German and 20 students without a knowledge of any Germanic language other than English. In the event, however, only 13 volunteers in the former category and 7 in the latter category actually presented themselves on the day of the experiment, which limits somewhat the generalizability of our findings.

The experiment was conducted in a language laboratory. First, each of the two groups was assigned a separate area in the laboratory. We then explained that the purpose of the experiment was to see how much

they could understand of a text spoken/written in a
language they did not know. Next, all subjects were
given copies of a questionnaire consisting of twenty
statements in English relating to different parts of
the text. Fourteen of the statements had a blank
to be filled in, while six required subjects to choose
one of three alternatives to complete the meaning
(see Appendix). Subjects were given five minutes to
study the questionnaire. Copies of the Dutch text
were then distributed, and subjects were given
individual control of their cassette recorders, in
each of which there was a pre-recorded audio cassette
of the spoken version of the text. Subjects were
allowed thirty minutes in which to extract from the
printed and spoken forms of the text the information
required to complete the questionnaire. Finally,
they were asked to write on the reverse of their
questionnaire

a) their impression of the difficulty of the
exercise;

b) how they thought they went about the task
of understanding the text and answering
the questions;

c) which they thought more helpful, the cassette
or the typescript.

3.   Results of the experiment

3.1 Comprehension of the text

Tables 1 and 2 summarize subjects' responses to
the questionnaire. Table 1 shows the proportions of
subjects in the two groups answering each question
correctly, and Table 2 shows the proportions of
subjects in the two groups answering each question
correctly or nearly correctly ('nearly correct'
answers were semantically close to the correct
answer, or true but unfocussed, or - in the case of
multiple-choice questions - arose when subjects chose
two options, one of which was correct). Both tables
show that although subjects with no knowledge of
German understood some of the text (the average proportion giving correct answers is 0.35, while the
average proportion giving correct or nearly correct
answers is 0.45), subjects with a knowledge of German
understood more of the text (the average proportion
of this latter group giving correct answers is 0.64,
while the average proportion giving correct or nearly
correct answers is 0.75). Subjects with a knowledge
of German performed better than those with a knowledge of no Germanic language other than English in
respect of seventeen of the twenty questions. At the
same time, the two graphs in Table 1 move in the same
direction in respect of all questions except 2, 6, 7,
10, 11 and 20; while the two graphs in Table 2 move in
the same direction in respect of all questions except

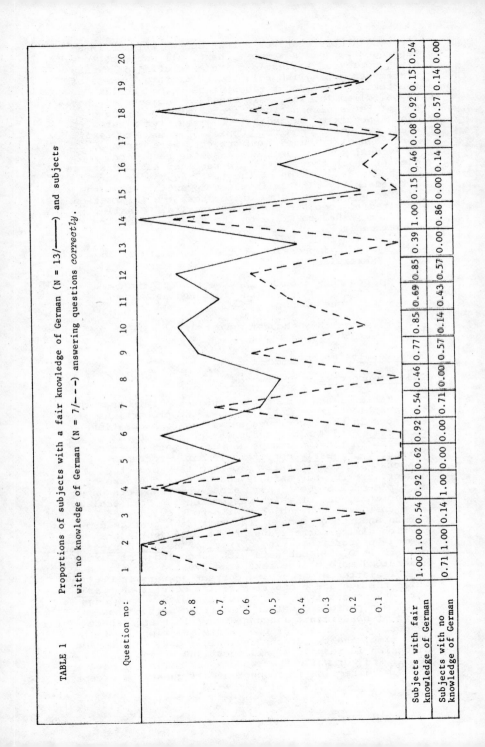

TABLE 1   Proportions of subjects with a fair knowledge of German (N = 13/————) and subjects
with no knowledge of German (N = 7/– – –) answering questions *correctly*.

Question no:	1	2	3	4	5	6	7	8	9	10	11	12	13	14	15	16	17	18	19	20
Subjects with fair knowledge of German	1.00	1.00	0.54	0.92	0.62	0.92	0.54	0.46	0.77	0.85	0.69	0.85	0.39	1.00	0.15	0.46	0.08	0.92	0.15	0.54
Subjects with no knowledge of German	0.71	1.00	0.14	1.00	0.00	0.00	0.71	0.00	0.57	0.14	0.43	0.57	0.00	0.86	0.00	0.14	0.00	0.57	0.14	0.00

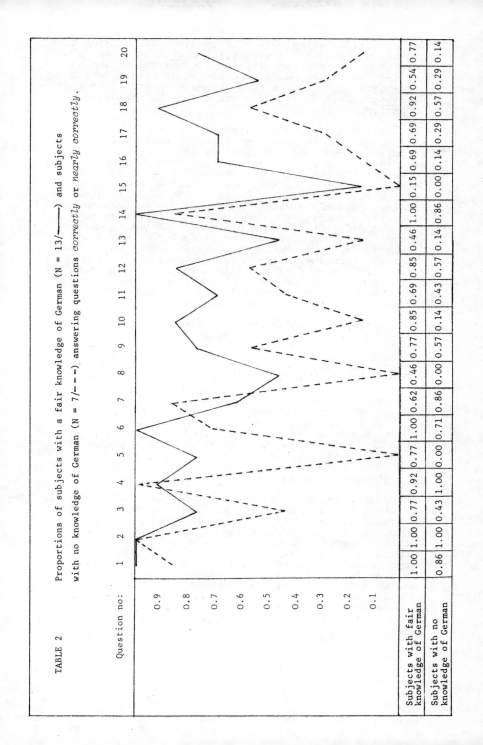

TABLE 2   Proportions of subjects with a fair knowledge of German (N = 13/————) and subjects with no knowledge of German (N = 7/- - - -) answering questions *correctly* or *nearly correctly*.

Question no:	1	2	3	4	5	6	7	8	9	10	11	12	13	14	15	16	17	18	19	20
Subjects with fair knowledge of German	1.00	1.00	0.77	0.92	0.77	1.00	0.62	0.46	0.77	0.85	0.69	0.85	0.46	1.00	0.15	0.69	0.69	0.92	0.54	0.77
Subjects with no knowledge of German	0.86	1.00	0.43	1.00	0.00	0.71	0.86	0.00	0.57	0.14	0.43	0.57	0.14	0.86	0.00	0.14	0.29	0.57	0.29	0.14

2, 7, 10, 11, 17 and 20. Thus in general the responses
to the questionnaire suggest (a) that a knowledge of
German contributed significantly to an understanding
of the Dutch text, and (b) that the difficulty which
two-thirds of the questions presented relative to one
another had to do with factors other than language
distance.

All subjects in both groups answered question 2
correctly: the sense of 'mijn grootmoeder - mijn
moeders moeder' was perhaps easy for any Anglophone
to deduce from either the printed or the spoken
version of the text. Subjects with no knowledge of
German answered questions 4 and 7 better than subjects
with a fair knowledge of German. The blank in question
4 was given in the printed text as '4': perhaps those
subjects without German seized on the figure as an
obvious aid, whereas some of those with a knowledge of
German could not identify the context adequately and
suspected a trap. Question 7 was multiple-choice, and
the difference between the two groups may simply be
due to different degrees of luck in guessing correctly
the English equivalent of 'al een tijdje aan de gang'
(a phrase perhaps not immediately penetrable to subjects with a naive knowledge of German).

No subject without German answered questions 5,
6, 8, 13, 15, 17 and 20 correctly (Table 1). The
key Dutch words that they thus failed to understand are
(in order): voorbeeld, dorpjes, prachtig, vooroordeel,
bezettingen, onderzoek, trouwen. It is worth noting that
although these items have readily identifiable German
cognates, fewer than half the subjects who had German
answered questions 8, 13, 15 and 17 correctly (Table 1).
No subject without German provided even a partially
correct answer to questions 5, 8 and 15 (Table 2):
it seems likely (see Appendix) that context is less
helpful in answering these questions than in answering
questions 6, 13, 17 and 20.

3.2 Subjects' perceptions

The two groups' reported impressions of the
difficulty of the comprehension task are summarized
in Table 3, which clearly shows that subjects with
German tended to find the task easier than subjects
with no German. Some confirmation that subjects'
impressions concerning the difficulty of the task
were related to their actual performance is provided
by the average scores for the twenty questions
achieved by (a) all subjects reporting that they
found the task hard - 10.7; (b) all subjects reporting
a mixed reaction - 11.9; and (c) all subjects
reporting that they found the task easy - 14.4.

TABLE 3

	Group with German (N = 13)	Group without German (N = 7)
Found task easy	0.69	0.00
Had mixed reactions	0.23	0.71
Found task difficult	0.08	0.29

The strategies reported by subjects as having been used in the performance of the comprehension task were: looking for similarities between forms in the text and forms in other languages to which they could attach meanings; using portions of the text which they had understood to contextualize and thus interpret other portions of the text; gleaning as much contextualizing information as possible from the questionnaire; and using the rewind facility on the cassette recorder to maximize any assistance available from the spoken version of the text. All of these were mentioned by subjects from both groups, but only one was mentioned by more than a minority of either group; this was the strategy of looking for help from other languages, which was reported by 0.85 of the group with German and by 0.71 of the group with no German.

Of those subjects in the group with German who reported having used this strategy, all said they had drawn on their knowledge of German, 0.73 mentioning only German as a source of help, 0.18 mentioning English as well as German, and 0.08 mentioning English, French, Latin and Greek as well as German. Of those subjects in the group with no German who reported having used this strategy, all said they had drawn on their knowledge of English, 0.80 mentioning English alone and 0.20 mentioning French as well as English. In other words, subjects who were aware of tapping linguistic resources already at their disposal seem for the most part to have concentrated their attention on one particular language; and it turns out that the language focussed on by each group was, of the languages known to members of that group, the one which was closest to Dutch and thus likely to give most help in interpreting a Dutch text. Moreover, no subject who reported having used the transfer strategy failed to mention the language in his/her repertoire which was closest to Dutch. Table 4 shows that subjects reporting that they had made conscious use of German were more likely to find the task easy than other subjects.

265

TABLE 4   Subjects' perceptions of the difficulty of
          the task cross-tabulated with the use they
          made of available linguistic resources

	Found task hard	Mixed reaction	Found task easy
German (8)	0.13	0.13	0.75
German/English (2)	----	0.50	0.50
German/English/French/ Greek/Latin (1)	----	----	1.00
English (4)	----	1.00	----
English/French (1)	1.00	----	----
No mention of use of available linguistic resources	0.25	0.50	0.25

With regard to the question of which version of the
text, spoken or written, had been found more helpful,
the divergences which emerged amongst subjects (see Table
5) did not correlate to any significant degree with
differences in language background. This suggests that
subjects' perceptions in this matter were unrelated to
the language distance factor and dependent on other
factors such as perhaps previous language learning
experience and cognitive style.

TABLE 5

	Group with German (N = 13)	Group without German (N = 7)
Found spoken version more helpful	0.46	0.43
Undecided as to which version was more helpful	0.00	0.14
Found written version more helpful	0.54	0.43

4.   Conclusion

In our description of the administration of the
experiment we suggested that the generalizability of
our results would be limited by the relatively small
numbers of subjects and by the disproportion between
the two groups. Nevertheless, it is difficult not to
construe the results as confirming the hypothesis

that the task of coming to grips with the comprehension
of utterances in an unfamiliar language is facilitated
if one can draw on knowledge of related languages, and
that the closer the relation between the languages one
knows and the unfamiliar language, the greater will be
one's degree of understanding of utterances in the
latter. The results seem also to indicate that language
distance is something about which swift, conscious and
accurate judgments are apt to be made, to the extent
that if one happens to know more than one language
which is related to the unfamiliar language, one is
likely to draw in a quite focussed and self-aware
manner on the resources of that language which is most
closely related to the unfamiliar language.

It seems to us that it would be well worth investigating this phenomenon further, and that if the
findings of the exploratory study can be more firmly
established, they may have interesting pedagogical
implications. For example, they may suggest possibilities for the devising of programmes which would
seek rapidly and economically to build a receptive
competence in (say) Dutch or Italian on (respectively)
'school German' or 'school French'.

APPENDIX

A. DUTCH TEST

Ik ben een Nederlands meisje. Op 16 maart 1953
werd ik in Eindhoven geboren. Mijn ouders noemden mij
Wilhelmina Francina Maria. Wilhelmina naar mijn
grootmoeder - mijn moeders moeder; Francina naar de
tante, die mij ten doop hield; en Maria, omdat mijn
moeder dacht, dat Maria haar het leven had gered.

Ik werd geboren in een ziekenhuis, net zoals mijn
zusje en de broer, die daarna kwam. Mijn jongste broer
is thuis geboren. Toen mijn jongste broer werd geboren
woonden mijn ouders in hun derde huis na hun trouwen; en
toen hij 4 maanden was, zijn we weer verhuisd.

Eindhoven is een interessant voorbeeld voor
industriële groei. Rond het eigenlijke Eindhoven lagen
5 dorpjes dicht bijeen: Gestel, Stratum, Strijp, Tongelre
en Woensel. Behalve in Strijp, hebben we overal gewoond;
het laatst in Gestel.

Toen Eindhoven door de uitbreiding van de Philips-
fabrieken en de Daf-automobiel fabrieken steeds meer

mensen aantrok, groeide het uit, totdat het vroegere
dorp Eindhoven het winkelcentrum werd en de vijf dorpjes
helemaal werden opgenomen in de grote stad. Toen ik
vijf jaar was en we naar Gestel verhuisden, was dit
proces al een tijdje aan de gang, maar er was nog steeds
weinig buiten de ring van dorpjes gebouwd. Het was een
prachtig gebied om 's Zondags te gaan fietsen tussen
de landerijen door en door de bossen.

Ik ben naar een lagere school gegaan in Gestel,
waar alleen maar meisjes opzaten. Daarna ging ik
naar de H.B.S., de Hogere Burger School. Daar waren
meer jongens dan meisjes op, want men had twee jaar
daarvoor van de oorspronkelijke jongensschool een
gemengde school gemaakt.

Veel mensen vonden het vreemd, dat ik naar die
school ging en vroegen of ik dan bruggen wilde gaan
bouwen of zo. Ik wilde alleen maar naar een school,
waar ik nog alle kanten mee uit kon; en niet naar
die 'meiden' school, waar je geen wiskunde en schei-
kunde en natuurkunde kreeg. Ik heb dan ook de
B-richting gekozen met de exacte vakken.

Na het examen wist ik nog niet wat ik wilde doen,
want de schooldekaan had me afgeraden naar Wageningen -
naar de landbouwhogeschool - te gaan. Achteraf denk
ik, dat dat wel een vooroordeel van hem zal zijn
geweest: dat meisjes geen landbouwvakken kunnen doen.

Dus ging ik naar de kweekschool voor onderwijzers.
Na een jaar ging ik daar weg om in Nijmegen aan de
universiteit antropologie te gaan studeren. Het was
een hele interessante periode in mijn leven en ook in
de geschiedenis. Ik viel midden in de democratiserings-
beweging in de universiteiten en heb zelf ook nog actief
deelgenomen aan twee bezettingen.

Terwijl ik voor mijn doktoraalexamen studeerde
werkte ik op de bibliotheek van het antropologisch
instituut en verder als studentassistent bij verschillende
docenten. In het laatste jaar heb ik in het Max Planck
Instituut gewerkt aan een psycholinguistisch onderzoek.

Voor mijn leeronderzoek ben ik naar Ierland gekomen,
waar ik mij in Killorglin drie maanden heb proberen in
te leven in de gemeenschapsontwikkelingsprocessen. Daar
ontmoette ik veel mensen, die goede vrienden zijn geworden.
Bovendien ontdekte ik, dat Ierland nog tamelijk onver-
vuild was, frisse lucht had en voldoende ruimte voor
iedereen.

Toen ik danook het jaar daarop terugkwam, en ook
nog eens mijn huidige levensgezel 'ontdekte', stond
het vast, dat ik zeker een paar jaar in Ierland zou
proberen te wonen en werken. Na mijn afstuderen
solliciteerde ik hier en in Nederland, en ik was zo
gelukkig hier het eerst een baan aangeboden te
krijgen.

Nu woon ik hier bijna twee jaar in Dublin en
hoop het volgend jaar in Kerry werk te vinden, zodat
ik eindelijk mijn man tevreden kan stellen en met hem
kan trouwen.

B. QUESTIONNAIRE

1. The speaker was .... in Eindhoven.
2. She is called Wilhelmina after her ....
3. Her youngest brother was born at ....
4. When he was ..... months old the family moved house.
5. Eindhoven is an interesting ..... of industrial growth.
6. At one time Eindhoven proper was surrounded by
   five ......
7. When she was five years old the growth of Eindhoven was
   just beginning/already under way/substantially complete.
8. The scenery around Eindhoven was ugly/beautiful/depressing.
9. In her primary school there were only ....
10. Her secondary school had originally been mixed/girls
    only/ boys only.
11. She went to this school because she wanted to study
    languages/science/music.
12. She was advised against going to the regional
    technical college/architectural college/agricultural
    college.
13. Afterwards she thought that this advice had been the
    result of ......
14. Eventually she went to the university at Nijmegen
    to study ......
15. There she was actively involved in two ....
16. While studying for her higher degree she worked as
    a research assistant for various ......
17. In her last year she worked on a psycholinguistic ......
18. When she first came to Ireland she stayed for three
    weeks/months/years.
19. She discovered that Ireland is still fairly ......
20. She hopes to find a job in Kerry so that she can ......

REFERENCES

Cohen, A.D. (1983a), 'Introspecting about second language learning', Studia Anglica Posnaniensia 15, pp. 149-56.
Cohen, A.D. (1983b), 'Researching second-language learning strategies: how do we get the information?', paper presented at the Annual TESOL Convention, Toronto, March.
Cohen, A.D. and C. Hosenfeld (1981), 'Some uses of mentalistic data in second language research', Language Learning 31.2, pp. 285-313.
Glahn, E. (1980), 'Introspection as a method of elicitation in interlanguage studies', Interlanguage Studies Bulletin 5.1, pp. 119-28.
Jordens, P. (1977), 'Rules, grammatical intuitions and strategies in foreign language learning', Interlanguage Studies Bulletin 2.2, pp. 5-76.
Kellerman, E. (1977), 'Towards a characterization of the strategy of transfer in second language learning', Interlanguage Studies Bulletin 2.1, pp. 58-145.
Kellerman, E. (1979), 'Transfer and non-transfer: where are we now?', Studies in Second Language Acquisition 2.1, pp. 37-57.
Oller, J. and S. Ziahosseiny (1970), 'The contrastive analysis hypothesis and spelling errors', Language Learning 20.2, pp. 183-9.
Ringbom, H. and R. Palmberg (eds.) (1976), Errors made by Finns and Swedish-speaking Finns in the learning of English, AFTIL vol. 5, Publications of the Department of English, Åbo: Åbo Akademi.
Schacter, J., A. Tyson and F. Diffley (1976), 'Learner intuitions of grammaticality', Language Learning 26.1, pp. 67-76.
Singleton, D.M. (1981), 'Alien intrusions in learner French: a case study', paper presented at the autumn seminar of the Irish Association for Applied Linguistics, October; to appear in Teanga: Journal of the Irish Association for Applied Linguistics 3 (1983), pp. 87-128.
Singleton, D.M. (1982), 'Language distance and language transfer: a case study', paper presented at a 'Language and Linguistics' seminar sponsored by the Centre for Language and Communication Studies, Trinity College, Dublin, November.
Sjöholm, K. (1976), 'A comparison of the test results in grammar and vocabulary between Finnish- and Swedish-speaking applicants for English 1974', in Ringbom and Palmberg (eds.) (1976), pp. 54-137.
Whinnom, K. (1971), 'Linguistic hybridization and the "special case" of pidgins and creoles', in D. Hymes (ed.), Pidginization and creolization of languages, Cambridge: Cambridge University Press.

LANGUAGE VARIATION AND FOREIGN LANGUAGE TEACHING : ISSUES AND ORIENTATIONS

Albert Valdman
Indiana University
Bloomington

INTRODUCTION

Currently the attainment of near-native communicative competence ranks highly as an objective in
foreign language (FL) teaching (Savignon 1972). To
reach that level of performance in the target language
a learner must at least attain near-native fluency. The
latter is defined by Fillmore (1979) in terms of four
sets of competencies: the ability to talk at length
with few pauses; the ability to talk in coherent,
reasoned and 'semantically dense' sentences, the ability
to have something to say in a wide range of contexts,
and the ability to be creative and imaginative in
language use. But in addition to demonstrating these
four sets of abilities, which require bringing into play
linguistic rules and rules for the organization of
discourse, the learner must control at least part of
the range of variability of native speakers. For if
the fiction of the ideal speaker-listener with
homogeneous speech and a static underlying system has
enabled linguists to discover linguistic rules, it does
not serve as a useful model to account for the
functioning of language in a social context. The static
Chomskyan model of language (Chomsky 1965) is pre-
dicated on the assumption that the function of language
is to communicate meaning. But the referential function
is but one of the many human needs that natural languages
serve. As the Biblical account instructs us, shibboleths,
the use of linguistic markers to assign or proclaim
membership in particular human groups, may on many
occasions have determining effects on linguistic interactions. Meaningful communication cannot take place
without attention being paid to all aspects of the
communicative context characterized by the model
presented in (1):

(1) SOCIAL FACTORS IN COMMUNICATION

Content	Communicative Context		Form
Semantic notions	Who speaks?		Imperfect Future
Functional notions ⟹	To whom? In the presence of whom?	Partici-pants	Possessive pronoun
(speech acts)	About what? Why? Toward what ends? With what means? Where?	Topic Intention ⟹ - Channels Setting Setting	-
Participants	Status Age Role Function Mood		

In communicative interactions identification of specific participants, topics, intentions, channels, and settings is not effected by referentially contrastive linguistic features (for example, the opposition between phonemes x and y or the choice between two verbal categories) but by the choice among variants of linguistic features or by linguistic differences that, precisely, do not have referential meaning. Subtle dosage of given variants or subtle shifting among synonymous features serve as powerful cues as to: Who speaks?, To whom?, In the presence of whom?, About what?, Why or toward what end?, Under what circumstances?, and Where? The attainment of near-native linguistic competence also requires the acquisition of native speakers' ability to shift among variants in order to produce speech congruent with the social and situational aspects of the communicative setting.

To lead to the attainment of near-native communicative competence in the target language a teaching syllabus should lead learners to attainment of the three following sets of abilities in the area of language variation:

1. To express themselves with ease and accuracy and in a manner appropriate to particular communicative situations;
2. To understand authentic discourse, that is to say, natural discourse reflecting the full range of social settings in which speech is imbedded. Specifically, this requires learners to understand a broad range of variation within the target language. In addition to the homogeneous standard variety of the TL, learners should be able to adjust to various regional dialects and sociolects, to different registers (reflecting the professional specialization of participants), styles and language levels (reflecting the relationship among participants in linguistic interactions, topics discussed, etc.);

272

3. To identify stereotypic features marking the
   various levels of variation and to be aware of
   their sociolinguistic implications.

Traditionally, learners have been exposed to a
homogeneous standard variety of the TL until they have
acquired a high level of fluency. It is not until
advanced levels of study that they are provided with
more authentic and hetereogeneous speech samples on the
basis of which they can acquire the three-pronged set
of abilities characterized above. Thus, even advanced
learners evidence highly stilted speech when forced to
engage in face-to-face communication taking place in a
natural setting. My contention is that, to the contrary,
the ability to handle language variability, like all
other aspects of communicative competence, should be
acquired progressively. Authentic speech samples and
examples of natural discourse should be provided early
in the training programme and language variation should
be treated both inductively and deductively as a fully
integrated element of the teaching syllabus.

In this paper, I will consider the problem of the
determination of a suitable target norm for foreign
language learners. The stress placed on the adjective
foreign reflects my contention that the definition of
a suitable target norm raises different issues in the
case of the learning of a foreign tongue in a formal
context than it does in the learning of a second
language under whatever conditions and in the
acquisition of a host language by migrant workers. I
will discuss first the special constraints imposed by
the formal classroom context. Next, I will consider
the issue of native speakers' attitudes towards
variation in foreigners' approximative terms
(interlanguage). These considerations will lead me
to propose that the most suitable target norm for FL
learners is neither the homogeneous, highly standardized
norm selected traditionally nor the full range of
variation evidenced in authentic speech samples, but a
pedagogical norm. The notion of pedagogical norm will be
discussed and its incorporation in teaching materials
illustrated. I will discuss the selection and ordering
problems posed by a highly variable aspect of the mor-
phosyntax of a highly codified language of wider
communication, interrogative structures in standard
French.

1. The constraints of the formal classroom context

Even in FL courses that focus on the attainment of communicative competence and which, accordingly, give a high priority to the simulation of natural communicative activities, authentic interactions are impossible. In the classroom environment language is diverted from its primary function, which is to relate linguistic and non-linguistic objects in a social context, to assume meta-linguistic and epilinguistic functions. Much time is devoted to talking about the language taught and language in general. Even when learners are asked to talk about the here-and-now in communicative-oriented courses, the main objective of the activity is to rehearse specific linguistic structures or discourse strategies rather than to transmit meaning or express genuine communicative needs. Such simple protocols as What's the weather like today? or What time is it? are not directives, for students realize that by a simple glance through the window or at his or her watch the instructor would satisfy the need for the putative information requested. Even in simulated communicative situations learners realize that their responses are evaluated just as much, if not more, for their conformity to TL structural norms as for their informational content. As A. Trévise points out (1979, p. 49), in the classroom context learners' utterances are characterized by a two-level enunciation. Behind the message conveyed lurks an implicit request for evaluation or feedback: 'Am I making myself understood?'; 'Am I using such or such a grammatical construction correctly?'. This accounts, for instance, for the tentative rising intonation that learners often super-impose on declaratives.

2. Native speaker attitudes toward variation in learner interlanguage

Since it was first put forward in 1972 L. Selinker's notion of interlanguage has stimulated much theory construction and empirical research in applied linguistics. While research has centred on psycholinguistic aspects of interlanguage, in recent years workers in the field have begun to investigate the relationship between characteristics of interlanguage - the nature of inter-linguistic systems, the variability of interlanguage, its patterns of longitudinal development, etc. - and the nature of the social interaction between various categories

of learners and speakers in the surrounding environment
(d'Anglejan 1983; Dittmar and Klein 1979). Two other
recent orientations in the study of interlanguage
promise to yield useful insights on the issue at hand;
relevant theoretical issues and empirical research in
these domains are discussed and reviewed by d'Anglejan,
Ryan, Long, and Eisenstein in a forthcoming special
issue of Studies in Second Language Acquisition. The
first orientation involves the observation of modifications of input effected by native speakers in the
course of natural communicative interactions with
foreign speakers. Long (1983) notes that only under
very special conditions do native speakers resort to
ill-formed discourse, foreigner talk, that mirrors
the interlinguistic level of non-fluent foreign learners.
Generally they make use of a special foreigner register
free of structural deviations. This register features
mainly modifications in the organization of discourse:
shorter utterances, fewer sentences or phrases per T-
units, etc. rather than special structural adjustments.
The fact that in this special register lexical choice
is more restricted and fuller alternants of morphemes
are used would suggest that it might also entail closer
adherence to the standard norm on the part of native
speakers and avoidance of sociolinguistically marked
alternants. However, to my knowledge, no study is
reported that focuses on departure from normal patterns
of language variation in interactions between native
speakers and foreign learners.

The second orientation involves the study of native
speaker attitudes and reactions toward various interlinguistic features: pronunciation accent, grammatical
errors, violations of sociolinguistic rules. One strand
of this research orientation has adopted a pedagogical
perspective. By determining the relative degree of
severity with which native judges view certain types of
errors (global versus local, higher-level versus low-
level, etc.) it is hoped that general principles will
emerge that might guide syllabus design, the preparation
of materials, and instructional practices. Another
strand (Ryan 1983) attempts to determine the social
psychological mechanisms that underlie native speakers'
evaluation of interlinguistic features. Available studies
motivated by this latter objective indicate clearly that
the evaluative dimensions of social class and group
solidarity at the intergroup level and of overall
judgment of competence and intelligence and negative affect
at the ingroup level interact in complex ways.

Socio-psychologically oriented studies of native speaker attitudes have not yet been extended to the area of language variation and the definition of sociolinguistically acceptable target language norms. From the only available exploratory study (Swacker 1976) it would appear that native speakers tend to downgrade foreigner speech that diverges markedly from the standard norm. Swacker observed that native speakers of East Texas English reacted negatively to a reading sample from an Arabic accented speaker whose speech contained local pronunciation and grammatical features. A higher rating was given to another Arabic accented speaker whose English was free of local linguistic features. She concluded that certain regional markers may be acceptable when found in the speech of native speakers but are offensive in the mouth of foreigners. Swacker does not specify whether the local features studied also symbolize lower social status.

In the absence of a substantial body of empirical data we must resort to extrapolation from other areas of interlinguistic research to seek principles for the determination of TL norms suitable for foreign learners. If it can be shown to hold for all types of foreign accented speech, the negative reaction of native speakers toward the use of local variants by foreign speakers may be accounted for in terms of the group solidarity evaluative dimension. Foreign accents and other interlinguistic features are highly salient markers of membership in outgroups. Their presence in the speech of a foreigner would preclude features symbolizing ingroup membership, such as regionally or socially marked variants. Appeal to the notion of the linguistic market (Bourdieu 1977) also supports the selection of a highly standardized TL norm for foreign learners. The learning of the TL may be viewed as an economic investment whose value would be depreciated if the variety mastered contained stigmatized features. In the case of formal classroom learning, those who have learned the TL through that process would rank high on the linguistic market scale. They would be conferred high social status which implied mastery of the prestigious standardized form of both the TL and their own native language. This application of the notion of the linguistic market accords well with the sentiment, often expressed by native speakers, that educated foreign speakers speak the TL 'better' than they do. When called upon to justify their sentiment, these speakers will mention the absence of TL alternants associated, rightly or wrongly, with depreciated social status, for example, the use in English of It is I instead of It's me or I'm going to instead of I'm gonna.

3. The notion of pedagogical norm

Standardization represents an attempt to reduce the
variability inherent in all natural languages within
the context of the upgrading of a vernacular tongue so
that it may assume wider functions, in particular the
vehicluar function (communication with outgroups) and
the referential function (the vehicle of a respected
body of cultural texts and/or the symbol of the
cultural and ethnic unity of the ingroup). Standardization often takes place when a vernacular is
graphized and modernized. Communities differ with
respect to the degree of standardization expected in
the use of their languages. For instance the English-
speaking communities accept considerable local variation;
little stigma, if any, attaches to the use of, say,
Indian English instead of RP on the part of Indians. On
the other hand, Parisian French is accepted as the
universal standard in all Francophone regions, and users
of other varieties readily defer to it.

Standardized varieties also differ with respect to the
degree of idealization they have undergone. This term
refers both to the degree of uniformization effected
and the distance between the codified norm and the
observable linguistic behaviour of subgroups whose speech
underlies the norm. French provides an extreme example
of a highly idealized standard language.   In 1647 C.
Vaugelas (1647) proposed as a model for linguistic
distinction and elegance, a variety he termed <u>bon usage</u> which
he defined as:
> La façon de parler de la plus saine partie de
> la Cour, conformément à la façon d'écrire de
> la plus saine partie des auteurs de temps
> (The manner of speaking of the most wholesome
> part of the Court, in conformity with the
> manner of writing of the most wholesome part
> of writers of the time)...

The Belgian linguist, J. Hanse (1949) provides a
definition of present-day standard French that differs
little from that given three centuries ago by his
illustrious predecessor:

> [..] le français parle par l'homme instruit et
> cultivé, le français écrit par les bons auteurs
> modernes [..] par ceux qui ont prouvé leur
> connaissance de la langue et de ses finesses,
> mais aussi leur amour de la clarté et leur
> conscience de la valeur sociale du language, et
> enfin le français défini par les meilleurs
> grammairiens. ([..] the type of French spoken
> by educated and cultivated people, the type of

French written by good modern authors [..] by
those who have demonstrated their knowledge of
the language and of its fine points, but also
their love of clarity and their feel for the
social value of language, and finally the type
of French defined by the best grammarians).

This idealization of the standard norm goes hand in
hand with the depreciation of vernacular varieties,
particularly those containing features associated rightly
or wrongly with speakers enjoying low social status. In
the French-speaking world, for example, socially stigmatized vernacular varieties, français populaire, are
characterized variously as a variety that pilfers words
from other languages and adulterates the meaning of
French words (Nisard 1872, p. 128), whose grammatical
forms and constructions do not obey any norm (Stourdé
1969, p. 22), and where a deterioration of syntax
corresponds to a heavy reliance on suprasegmental
features (Bonin 1978, p. 97).

To summarize, a standardized norm represents a
fictitious construct resting as much on ideological
as on empirical grounds. Its suitability as a TL norm
for foreign learners is a matter that may be determined empirically on the basis of the following
criteria: (1) to what extent it reflects actual native
speaker behaviour in genuine communicative situations;
(2) to what extent it conforms to native speakers'
idealized views of their behaviour; (3) to what extent
it matches the behaviour that native speakers deem
appropriate for particular categories of foreign learners.
From a pedagogical point of view, the standard norm has
a serious drawback; it fails to accommodate to learner
interlanguage and, in this way, it may be relatively
difficult to acquire. More useful in imparting the
desired standard norm to foreign learners is the
notion of pedagogical norm. The latter is established
on the basis of the three criteria used to define the
sociolinguistically acceptable TL norm but, in
addition, it takes into consideration acquisitional
factors. Given alternative strategies leading to the
teaching of the TL norm, the one to be preferred in
the formal teaching setting is the one that coincides
with some interlinguistic stage. The notion of
pedagogical norm and the process by which it is defined
will be illustrated by its application to the
establishment of a sociolinguistically acceptable TL
norm for French interrogative structures for English-
speaking formal learners.

5. A pedagogical norm for French interrogative structures

5.1 Variation in French interrogative structures

The objective of this illustration of the notion of
pedagogical norm is to show how lawful and patterned
language variation may be introduced in beginning and
elementary level FL courses so that learners may
eventually acquire stylistic manoeuvre, that is, the
ability to behave linguistically in a manner congruent
to the total communicative setting. One key aspect of
that total communicative setting is that they must
adhere to social constraints set by host community
speakers on the sort of verbal range appropriate for
foreign speakers in general and for formal learners in
particular.

In French questions may be formulated in a variety
of ways. If we limit our consideration to nuclear
(non yes/no) questions, there are five synonymous
constructions (Valdman 1972). Consider the examples
in (2):

(2a)	INVERSION	Où va Jean?	Où va-t-il?
		Où Jean va-t-il?	Lui, où va-t-il?
(2b)	EST-CE QUE	Où est-ce que Jean va?	Où est-ce qu'il va?
(2c)	PRONOMINAL-IZATION	Jean va où?	Il va où?
(2d)	FRONTING	?Où Jean va?	Où il va?

The question mark preceding Où Jean va? indicates
that many speakers of French would consider it ill-
formed but, while they may question their 'correctness'
or 'appropriateness', they will not label any of the
other variants as categorically ungrammatical.

The imparting of some degree of communicative ability
requires the presentation of variants in a way that will
enable the learner to acquire the ability, not only of
producing grammatically correct sentences, but also of
producing sentences that are pragmatically appropriate
and socially acceptable; French speakers do not use
the various interrogative structures in a random way.
The four constructions no doubt differ with regard to
presuppositions, to speech levels, etc., although
currently available descriptions of the language do not
provide rules that are sufficiently delicate to enable
the syllabus designer and textbook writer to make
categorical statements with confidence.

5.2. Observations of actual native usage and speaker perception of frequency of use

There exist numerous analyses of French interrogatives. Most of these consist of arguments in favour of some particular syntactic model, and they fail to provide crucial information about the discursive properties of each of the four apparently synonymous constructions. With respect to the sociolinguistic dimension there exist several investigations of the correlations between interrogative variants and social class and level of formality in French. Behnsted (1973) collected a large number of nuclear questions in the course of interviews with speakers representing the working class (français populaire) and the middle class. Behnsted assumes, wrongly in my opinion, that only the latter would show significant stylistic variation. Accordingly, he distinguishes between informal style and formal style variants of Standard (i.e. middle class) French but posits invariant behaviour on the part of speakers of français populaire.

The data presented by Behnsted, see (3) below, shows that the main line of cleavage in French does not demarcate working class from middle class usage but informal from formal style. In both putative sociolects INVERSION occurs with low frequency in informal style (respectively, 9% vs. 5% in working class vs. middle class French). The fact that emerges clearly from Behnsted's survey of French speakers' actual behaviour is that PRONOMINALIZATION and FRONTING account together for nearly 80% of all instances of interrogative structures occurring in a representative sample of informal Standard French; we will see, below, that those are precisely the interrogative constructions subject to social depreciation and which, furthermore, are studiously avoided by textbook writers. The only interrogative constructions occurring in français populaire that are excluded from Standard French are morphophonological variants of EST-CE QUE: e.g., Où c' que tu vas?, Où qu' tu vas?, Où c'que qu' tu vas?, etc. Indeed, FRONTING AND PRONOMINALIZATION occur more frequently in informal Standard French than in français populaire.

(3) FRENCH INTERROGATIVE CONSTRUCTIONS

	production			perception
	Fr. Pop.	Fr. St. I.	Fr. St. F.	
Pronominalization Tu vas où?	12%	33%	25%	20%-
Fronting Où tu vas?	36%	46%	10%	30%-
Est-ce que Où est-ce que tu vas?	8%	12%	3%	20%(+)
Est-ce que variants Où c'est que tu vas?	45%	4%	-	
Inversion Où vas-tu?	9%	5%	62%	30%(+)
	N-587	N-446	N-436	

280

In addition to tabulating the percentage of
occurrence of the four interrogative constructions in
his corpus Behnsted asked his middle class subjects to
estimate the distribution of the constructions relative
to each other. As the figures in the last column of
(3) indicate, they tended to underestimate the frequency
of occurrence of the stigmatized constructions
(PRONOMINALIZATION and FRONTING) in informal speech and,
on the other hand, overestimate the frequency of
occurrence of the more standard features (EST-CE QUE and
INVERSION). The middle class speakers' perception of
frequency of use reflects directly the sociolinguistic
value of the interrogative alternants and, partly, their
level of formality. As they shift from informal to formal
speech contexts, middle class speakers dramatically
increase their use of INVERSION, moderately that of
EST-CE QUE, and reduce considerably the number of FRONTING
constructions.

5.3. Acquisitional order

As would be expected learners of French produce a
wide variety of deviant replicas of the various interrogative structures to which they are exposed. Intrasystemic
considerations and contrastive analysis would suggest that
EST-CE QUE would rank as the structure most easy to
acquire (Valdman 1972). From a surface structure point of
view it involves simple juxtaposition of an interrogative
marker whereas its competitors require syntactic per-
mutations and copy of propositional elements. INVERSION
stands out as the most complex syntactically since it is
subject to numerous constraints. For English learners,
EST-CE QUE appears to provide the best surface structure
match to the canonical native structure:

(4)   Where │ does   │ John   work?
       ⇕   │   ⇕   │ ⬆   ⬆
       Où   │ est-ce que│ Jean   travaille?

Note in particular that, in a sense, both the inserted
auxiliary <u>do</u> and the adjoined <u>est-ce que</u> serve as semantically vacuous 'dummy' elements.

Observation of errors made by beginning American
learners do not confirm the predictions based on structural
considerations and contrastive analysis. Beginning
learners exposed to INVERSION and EST-CE QUE models exclusively produced FRONTING replicas in greater proportion
in tasks that required question construction. These

replicas may in fact be considered interlinguistic
features since the model was absent from the input,
(Valdman 1975, 1976).

5.4. A pedagogical norm for French interrogatives

On the basis of the preceding considerations,
I offer the following principles for the selection and
ordering of French interrogative variants for purposes of
the formal teaching of French as a FL. INVERSION, which
in present pedagogical practice ranks as the primary
target construction, is highly marked for formality; it
is characteristic of monitored spoken styles and of
written discourse. The data from native speakers' perception of frequency of use adduced by Behnsted suggest
that they would no doubt assign INVERSION highest
linguistic market value and that they would give it
highest rank for inclusion in a TL norm for foreigners.
However, because of its association with formality it
would be inappropriate to set it up as target feature
in courses designed to impart communicative ability.
In addition, the numerous syntactic constraints that
attach to it render it difficult to acquire and use
accurately. The role of primary target feature should
instead be assigned to EST-CE QUE since it is at the
same time sociolinguistically neutral and structurally
simple.

There are cases where EST-CE QUE is perceived as
awkward or lacking in euphony, e.g. in questions containing a nominal NP and certain verbs or interrogative
adverbs. Compare: Où est-ce que vos parents travaillent?
and ?Où est-ce que vos parents vont? (Où vont vos parents?);
Où est-ce que vous allez? and ?Comment est-ce que vous
allez? (Comment allez-vous?). Such cases may be taught
as lexicalized protocols. Where dictated by pedagogical
considerations FRONTING or PRONOMINALIZATION may be used
as preliminary steps. In more advanced levels these two
constructions, particularly the former, must be identified
as more appropriate for informal use. Explicit statements
need to be made about the sociolinguistic correlates of
the various constructions and about their stylistic
function. Their use in contrived texts must reflect
their distribution in authentic, unedited speech samples
so that learners may be led to induce their pragmatic
and sociolinguistic value. In (5) I offer a pedagogical
progression illustrating order of introduction of the
four variant constructions in speech and writing. Note,
too, that a distinction is made between the learner's
active (productive) and passive (receptive) capabilities.

(5)

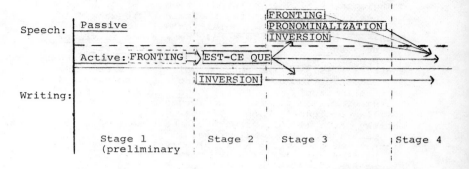

REFERENCES

d'Anglejan, A. (1983), 'Introduction to special issue on
    native speaker reactions to learner speech', Studies
    in Second Language Acquisition 5.2 (forthcoming).
Behnsted, P. (1973), Viens-tu?, est-ce que tu viens?,
    tu viens? - Formen und Strukturen des direkten
    Fragesatzes im Französischen, Tübingen: Gunter Narr.
Bonin, T. (1978), 'The role of colloquial French in
    communication and implications for foreign language
    instruction', Modern Language Journal 52, p. 97.
Bourdieu, P. (1977), 'L'économie des changements
    linguistiques', Langue française 34, pp. 17-34.
Chomsky, N.A. (1965), Aspects of the theory of syntax,
    Cambridge, Mass.: MIT Press.
Dittmar, N. and W. Klein (1979), Developing grammars,
    Heidleberg - Berlin - New York: Springer.
Eisenstein, M. (1983), 'Native reactions to non-native
    speech', Studies in Second Language Acquisition 5.2
    (forthcoming).
Hanse, J. (1949), Dictionnaire des difficultés grammaticales
    et lexicologiques, Paris, Bruxelles: Bause.
Long, M.H. (1983), 'Linguistic and conversational
    adjustments to non-native speakers', Studies in
    Second Language Acquisition 5.2 (forthcoming).
Nisard, C. (1872), Étude sur le langage populaire,
    Paris: Franck.
Ryan, E.B. (1983), 'Social psychological mechanisms underlying
    native speaker evaluations of non-native speech',
    Studies in Second Language Acquisition 5.2 (forthcoming).
Savignon, S. (1972), Communicative competence: An
    experiment in foreign language teaching, Philadelphia:
    Center for Curriculum Development, Inc.
Selinker, L. (1972), 'Interlanguage' International Review
    of Applied Linguistics 10, pp. 209-31.
Stourdze, C. (1979), 'Les niveaux de langue', Le Français
    dans le Monde 69, pp. 18-21.
Swacker, M. (1976), 'When (+native) is (-favourable)',
    Lektos, special issue. ERIC ED 135-254.
Trévise, A. (1979), 'Spécificité de l'énonciation
    didactique dans l'apprentissage de l'anglais par
    des étudiants francophones', Encrages 1, pp. 44-52.
Valdman, A. (1972), 'Language variation and the teaching
    of French', in G. Todd (ed.), Current issues in the
    teaching of French, Philadelphia: Center for
    Curriculum Development, Inc., pp. 87-108.
Valdman, A. (1975), 'Error analysis and pedagogical
    ordering', in S.P. Corder and E. Roulet (eds.),
    Some implications of linguistic theory for applied
    linguistics, 105-26, Paris: Didier; Brussels: Aimav,
    pp. 105-126.
Valdman, A. (1976), 'Variation linguistique et norme
    pédagogique dans l'enseignement du français langue
    seconde', Bulletin de la Fédération Internationale
    des Professeurs de Français 12-13, pp. 52-53.
Vaugelas, C. (1647), Remarques sur la langue française,
    Paris: Droz, éd. Streicher, 1936.